Transforming Summar

GW01425194

Sweeping changes are being introduced into the lower-tier magistrates' courts in England and Wales in efforts to modernise the system and speed up case processing. They concentrate on delivering prompt justice within a modern, efficient and technologically advanced system. But these transformations are fundamentally changing the way justice is delivered. This book analyses criminal court streamlining processes and argues that there are areas where due process protections are being undermined.

Transforming Summary Justice reports empirical research carried out with lay magistrates and criminal justice professionals. Views and experiences drawn from magistrates are valuable because of the central role they perform in lower court justice. Further, magistrates provide a wider understanding of the context in which the lower criminal courts operate and enable a critical appraisal of this unique style of 'lay justice'.

This book is directed at students of criminology, criminal justice and socio-legal studies, who will find the debates stimulating and useful to engage with in contemporary analyses of criminal court justice. It will also be of interest to justice and legal professionals who are seeing swingeing alterations to the field in which they work. The book will have appeal in other common-law jurisdictions, where similar modifications to lower court justice are occurring, and also across Europe, where lay involvement in legal decision-making is being debated and becoming accepted practice.

Jennifer Ward is a senior lecturer in criminology at the School of Law at Middlesex University, London.

Routledge Frontiers of Criminal Justice

Transforming Summary Justice

Modernisation in the lower criminal courts

Jennifer Ward

Routledge
Taylor & Francis Group

LONDON AND NEW YORK

First published 2017 by Routledge

2 Park Square, Milton Park, Abingdon, Oxfordshire OX14 4RN
52 Vanderbilt Avenue, New York, NY 10017

Routledge is an imprint of the Taylor & Francis Group, an informa business

First issued in paperback 2019

British Library Cataloguing in Publication Data
A catalogue record for this book is available from the British Library

Library of Congress Cataloging in Publication Data
Names: Ward, Jennifer R., author.
Title: Transforming summary justice : modernisation in the lower criminal courts / Jennifer Ward.
Description: Abingdon, Oxon ; New York, NY : Routledge, 2017. | Series: Routledge frontiers of criminal justice ; 41 | Includes bibliographical references and index.
Identifiers: LCCN 2016026278| ISBN 9781138846739 (hardback) | ISBN 9781315727288 (ebook)
Subjects: LCSH: Criminal justice, Administration of–England. | Criminal justice, Administration of–Wales. | Criminal courts–England. | Criminal courts–Wales. | Justices of the peace–England. | Justice of the peace–Wales.
Classification: LCC KD8309 .W37 2017 | DDC 345.42/0142–dc23
LC record available at https://lccn.loc.gov/2016026278

ISBN: 978-1-138-84673-9 (hbk)
ISBN: 978-0-367-22609-1 (pbk)

Typeset in Times New Roman
by Wearset Ltd, Boldon, Tyne and Wear

MIX
Paper from
responsible sources
FSC
www.fsc.org   FSC™ C013985

Printed in the United Kingdom
by Henry Ling Limited

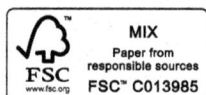

Contents

Tables

Acknowledgements

Several people need thanking for their input and support during my research and writing of this book, without whom it could not have been achieved. These are all the people who took part in the research who will not be named for purposes of anonymity, but to whom I am extremely grateful. My colleagues in the School of Law and Department of Criminology and Sociology at Middlesex University require particular thanks for listening to my ideas, but especially for their encouragement and support over the research period and over the time of writing. Their kindness and reassurance have been particularly helpful during the final weeks. Very special thanks go to John Baldwin, who read chapters of the manuscript. The comments provided were enormously helpful in moving the arguments forward. There are several people in New Zealand who need thanking. Sincere thanks go to Philip Harkness, whose PhD and book research on justices of the peace (JPs) in New Zealand sparked my interest in conducting a similar study on this side of the globe and who put me in touch with several jurists in New Zealand, who were interviewed in an earlier stage of the research. I am very thankful to Chris Brace, chief executive of the Magistrates' Association, who from the beginning has been in full support of the study and helpfully connected me with active magistrates willing to take part. Sally Westoby was an important contact in the early stages, whose experiences as a magistrate helped shape the enquiry at the start. I am grateful to Judy Kemp for our many conversations, for the magistrate contacts and for her continued encouragement. Further thanks are due to the School of Law at Middlesex University for providing funds through the small research grant awards. The financial assistance has been most helpful and I am appreciative of it.

While thanks are needed, there are also apologies and these go to my friends and family for the distance I kept while I concentrated on writing.

Thanks most of all go to my partner Nick Kemp.

1 Introduction

> Efficiency is one of the highest cultural values of modernity.... To be efficient is to be modern.
>
> (Clegg, 1990, cited in Fix-Fierro, 2003)

Sweeping alterations are being introduced into the lower criminal courts in England and Wales in efforts to modernise the system and respond to the changing demands of contemporary society in progressing to the future (Leveson, 2015a; Ministry of Justice, 2014d). Notwithstanding the deep financial restructuring in place in the United Kingdom (UK) since 2010 and its impact on the delivery of all public services, ambition for change within the criminal courts is linked to the government's commitment to operate an up-to-date, modernised court service fit to function in the twenty-first century. This focuses on delivering prompt justice within a modern, streamlined, economically efficient and technologically advanced system. Reducing delay in court case progression and enhancing the swift transfer of casefile information between the courts and the interconnected agencies of the police, the prosecution, probation and the prisons are central.[1]

Along with these modernising transformations, the role of volunteer lay magistrates is being discussed, with suggestions that greater use should be made of their professional expertise and existing skill sets (Green, 2014; Chambers *et al.*, 2014; Ministry of Justice, 2012). England and Wales is unique in its reliance on lay justices in presiding over the majority of all lower criminal court proceedings, a style of court administration that has been in place for many centuries and which successive governments have pledged their support for. However, the role of the magistracy is periodically under discussion (Civil Liberties Trust, 2002; Auld, 2001). In 2014, Damian Green, then government minister for 'Policing, Criminal Justice and Victims', in a speech following publication of the report *Future Courts* (Chambers *et al.*, 2014), set out ideas for reshaping the magistracy and aligning it to 'the future demands of the 21st century'. Green's speech praised the participation of lay justices, while at the same time calling for better use to be made of the position of magistrates as members of the community. Making reference to the concept of community justice that has historically run through magistrates' court justice, innovation alongside local communities was encouraged. Green candidly stated that he aspired to shape a more diverse magistracy and attract younger members. Green's visions for reform built on proposals set out in the earlier government White Paper, *Swift and Sure Justice* (Ministry of Justice, 2012), that suggested new and expanded roles for magistrates and the preliminary ideas for involving them in dispensing justice outside traditional courtroom settings in community-based locations.

It is against an altering criminal court backdrop that this book has come to fruition. The book has two main areas of focus. The first concentrates on particular modifications that have been made to summary justice in the lower criminal courts over the last few years. These include: the ongoing promotion of 'speedy justice' initiatives that aim to quicken the pace of court case processing; the widespread closure of criminal courts across England and Wales, reducing the number of courts where courtroom judging takes place; the enhanced encouragement of early guilty pleas; the introduction of 'virtual courts' in some areas, where defendants appear in court over live video link from police stations; and amendments to legal aid provision that sees fewer defendants eligible for state-funded representation in courtroom proceedings. These changes are contextualised within the concepts of 'managerial' and 'technocratic justice' and the enduring commitment to neo-liberal economics that has been pursued in the UK since the 1980s (Ward, 2015; Bell, 2011). Indeed similar changes are evidenced in other criminal justice systems, and likewise for the purposes of modernised service delivery and achieving economic efficiency savings (Pen, 2015). These concepts are further explained later in this chapter. An important question that sits beneath 'managerialist' alterations relates to whether challenges are presented to the longstanding principles of due process that are central to the delivery of fair justice within the UK criminal court system.

The other focus of the book is on volunteer lay magistrates and the role that they play in dispensing justice in the lower criminal courts of England and Wales at this time of transformation (Morgan, 2012). Empirical evidence is drawn from interviews with serving magistrates, carried out in focus group and individual one-to-one interviews. The empirical research findings are framed within conceptualisations of lay justice and the value of a lay involvement in legal administration and links to the broader, growing international movement in favour of citizen participation in criminal court and legal decision-making (European Academy Berlin, 2012).

Many social research studies have been conducted within the lower criminal courts in different jurisdictions that shed light on court process and procedure and illuminate the interactions and dynamics of power between judicial agents and defendants. However, there is little recent research that incorporates the voice and experiences of magistrates in their courtroom working role. This is despite their large number and the fact that they oversee the bulk of all criminal court work in the English justice system. In 2015 there were just under 20,000 lay magistrates dispensing justice in the lower courts of England and Wales

(Courts and Tribunals Judiciary, 2015). It is a well-cited statistic that 95 per cent of all criminal prosecutions begin and end in the magistrates' courts. In 2014, over a million defendants were proceeded against in these courts. This is alongside the range of powerful decisions lay magistrates are making, such as determining guilt or non-guilt in criminal trials, making bail and remand decisions, sentencing within a wide range of community and custodial options, imposing fines of up to £5,000 and granting police warrants to search private homes. Thus, the views and experiences drawn from magistrates as presented in this book are valuable for a wider understanding of the context in which lower criminal court summary justice operates, the substantial role lay magistrates play in justice administration and the consequent impact their role has on the lives of citizens and community members.

The main themes running through the following chapters are modernising transformations within the lower criminal courts (which are framed within notions of managerial and technocratic justice with due process protections considered alongside), the magistracy and the value of lay justice, and the embedding of social justice principles within the work of the lower courts and case processing.

The main focus of the book's content is the lower courts of the English justice system. However, the conceptual themes and theories advanced are applicable across jurisdictions since they are universal developments in criminal court justice administration and are recognisable in other countries, such as, the introduction of video link technology in courtroom proceedings, rehabilitative sentencing and alternative dispute resolution in the form of specialist problem-solving courts. As such they are not geographically bound concepts, although common-law jurisdictions operating similar adversarial justice systems will recognise more the streamlining alterations focused on.

Different countries apply different approaches to processing criminal cases, which can broadly be distinguished as continental European inquisitorial systems and the adversarial justice systems established in the former British colonies. For example in the United States (US), Canada, Australia, New Zealand (NZ), Hong Kong, South Africa and India, which these days mainly operate in revised forms from that were implemented under the former administration but are similar in criminal justice process and procedure.

Modernisation in the lower criminal courts

Criminal court transformations in the English justice system can be taken back some years to the public service modernisation project of Tony Blair's 'New Labour' government, in power in the UK from 1997. Under his leadership radical alterations were made to the delivery of all public services, including the criminal justice system. Criminal justice reforms continued unabated through the Labour term, with the period now renowned for its heightened toughening of law and order legislation and the criminalisation of a wide range of social activities.

The Conservative/Liberal Democrat coalition that came to power in 2010 continued with significant criminal justice reform, which was also influenced by a particular political and economic ideology. The coalition government entered power with bold ideas for change. In the first instance, there was determination for less and better use of prisons (Ministry of Justice, 2010), and policy documents stated the need for modernisation and replacing outdated systems of delivery. But many of the changes can also be located in the timing of the global financial crisis and the swingeing cuts to public-sector budgets that have come under the austerity politics the Conservative Party has remained committed to.

The recent time period has seen accelerating changes which can be argued as fundamentally altering the way justice is delivered. Some legal and criminal justice scholars, practitioners and civil libertarians have argued that swift justice in the form being pursued has the potential to undermine fair justice. Concerns have been expressed that important due process principles are being weakened and causing problems to the system of fair justice that the UK prides itself for (Chakrabarti, 2014; Morgan, 2008).

To place parameters around my discussions of lower criminal court transformations, the early 2000s can be taken as a starting point. Various important changes occurred at earlier points, but the early 2000s can be taken as a beginning, since this was the period immediately following New Labour's entry into power and when many changes to civil and public life were made. This was nowhere more pronounced than in the area of crime control and criminal justice policy making. The early years of New Labour saw the introduction of the Criminal Justice Act 2003, which brought multiple and also questionable changes to criminal justice procedure, such as the introduction of 'hearsay' and 'bad character' evidence into the trial process, as well as the introduction of caveats to the 'right to remain silent' principle. Indeed, some critics argued that these shifts were examples of a move towards a criminal justice system that was more concerned with crime control and enhancing prosecution powers than ensuring that due process protections were upheld (Sanders *et al.*, 2010). The Criminal Justice Act 2003 also re-categorised criminal offences enabling more cases to be dealt with in the swifter-moving lower-tier magistrates' courts. Offences previously categorised as 'indictable' offences tried only within the higher Crown Courts were reassigned to the 'triable either way' (TEW) category meaning they could be allocated either to the Crown Court or to the lower courts. Various ongoing modifications have limited the rights of defendants to choose which of the courts their case is heard in.

The New Labour government came to power with a particular political ideology of 'communitarianism', which was dominated by a 'rights and responsibilities' agenda in which communities were encouraged to take a personal stake in society in tandem with the obligations to be met by government (Etzioni, 1993). In regard to criminal justice, strong messages of 'closing the justice gap' were delivered, which meant bringing more offenders before the courts and removing the obstacles that hindered convicting the guilty (Sanders *et al.*, 2010), and 'rebalancing the justice system' so that greater attention was paid to the needs of crime victims (H. M. Government, 2002). The period was also important for

Blair's 'third way' politics, which mixed private-sector funding with public state-run services and promoted tightly managed, economically efficient service delivery (McLaughlin *et al.*, 2001; Newburn, 2007).

The early 2000s are also noteworthy in respect to criminal justice alterations because it was the period that Lord Justice Auld's large-scale review of the criminal courts in England and Wales was carried out (Auld, 2001). The remit of the review was for a broad and thorough examination of the workings of the criminal courts. Themes of efficiency, streamlining and modernisation were present in the review's purpose, along with evaluating where improvements could be made in delivering justice fairly, prioritising the rights of crime victims and promoting public confidence. The report stated the review was appraising the courts so that they were:

> modern and in touch with the communities they serve; efficient; fair and responsive to the needs of all their users; co-operative in their relations with other criminal justice agencies; and with modern and effective case management to remove unnecessary delays from the system.
>
> (Ibid.: 1)

Thus, the early 2000s can be seen as a period underpinned by a particular political ideology that saw various alterations to criminal justice service delivery being addressed within notions of modernisation, efficiency and fair justice.

A new, invigorated approach to the criminal justice system was heralded in soon after the Conservative/Liberal Democrat coalition government came to power in 2010. This was set out in the Green Paper *Breaking the Cycle: Effective Punishment, Rehabilitation and Sentencing of Offenders* (Ministry of Justice, 2010) soon after the election and it established the course for a different penal policy than that which had come before under New Labour. The vision was based on a future of projected austerity and financial cuts that were foreseen to all public services including the Ministry of Justice and H. M. Courts Service[2] budgets. This was in the shadow of the global economic downturn and the impact on the nation's finances, but was also linked to the Conservative Party's belief in the 'Big Society'. The Big Society was articulated in the run-up to the 2010 general election as the Conservative Party's key social policy idea. The Big Society as visualised by the Conservatives was for a 'smaller state' with less interference in social and economic governance and giving way to more local innovation in the design and delivery of community and social services. Devolving responsibility and solutions down to local communities was a key defining construct with principles of 'localism' and promoting community involvement (Jennings, 2012). The place of volunteering and building civil society was central to the Conservative Party's image of the 'Big Society' (Edwards, 2012: 2). At the level of the criminal justice system and crime policies this translated into the preference of relying less on imprisonment and more on searching for innovative community-based alternatives delivered by social enterprises, charities and local voluntary organisations.

The severe fiscal tightening and austerity politics in place since the Conservative government came to power in 2010 has meant funding cuts to all public services. The government's commitment to reducing the national fiscal deficit through reductions in public spending has seen a sustained overhaul of the criminal court estate, with different working approaches devised. According to the financial analysis in the report *Future Courts* by the independent Policy Exchange think tank, between the years 2012 and 2016 the court service was faced with a 37.8 per cent reduction to its budget (Chambers *et al.*, 2014)

Alongside the Conservative Party's bold ideas for reforming the criminal justice system and offender rehabilitation and its ambitions for a lowered prison population (Prison Reform Trust, 2011) came ideas for transforming lower criminal court justice. Not long after taking power the White Paper *Swift and Sure Justice* (Ministry of Justice, 2012) was published. This set out pathways for reform and pinpointed areas for modification. The document highlighted the delays within the system being caused by the large numbers of people processed in the magistrates' courts. It was seen that many low-level cases could be dealt with out of court, and that outdated paper-based systems slowed down the timely flow of information between parties and needed revising. Moreover, expanded roles for lay magistrates were considered. These alterations continue to progress and radical transformations in criminal court delivery and case processing can be seen. These are laid out in detail in the following chapter and are transformations that permeate the findings presented though out the book.

Managerial justice and the criminal courts[3]

The concept of managerial justice is central to my analysis of the alterations that are being made within the lower criminal courts. Indeed, several commentators writing on criminal justice and on the increasing priority for services and facilities to be run as streamlined, economically efficient systems link it to the concept of managerial or technocratic justice (Pen, 2015; Bohm, 2006; Freiberg, 2005; Jones, 1993).

Definitions of managerial or technocratic justice incorporate the way business models of management and administration have been incorporated into the operation of criminal justice institutions, in efforts to bring about tightly managed and improved services. Commentators' descriptions of managerial justice emphasise that the three buzzwords, efficiency, effectiveness and economics, are at the core (McEwan, 2011; Raine and Willson, 1993, 1995; McLaughlin *et al.*, 2001). Newburn (2007), in writing on managerialist approaches to public service delivery from the late 1990s in the UK, commented that managerialism introduced the same business acumen seen within private sector-run companies into state-run organisations. He says, 'The perceived attributes of the well-run private sector company (of high efficiency, of explicit accountabilities, of clear objectives, and of measured performance) have increasingly been applied to management in the police, prison and probation services and other agencies' (Raine and Willson, 1993, cited in Newburn, 2007: 553).

Several criminal justice scholars have charted managerial justice developments in the UK and in other jurisdictions, where similar trends are evident, for example in the United States (US), Australia and New Zealand. These typically highlight swift justice initiatives such as tightening criminal court process and procedure, the incentivising of guilty pleas, and the growth in out-of-court administration penalties, all of which bring swifter case processing into lower court practice. Bohm (2006), in writing about 'bureaucratisation' and swift justice in the US, refers to it as the 'McDonaldisation of justice' or 'McJustice' to conjure the image of the conveyor belt and the fast-paced processing of lower court criminal cases. Pen (2015) refers to the technocratic justice landscape of Australia's lower criminal courts. He notes the increased incentivising of guilty plea entries and the growth in out-of-court administration penalties as examples of technocratic justice. These writings often emphasise concerns with the efficient management priorities in the way they too often sacrifice the needs of defendants and impact worryingly on 'vulnerable' defendants (McEwan, 2013; Baldwin and McConville, 1977).

Various critics writing on bureaucratic efficiency in regard to the criminal justice system raise concerns (Corcoran, 2014). Raine and Willson (1993, 1995) questioned whether economic efficiency principles can legitimately be applied to criminal court process. They argued that the application of performance measures in the form of speeding up case progression undermined principles of due process. They pointed out that there are elements of the criminal court process that cannot be put through expedient 'managerialist' values and referred to the 'legality condition', which demands court case processing is 'highly structured, predictable and disciplined' (ibid.: 37). Raine and Willson stressed that managerialism is not as straightforward to achieve in the courts as it might be in other public services. Moreover, they referred to the human rights protections enshrined in European statutes that relate to the fair treatment of accused defendants, such as the 'right to trial' for those who plead not guilty (ibid.: 36) and the right to legal representation. They question managerialism in criminal justice for its capacity to jeopardise human rights and justice, asking, 'Might the steady progress made over many decades regarding human rights be put at risk by managerialist pressures?' (ibid.: 36).

Bell (2011) also connects transformations in the criminal justice system to managerialist public-sector reform. Her work focuses on the dominance of neo-liberal economics by successive governments. She links this, as several authors have, to the enhanced punitiveness of criminal justice policy. A number of researchers associate neo-liberal economics with the punitive crime responses that emerged in 'advanced liberal democracies',[4] such as the expansion in prison populations, the gradually privatising prison estate, the growth in CCTV monitoring and the development of new technologies for assessing increasing categories of 'dangerous' offenders (Stenson and Edwards, 2001). Links are also made between neo-liberalism and the criminal justice roles drawn into the private commercial sector, such as prisoner transport services and, now in the UK, community offender rehabilitation services (Corcoran, 2014). Bell states that 'the penetration of the market logic of neo-liberalism into the criminal justice system and the spread of management ideology has gradually altered the culture of criminal justice services which have become increasingly concerned with narrowly-defined targets' (Bell, 2011: 5).

The earlier arguments of Cook (2006) drew on New Labour's approach to the criminal justice system of managerialism, stating that it 'undermined the independent justice ends of the different criminal justice agencies and that it effectively fetters them to politically determined priorities and policy goals' (ibid.: 177).

Managerial and technocratic justice reforms are at the heart of the changes we have seen in the criminal courts and the alterations that are being cemented in place today, such as the speedy justice initiatives, the enhanced encouragement for early guilty pleas, courthouse closures and the introduction of virtual courts. These can be argued as a radical escalation of the managerialist project, in which due process procedures become questioned, with legitimate reasons for concern. As such, a main theoretical underpinning of the material presented in this book is neo-liberal economics and the application of managerialist models within lower criminal court justice.

The application of neo-liberal economics and its impacts is seen across many advanced liberal democracies. Due to the different values embedded within adversarial systems of justice and continental European inquisitorial styles, comparative analysis is made difficult. But it is the case that criminal court streamlining, in the form of speedy justice initiatives, the expansion in offences categorised as administration offences deemed fit for paper-based and electronic form filling and the pervasiveness of out-of-court penalties, are evidenced in other jurisdictions and for similar purposes of managerialist efficiency and economic savings.

Procedural due process

As is being emphasised, a key concept that can be closely tied to the concepts of managerial justice and which is applied throughout my arguments of criminal court transformation is the issue of procedural due process. A central question asked throughout this book, which shapes my final arguments, is whether due process protections are being undermined by the streamlining processes unfolding within lower criminal court justice. The term 'due process' in relation to criminal justice procedure is usually applied within discourses and interpretations of 'fair justice' and what an accused suspect can expect in terms of system safeguards when faced with criminal prosecution. However, the terms surrounding fair justice vary and are variously applied. The terms 'procedural justice', 'procedural fairness' and 'procedural rights' are used in reference to the fairness of the criminal justice process. Moreover, the work of Tyler (2000, 2008, 2010) has become a dominant reference on the subject. Tyler has conceptualised procedural justice in the way it can be understood in policing, in court decisions and in the 'correctional services'. Tyler draws on principles of social psychology to note that if defendants perceive their experience of procedures within the criminal courts as fair and just they are more likely to comply with the sanctions handed out to them, even if they are not penalties they welcome. Tyler writes about legitimacy within the criminal courts (Tyler, 2008) and argues that court processes deemed fair by the people who experience them are important in terms of adherence and compliance with criminal sanctions. Indeed, Tyler has written extensively on procedural justice and his work is referred to by many authors in critiques of criminal justice process and legitimacy (Kaiser and Holtfreter, 2016; Jacobson *et al.*, 2015; Donoghue, 2014b).

Procedural due process in the way it is applied to my arguments differs from Tyler's application, although my analysis is strongly aligned to his interpretations of fair procedure. I adopt the term 'procedural due process' and apply it in terms of defendants' rights within criminal court processes and procedure. In this way, interest is placed on how it applies to processes and procedures that are – or are not – granted to defendants in the lower criminal court system, such as the right to be tried in an impartial hearing in open court, the right for the accused to know the case against them, the right to legal assistance etc. Galligan (1996) writes about due process and fair procedures. His theories relate it to a doctrine applicable within administrative contexts. Galligan states '... the duty to provide fair procedures comes into play whenever a person is affected by an administrative process' (ibid.: 316) and highlights this in regard to people experiencing legal processes. He says 'procedural fairness is very much concerned with the way persons are treated in legal processes' (ibid.: 52) and that 'legal procedures are fair procedures to the extent that they lead to or constitute fair treatment of the person or persons affected' (ibid.: 52). Galligan argues from the standpoint of political morality and the legal process, referring to the 'hearing principle', the right to be heard, elements such as notice and disclosure, and the right to legal defence.

Heffernan (2000) similarly makes reference to procedural due process in his writing on law administration. His explanation states 'It is concerned with the steps government officials follow when investigating and prosecuting people suspected of committing crimes' (ibid.: 51). Heffernan says that procedural justice is concerned with the fairness of investigative and adjudicative procedures' (ibid.: 51). In the US, from where Heffernan writes, the procedural rights are the same as in the UK and include the right to legal counsel, to receive notice of the criminal charges, to confront adverse witnesses, to be tried by a jury and to not be compelled to self-incriminate (ibid.: 52).

Some jurisdictions have constitutional documents setting out the rights of citizens before the law. The US for example has had a written constitutional charter since 1789. The different articles state the general and judicial rights of citizens, for instance that 'no person be deprived of life, liberty, or property without due process of law' (Brennan, 1985). The UK does not have a published 'penal code' but the principles of fair judicial procedure are enshrined in the UK's democratic governance and application of the 'rule of law'. This dates back to the historic agreements of impartial justice settled in Magna Carta of

1215 (Klug, 2015; Bingham, 2010) and, these days, procedural due process rights as they relate to criminal court process are enshrined in the Human Rights Act 1998. This incorporates values drawn from the European Convention on Human Rights (ECHR) and Article 6 ('the right to a fair trial') contains the protections most relevant to procedural due process in criminal court case hearings. It lists the rights people charged with a criminal offence can expect as being promptly informed, and in detail, of the accusation against him or her, the right to adequate time and facilities to prepare a defence, and the right to defend him/herself, or have legal representation in confronting opposing witnesses. Specifically, the Article leads with the statement 'In the determination of his civil rights and obligations, or of any criminal charge against him, everyone is entitled to a fair and public hearing within a reasonable time by an independent and impartial tribunal established by law' (H. M. Government, 1998: 23).

In addressing the various and escalating changes that are being implemented within the lower criminal courts of the English justice system, questions of whether procedural due process as it relates to accused defendants are being undermined and leading to injustices are asked throughout.

Lay justice in the lower courts

A main focus of my research is on the magistracy and the participation of 'ordinary' citizens in the administration of court justice. As such, a theoretical strand of analysis is the value of lay citizen involvement in criminal law decision-making. Successive governments of the UK have committed to retaining this style of court justice, but, along with the transformations taking place in the lower courts, the magistracy and lay justice are the focus of modernising reforms. It is well-documented within analyses of national criminal court systems that the English approach is unique in its extensive use of lay members of the public to dispense the majority of criminal court work and that this style is not replicated elsewhere across the globe (Donoghue, 2014a; Auld, 2001). Indeed this draws comment from judicial corners, specifically continental European justice systems, which rely mostly on the expertise of legal professionals to conduct criminal court adjudication (Malsch, 2009). In Auld's review of the English criminal courts, he stated that 'no country in the world relies on lay magistrates sitting usually in panels of three, to administer the bulk of criminal justice' as we do in England and Wales (2001: 94). Yet, the conclusions of Auld's review supported belief in this style of citizen involvement in justice administration, and with it accepted that 'the resolution of guilt should continue to be the responsibility of lay magistrates and juries' (Auld, 2001: 13). However, scope for improvement in reflecting the cross-section of society was noted. The issue of diversity among magistrates and thus their community representativeness continue to be criticisms directed at the magistracy (Gibbs and Kirby, 2014). This point is critiqued within my analysis.

Involving lay people in court justice has a long history in the English system, dating back to the development of constitutional parliamentary structures and processes of democracy. The sealing of Magna Carta in 1215 is signified as a defining point in this history, when the sole authority of the monarchy was tempered by the introduction of written rules of law and the right of accused citizens to be tried by their peers (Klug, 2015). The fundamental principles of the rule of law established in Magna Carta underpin justice systems and legal rules across the world.

There are forms of lay participation in other criminal court systems where ordinary people participate in criminal legal decision-making. These are often in mixed tribunals with lay people involved alongside legal professionals (Hans, 2008; Malsch, 2009). In comparison, lay magistrates in the English justice system hold much greater judicial powers than in other jurisdictions. This is in their role of adjudicating in guilt and non-guilt and in the powers they hold in criminal sentencing.

Lay justice in the form of the magistracy is presented as local justice delivered by selected members of the local community to perform in criminal court decision-making. Thus it is conceived of as ordinary members of the public bringing common sense into the navigation and interpretation of the technicalities of the criminal law. Systems of lay justice are held as an example of 'participatory democracy' or 'active citizenship'. Malsch's (2009) research on lay participation in European criminal justice systems says that the democratic argument is in general the strongest one in its favour. Drawing on definitions of democracy, Malsch locates lay participation in legal court decision-making to be illustrative of 'representative democracy'.

The main arguments established in favour of lay legal participation is that it neutralises judicial power and by doing so increases public confidence and enhances transparency and the legitimacy of justice systems. It counterbalances systems that operate on judicial power held in the hands of professional experts who Malsch suggests have been taught 'justice' and may be inclined to bureaucratic decision-making (Malsch, 2009: 4). Malsch's critical review of lay participation in European justices systems rehearses the arguments in favour and finds the view that judging should not be the task of a small 'elite' of professional legal experts. Donoghue (2014a), similarly writing on lay participation specifically in connection to lay magistrates in the English system, presents the existing argument that value lies in magistrates not being legal professionals and that this holds 'technocratic advantage' over guilt and non-guilt decided by a single professional judge. Thus, she says, it provides 'an important check on professional power' (ibid.: 930).

Arguments against the involvement of ordinary lay people lie in the steadfast belief that legal decision-making should be left to legal professionals (Savage and Bretherwick, 2011); that the lay involvement of everyday members of the public slows down the pace of case hearings due to the lack of legal knowledge, the need for explanation and the potential for emotion and opinion to get in the way of judgements (Malsch, 2009). Much of the argument that Malsch draws on relates to lay jurors sitting in a judge-and-jury format called to serve on a one-off basis. This is different to the input of lay magistrates in the English system, who are a core component of the judicial family and are trained to perform impartially in their regular court judging role.

The argument I build in relation to lay justice asks, along with the increasing professionalisation that we see within lower court justice, which is drawn out in the forthcoming chapters, are magistrates effectively lay legal professionals? Malsch (2009: 7) similarly questions the issue of when lay involvement in professional roles crosses over to professional status: 'where does the boundary lie between lay people and professionals' (ibid.: 4)? With my sample of long-serving magistrates, whose court work operates in accordance with tight legal rules, can it be considered that they are essentially lay legal professionals?

Donoghue's (2014a) work discusses the lay magistracy. She maintains that in order to continue an argument in favour of it, the precise value needs to be articulated. She contends, given the significance of the lay magistracy to the English legal system, that the lack of clarity in theorising its worth is surprising and adds that this limits the strength of arguments in favour of its retention (ibid.: 932). Donoghue argues that the lay magistracy is a valuable institution because it embodies 'citizen participation' in justice, but a more substantive justification is needed than a historical legacy (ibid.: 940). She states that there is strength in its preservation being constructed around the commitment to participatory democracy – 'the laity is an intrinsically valuable institution because the role of magistrates is an embodiment of society in the legal process which exists as a direct democratisation of that process' (ibid.: 930).

Lay justice in the international context

Lay involvement in criminal court legal decision-making is currently gaining traction in other jurisdictions (Pedroso and Trincão, 2008; Hans, 2008; Vidmar, 2002; Lempert, 2001). A number of European countries and other nations have introduced a form of trial by jury, with the general arguments for this shift located in notions of legitimacy, and for the power of citizen involvement in tempering the might of the state. In 2009, Japan reintroduced trial by jury, having had a 'judge-only' trial system since the First World War. Wilson (2007) discusses Japan and links this development to the growing distrust of untampered judicial power held in the hands of an 'elite'. Corey and Hans (2010), writing about the Japanese style of jury trial, refer to it as a 'lay judge system' but discuss that it is differentiated from jury trials elsewhere, where lay jurors decide on guilt. The Japanese system is a mixed tribunal and operates with three professional judges and six lay participants arriving at shared judicial decisions. Malsch from her research on lay participation found a variety of criminal justice adjudication systems across the European nations, with some instituting mixed tribunals of lay members working in tandem with legally qualified judges (Malsch, 2009: 6). She sets out how Spain reintroduced trial by jury in recent years and that France has accepted that citizen participation in law administration is a necessary requirement of democracy. Belgium, Malsch says, is 'modifying their system' and in the Netherlands, where law administration is resolutely carried out by legal professionals, a few politicians have advocated introducing a role for lay judges in criminal cases (ibid.: 1).

Moreover, there is action at the European level promoting the importance of lay people involved in dispensing justice. In 2012 the European Day of Lay Judges was initiated, receiving financial support from the European Commission. The foreword in the publication supporting the initiative stated 'The right of participation by the people in dispensing justice is an element of civil emancipation and a fundamental principle in any democratic society' (European Academy Berlin, 2012: 6).

Scholars writing on developments in lay local justice systems and the different form they take also include reference to judicial proceedings in 'transitional justice' in countries rebuilding themselves following internal conflicts, such as the courts in Croatia (Ivkovic, 1999, cited in Hans, 2007). Lay/local justice was the style applied in the community grassroots Gacaca courts in Rwanda following the 1990s genocide, which aimed at the resolution of the many untried cases (Schabas, 2005) and bringing justice and reconciliation to the local community level.

The purpose of including this brief international summary of the growth in citizen participation in legal decision-making is because these developments illustrate a growing belief in the contribution that a non-legally qualified element can add to the quality of the judging process. However, questions are also asked on whether the inclusion of lay people in judicial systems is merely 'window dressing'. Hans (2007) queries whether a 'patina of democratic participation masks authority that lies elsewhere', or whether it really does add to legitimate justice (Hans, 2007: 304). Also, some commentators raise human rights concerns in connection to judging that takes place in informal lay justice systems and the potential for issues of unchecked power (Jackson and Kovalev, 2006; Delgado *et al.*, 1985).

Indeed, as some countries shift from judicial systems operated by legal professionals to enhanced styles of lay justice others veer towards systems of professional justice. Harkness (2009, 2015), writing on the history of the lay magistracy in New Zealand, refers to the political move in the 1950s that transferred powers and decision-making from what was a lay justice system modelled on the English style to a professional judiciary. New Zealand's court structure maintains a lay involvement in lower court adjudication, but courtroom proceedings are primarily managed by legally qualified judges sitting alone.

The attention paid in this book to the participation and contribution of the lay magistracy adds to the discussion on international lay justice and the wider public benefits that citizen participation can bring to national democracies and state governance. It is possible to apply the positive arguments put forward in favour of the lay justice role performed by magistrates in the English justice system to this broader representative democracy ideal.

The interview material provided by the magistrates in the following chapters provides their views on the value of lay local justice and the contribution and strength they as members of the community bring to the criminal justice process.

Connected to this is my argument that we are witnessing an increasing professionalisation of lower court justice. This is in evidence in a range of ways, but particularly in the managerial changes occurring to court working practice and the expectations on the lay magistrates working within them. The introduction of more uniform approaches to court sentencing in the application of sentencing guidelines can be added. Others have identified this professionalising trend in lower court justice (Donoghue, 2014a; Herbert, 2004). With this my argument considers the point Malsch (2009) sets out: at what point does a lay person become a professional and are lay magistrates effectively lay legal professionals?

Conceptualising social justice within criminal justice

Another key theme applied within the material presented in the following chapters, which links closely to my empirical research, is the concept of social justice and its interconnection with criminal justice. Several writers connect social justice and indeed injustice to criminal justice. Here the conceptual framework in relation to these ideas and how it can be applied in my research are introduced. It is a fact that lower criminal court defendants are significantly represented by society's most marginalised people, whose lives and lifestyles of poverty, homelessness, drug and alcohol addiction, mental ill-health and vulnerability are entwined with offending activity.

Reference to social justice permeates much discourse on society, in philosophies on the ideal values of society and in the search for causes of societal failings. Social justice was a core value placed at the centre of New Labour's political ideology of 'communitarianism' and the rights and responsibilities agenda embarked upon under that government. To some extent, social justice ideals were evident in the Conservative Party's policy ideas on the Big Society, although the reality is a starkly opposite one. Barry (2005) is a renowned social justice theorist. He assesses that, despite much reference to social justice in political discourse, its meaning and application lack clarity. He states that there is an 'absence of an explicit conception of social justice in political life' (ibid.: 10).

Writings on social justice note various interpretations, but for the purposes of my discussions the meaning provided by Barry (2005) is useful. Barry, in his book *Why Social Justice Matters*, refers to the work of John Rawls, who defined social justice as 'the basic structure of society' (Barry, 2005: 16). Barry states that this basic structure can be understood as 'constituted by the major institutions that allocate (or bring about the allocation of) rights, opportunities and resources' (ibid.: 16). Essentially, what is considered in this interpretation is the way in which rights, opportunities and resources are distributed across society. Barry says that social justice is about the treatment of inequalities of all kinds and pays attention to how social injustice is brought about through differential resource allocation and opportunity.

Similarly, Heffernan and Kleinig (2000) discuss the definition of social justice/social injustice and broadly define it as 'the requisites of a justly constituted society' (ibid.: 1). Heffernan incorporates concepts of social justice into understandings of criminal justice. Heffernan (2000) offered three models of social justice but prioritised a 'social welfare model' in his connection of social justice to criminal justice. Heffernan considered the unequal distribution of resources and the concentration of poverty and disadvantage among court defendants. Within his theoretical arguments he asked questions of whether social conditions can be a source for the application of the 'excuse defence', most typically applied in cases of insanity (ibid.: 62). Central to the conceptualisation Heffernan draws on are the theories he cites of Judge Bazelon (Bazelon, 1976, cited in Heffernan, 2000: 55), who argued that court decision-makers should be allowed to consider the personal mitigation of what Bazelon called a defendant's 'rotten social background' in passing judgement. Heffernan writes that the 'rotten social background' defence Bazelon considered is rooted in experiences of disorderly childhood, poverty, fatherlessness, racial oppression and emotional illness, etc.

The collection of essays published in *From Social Justice to Criminal Justice*, edited by Heffernan and Kleinig (2000), address the ethical dilemmas in the administration of criminal law aligned to the disproportionate numbers of economically deprived people in the USA who come into contact with the criminal court system. Heffernan (2000) intersects social justice and criminal justice (ibid.: 49) and takes forward a theoretical discussion presenting the question of whether those who have been deprived of the fair distribution of resources in society should be allowed to use a justification or an excuse defence. Heffernan's work is central to the theory developed within my work, in the way that we can conceptualise elements of social justice within the context of the lower criminal courts.

Cook (2006) has also focused on the interconnectedness and interdependence of social justice issues within criminal justice. She focused on the discourse of social justice within New Labour's political leadership and their ambition to reduce social exclusion as a means of strengthening communities and embedding an appreciation of citizen rights and responsibilities. Cook's analysis combined the two policy domains of social policy and criminal justice policy. Cook (2006) noted the New Labour government's pledge to social justice, but also the different experiences of certain groups in respect to criminal justice with an emphasis on the disparity between the advantaged and the disadvantaged, between ethnicities and between the vulnerable and the successful. Barry (2005) also brought together the situation of particularly disadvantaged groups connected with criminal justice in his discussions of social justice and injustice. His book included a chapter titled 'The Making of the Black Gulag', which documented the explosive imprisonment trajectory for large numbers of African American young men from the 1990s.

In my research, themes of social disadvantage and criminal court justice are linked to concepts of rehabilitative sentencing and the introduction of specialist problem-solving approaches that are being developed across different jurisdictions and in the English justice system with certain groups of offenders, specifically drug-dependent and young offenders. These areas are discussed in detail in

Chapter 6. There is a vast literature on the different problem-solving court models, which connects to the growth in popularity in this style of justice, as evidenced in the drug and alcohol courts, mental health courts and family violence courts that have been developed across different jurisdictions. In drawing on the arguments of certain social justice critics, the idea is put forward in this book that the lower criminal courts can play a role in the embedding of social justice principles.

Much of the material presented in the following chapters has been generated through empirical research with lay magistrates and criminal justice professionals employed in different agencies of the English justice system. The following section sets out my research methodology.

Research methodology

The research has comprised different methods, including documentary analysis of criminal justice policy and legislation and statistical analyses of Ministry of Justice data sets recording court case profiles and sentencing outcomes. Research interviews were carried out through focus groups and in one-to-one interviews with 33 lay magistrates working in the adult and youth criminal courts of the English court system. Key informants working in different criminal justice agencies whose work intersects with the operation of the courts such as police representatives, lawyers and youth offending team staff were interviewed. They provided insights from their professional perspectives relating to the alterations occurring in lower court justice. Table 1.1 sets out the research sample.

Three focus group interviews were held, with six or seven magistrates participating in each group ($n=20$). An additional 13 magistrates were engaged in one-to-one interviews. In line with the broad aims of my research, the main questions put to the magistrates within the focus groups and individual interviews broadly focused on how the transformations to lower criminal court operation were impacting on their day-to-day work, what motivated them to perform in this voluntary judicial role, how they viewed their contribution to lay justice, some general views on crime and the predominant status of the people being processed within the lower criminal courts. The 13 individual interviews were set up to boost the overall sample, but were also undertaken to shape the involvement of more recently recruited magistrates. The research was going on at a point when there was activity within the recruitment of lay magistrates connected to the

Table 1.1 Research sample

Interviewees

Lay magistrates: 33
Professional judges: 2
Criminal defence lawyer: 1
Police professionals: 3
Youth Offending Team staff: 5

---

ambition to engage a more diverse magistracy with a younger representation. A dominant theme in discussions on the lay magistracy is its limited diversity (Gibbs and Kirby, 2014), with a general enthusiasm for enhancing this across a range of domains. Since I was conscious that there had been concerted efforts to recruit a younger and more varied group of volunteers to the lay magistracy, further sample selection was imposed to include those recruited to the lay justice role in the recent time period. Six of the 33 magistrates interviewed can be classified as younger, newer recruits to the magistracy and receive particular mention for some differences identified among them and their outlook.

A brief questionnaire collected socio-demographic information from each of the participating magistrates. This provided general, social, professional and personal background detail. The formal fieldwork period in which the focus groups and individual interviews were carried out was between May 2014 and December 2015. Aside from a small support grant, awarded through Middlesex University's School of Law, the research was conducted as an unfunded study.

The research interviews were carried out in three geographic areas of England. Three 'bench areas'[5] were chosen to represent a London bench (thereby including magistrates working in a large, busy metropolitan city court), a bench area of a smaller but largely populated English city, and a county bench area including magistrates sitting in courthouses in more sparsely populated regional areas. The bench areas were chosen for their difference in location and possible variance in the profile of serving magistrates, the nature of the cases being processed and the magistrates' experiences relating to the changes occurring to lower court justice, which might be more pronounced in some locations than in others. The overall sample size is small, thus making any real comparison difficult beyond subtle differences, but it is insightful for the range of lay justices experiences across the regions.

Anyone attempting to conduct research with members of the judiciary through official channels will be aware of the difficulties presented. This is in the lengthy permission process, but mostly in the resistance that can be experienced. Researchers with judicial actors have noted the problems in negotiating through the formal routes of the court service. Baldwin (2008) writes on the complications faced with researching the judiciary, with the authority of 'judicial independence' shielding them from the enquiring questions of researchers. Baldwin notes how the judiciary are not amenable to being researched, but that there appeared to be some loosening in access alongside the government's demand for evidence-based policy. Baldwin adds that there are some studies that have secured access to the judiciary but infers that it has been achieved through privileged access or by bending the rules – 'researchers have devised imaginative strategies in order to overcome the access problems' (ibid.: 376). Indeed, my application for a larger study, on the same topic as that written about in this book, remained for many months within the court access and permission system and was eventually rejected. Owing to the timeliness of my research enquiry, insofar as it coincided with the widespread reforms occurring to lower court justice, I decided to proceed with it but on a smaller scale and using a different access approach.

Thus, my route to recruit serving magistrates shifted to draw upon the assistance offered by the Magistrates' Association (MA), as well as using my own personal contacts. The Magistrates' Association is the independent organisation representing serving magistrates in England and Wales and access to the magistrates in the three bench areas was gratefully facilitated by them. According to the Magistrates' Association's website, membership of the association comprises 80 per cent of serving magistrates. The chairs of the three bench areas were used to organise the focus groups in their area.

In using this access approach, a convenience and purposive sampling frame was applied (Bryman, 2012), with those magistrates who were willing to participate being included. In line with the small sample size and convenience sampling methods, the sample cannot be considered representative of the serving magistrate population. However, male and female magistrates, magistrates serving in London and other parts of the country, from varied age profiles, different lengths of service and with a wide range of social and professional backgrounds were all included. More detail is given in Chapter 4 on the profile of the magistrates involved, but it is considered that those who took part and provided accounts of their experiences in light of the various transformations are a close reflection of the wider pool of serving magistrates. The experiences of my sample will not be unique.

Two focus groups were held at the premises of the magistrates' court in which the participating magistrates were employed and the other was carried out in an office of a local court service building. The 13 individual interviews were carried out in various locations at the convenience of the magistrates. These included their private homes, cafes, my place of work and one magistrate's place of work. Three of the 33 magistrates participated in a follow-up interview connected to their specialist and youth justice expertise. This is drawn out in Chapter 6 in my discussions of the way social justice elements are embedded within the context of lower criminal court work.

The criminal justice professionals who were interviewed included three police employees involved in virtual court styles of operation that had been established in their policing areas. Virtual courts function by arrested suspects being produced in court via live video link from police custody; this is an advancing style of court operation in the UK in this current modernising period. The head of a criminal defence legal firm was interviewed for his experience in representing legally aided defendants and insights on recent restrictions to eligibility. Two professional judges employed in different lower courts were interviewed. These were recruited through personal contacts. Staff from a local youth offending team were also interviewed for the sentence review work they were engaging in with young offenders. A group of youth court magistrates participating in one of the focus groups was a part of this initiative.

These interviews with criminal justice professionals were carried out in their various places of work. The police professionals were interviewed on police station premises, which enabled workplace observation and an introduction to the video link technology being used to remotely connect defendants from police custody to the courts. The legal defence manager was interviewed at his offices with the busy bustle of legal defence advocacy work going on in the background. The two district judges were interviewed in the courts they work in. These court- and work-based interviews added an ethnographic element to the research and provided a sense of the working environment in which law and justice adminis- tration goes on.

Courtroom observations also formed an important method in my research. Observations were carried out in different London magistrates' courts, with repeat observations in one busy north London court. These are drawn upon and descriptively analysed in Chapter 3. Courtroom observations are a rich method and provide opportunities to see court justice in action. The observational material provides a lived experience of the courthouse as a crime control institu- tion, as well as the way rules, rituals, power dynamics and emotions are played out within the courtroom space. The observations were systematically docu- mented, noting detail on the type of offences coming before the courts, the general life circumstances of the people appearing within them, the overall atten- tion given to individual defendants in terms of the time given to their case hear- ings and the pleas entered and sentences dispensed.

In addition to the formal interview approach, my research has been informed through many informal conversations held over the years with people employed in criminal justice institutions, serving in court as lay justices or professional judges, in legal defence services and in the prosecution service. This has involved communications in the UK and abroad through personal contacts, 'snowballing' and attendance at various criminal justice conferences. The Crim- inal Justice Management conference held in London in 2015 was particularly useful for the opportunity to hear from parliamentarians and court executives on the UK government's onward strategy in moving forth with criminal justice modernisations, as well for the discussions it enabled with the lay magistrates in attendance and with people working in the Crown Prosecution Service (CPS) and in the criminal defence services. These are also embedded within the material set out in the forthcoming chapters.

Another dimension was added to the empirical data collection in the way I was able to become involved with an informal problem-solving justice initiative with young offenders in one of the court areas. As noted, a few magistrates in one focus group were involved with their local youth offending team (YOT) in implementing this problem-solving approach. Two review panels involving the input of the magistrates were observed. This initiative is explained in detail in Chapter 6, but between January and April 2015 a brief evaluation was carried out by myself and a criminology master's student at Middlesex University. The findings from this evaluation are published in Ward and Warkel (2015).

The book's content is located within a socio-legal theoretical framework in which the court observations and narratives of lay magistrates advance an appre- ciation of daily courtroom activity and illustrate the contribution they make to legal decision-making in the contemporary period; it explores their views, experiences and perceptions of the lay value they bring to justice administration.

My standpoint is one of a belief in citizen involvement in legal decision-making, and that there is much worth in lay justice and using ordinary members of the community to participate in court adjudication and sentencing.

Structure of the book

The following chapter is a critical review chapter setting out some of the key alterations occurring to summary justice within the lower criminal courts and that fit within notions of modernisation. It centres on speedy justice initiatives that promote quicker case progression; the closure and amalgamation of criminal courts across the English justice system; the enhanced encouragement for early guilty pleas; the growing development of virtual courts; and changes in eligibility for legal aid provision. Throughout this chapter it is asked whether due process protections are being undermined alongside modernisation and efficiency transformations.

Chapter 3 provides an overview of the magistrates' courts; the high volume and broad range of cases processed within them; the vast and varied decision-making roles magistrates hold; and the sentencing powers they preside over. It presents research material drawn from courtroom observations to give an impression of the lower courts in action and the real-life cases of the defendants appearing within them. It emphasises the function of the magistrates' courts as the 'workhorse' of the criminal justice system (Sanders *et al.*, 2010: 500) and the importance of taking an interest in justice administration within the lower court context.

Chapter 4 is the main empirical chapter. It draws on the interviews with lay magistrates and discusses their views on the changing nature of summary justice and on the role and value of lay citizen participation in legal decision-making. It includes general background information on the magistrates interviewed to illustrate their broad social and professional lives, what motivated them to take on this judicial volunteering role and their general experiences of performing judicial work in the lower courts of the criminal justice system.

Chapter 5 continues to draw on the magistrates' interviews and addresses what can essentially be interpreted as a changing occupational culture. It discusses how the altering work practices within the lower courts amount to the increasing professionalisation of lower court justice and looks at how magistrates are adapting to the enhanced expectations on them. The chapter moves to consider notions of lay versus professional justice and considers the contradictions that are being introduced into definitions of lay local justice.

In Chapter 6, notions of social justice as it can be connected to criminal justice are explored. In doing so, alternative styles of justice administration are discussed, such as the development of specialist and problem-solving courts across a number of jurisdictions including in the UK, the USA, Australia, New Zealand and elsewhere. Specialist problem-solving court approaches are being established in the English justice system, and a role for lay magistrates has been raised in association with them. The chapter leads into a discussion on social justice principles and how they can be applied and incorporated into understandings of the lower courts and the administration of justice within them.

The concluding chapter summarises the main arguments of the book and moves into revisiting and appraising whether a lay involvement in legal decision-making is a valuable style and whether some of the alternative approaches being put forward, such as specialist courts and problem-solving courts are useful ways to think about the future for criminal justice. My argument is that these are a more sensible form of court administration for certain offender types in the way they help to address the underlying causes of individual offending. The question of what price is justice is asked and a critical appraisal is made of the emphasis currently being placed on economic efficiency within the criminal courts. It argues there are aspects of court adjudication that should not be open to economic equation.

Notes

1 'Transforming Summary Justice' (TSJ) was launched as an initiative in the English criminal justice system in 2014 with the objective of coordinating the separate agencies in efficient case processing (H. M. Crown Prosecution Service Inspectorate, 2016). Although this book carries the same title, the TSJ initiative is not the focus.
2 The official title of the court service of England and Wales is Her Majesty's Courts and Tribunal Service (HMCTS). Throughout the text it is mainly referred to as the court service.
3 An earlier version of this section was published as Ward, J. (2015) Transforming Summary Justice through Police-led Prosecution and Virtual Courts – Is 'Procedural Due Process' Being Undermined? *British Journal of Criminology*, 55, 2, 341–358. I would like to thank the *British Journal of Criminology* and Oxford University Press for their kind permission to reproduce the text.
4 See for example Cavadino *et al.*, 2013, 2008; Wacquant, 2009; Lacey, 2008; Pratt *et al.*, 2005; Garland, 2001; O'Malley, 2008.
5 The bench areas, courts and magistrates are not identified.

2 Transformations to lower court summary justice

In keeping with the book's focus as set out in the introduction, this chapter provides an overview of some key alterations that are currently occurring in the lower criminal courts. Transformations within the courts have been various and multiple, and have been found in the different criminal justice agencies whose work intersects with the criminal courts: the police, the prosecution service, the legal defence profession and probation services. Summary justice alterations have been in a transformative state for some decades, but this chapter addresses changes in the present period which are fundamentally changing the way justice is delivered.

The chapter frames these changes within themes of public service modernisation and ambitions to run a criminal court system operating to the demands of the twenty-first century, which includes building streamlining and efficiency savings into the system. The changes described are the defining features of managerial justice. Managerial justice is the dominant model we have seen unfolding in the UK and elsewhere, and is evidenced in the many cost and efficiency savings being made to criminal court service delivery (Ministry of Justice, 2011b; The Conservative Party, 2010, 2015; O'Malley, 2008; Bohm, 2006; Freiberg, 2005; Raine and Willson, 1993).

The changes discussed in this chapter are the different speedy justice initiatives implemented over the years in efforts to quicken the pace at which cases move through the criminal court system: the amalgamation and closure of criminal courthouses as part of a court rationalisation project since 2011 and the introduction of virtual courts and the increasing use of live link technology in courtroom hearings (Ward, 2015; Mulcahy, 2008, 2011). The chapter focuses on changes within the English justice system, but similar modernising, streamlining and efficiency developments have been emerging in other jurisdictions (Haarhuis and Niemeijer, 2006), which are similarly located within models of managerial justice and reformed public service management. This can be seen in the growth of out-of-court administration offences in continental European countries, where some lower-range offences are assigned to office-based and online administration systems (Jehle and Wade, 2006), virtual court and live link developments in the Netherlands etc. It is not possible in this book to review the patterns of change in other jurisdictions, although reference is made to some throughout.

There are many interlinked ways in which streamlining criminal court process and procedure have been occurring, but the areas of change focused upon in this chapter are what can be considered dominant and significant with regard to the everyday working of the criminal courts and to the magistrates dispensing justice within them. The changes discussed in this chapter are also relevant to the interview data collected from serving magistrates, judges, police and other criminal justice professionals reported in the following chapters. The interviews with serving magistrates enquired into the changing demands placed upon them in their courtroom role, such as the requirements to ensure tighter case management, the impact of courthouse closures on them, as well as on defendants, and acclimatising to the enhanced use of digitised technologies being used within courtroom proceedings. In presenting these altered modernising and streamlined forms of criminal court process, this chapter examines the extent to which procedural due process is being adhered to. Attention is drawn by many critics to areas of the criminal justice system where 'crime control' mechanisms are being enhanced at the expense of due process protections (see Ward, 2015; Ashworth and Zedner, 2014; Chakrabarti, 2014; Hallsworth and Lea, 2011; Sanders *et al.*, 2010).

In order to place parameters around what have been multiplying alterations within the lower criminal court environment (Garside and Ford, 2015), the focus in this chapter is upon the areas mentioned and the current governmental discourse and ambition for developing and delivering public services within modern and efficient systems of management (Leveson, 2015a, 2015b).

Speedy justice

One area of change occurring to lower criminal court business which sits within processes of streamlining and economic efficiency and is indicative of managerial justice models is the implementation of speedy justice initiatives. Speedy justice initiatives introduce formalised approaches into the management of criminal court case processing in efforts to quicken the pace at which cases move through the system. They centre on reducing the number of times a case is adjourned on its way to trial, placing time limits on how long a case should take to reach conclusion from the point of arrest to either conviction or acquittal, and extracting guilty pleas from defendants who are guilty at the earliest possible stage in the process. All parties involved are encouraged to contribute to the ideals of speedy justice and swifter process, including the police, the prosecution service, defendants, defence lawyers and magistrates and judges.

Various campaigns have been implemented within the English court system over the years aligned to the concept of speedy justice. In 2007 the 'Criminal Justice: Simple, Speedy, Summary' (CJSSS) initiative was launched (Leveson, 2007; Department for Constitutional Affairs, 2006). In a form similar to CJSSS, in 2012 the 'Stop Delaying Justice' initiative was introduced, and further activity came in 2014 with alterations made to the Criminal Procedure Rules (CPR). This embedded tight and active case management into criminal court administration.

Specifically, CJSSS called for a reduction in the number of adjournments granted in cases, on average four to five per case, and time limits of between one day and six weeks were set for cases to reach completion. Similarly, the 'Stop Delaying Justice' initiative was rolled out across court service areas to reinvigorate tighter time frames between arrest and trial, and had principles of fairness at the core. This is in the way time delays in the justice process in the form of multiple and possibly unnecessary adjournments are considered unfair on crime victims as well as on innocent defendants.

Leaving aside arguments of cost burden, a dominant concern emerging with the delay and backlogs in the system is the issue of fair justice. Here, an emphasis is placed on the injustice to crime victims, witnesses and their families, if they are kept waiting for long periods to recall evidence in court and for perpetrators of crime to be brought to justice (Leveson, 2015a; Department of Constitutional Affairs, 2006). Over the years the needs of crime victims have progressively been strengthened, with greater attention paid to the way they experience the criminal justice process. Effectively addressing the needs of victims also helps ensure public confidence is maintained in the system. Delays in the system are also unfair for defendants who live with unresolved cases hanging over their head, especially if remanded into prison custody to await trial or bailed in the community with the imposition of restrictions like home curfews, denial of contact with family members and limitations on where they can reside. The H. M. Inspectorate of Prisons report *Remand Prisoners: A Thematic Review* (2012) notes that on average 15 per cent of the prison population are remand prisoners awaiting trial and that on average the time spent on remand is nine weeks. Finding ways to minimise delays is evidently of paramount importance.

The degree of importance placed upon the timeliness of court hearings for accused people is apparent in the constitutional documents of the USA. Feeley (1983) notes the 'right to a speedy and public trial' under the Sixth Amendment of the constitution (ibid.: 156). Feeley's book *Court Reform on Trial* gives his evaluation of various court reforms in the early 1980s in the American criminal justice system. The introduction of the 'speedy trial rules' and the Speedy Trial Act of 1974 is one reform focused on. In the same way as referred to in the more recent initiatives of the English justice system, these implemented tighter time management rules into statute and placed managerial oversight onto criminal case progression, with sanctions imposed for failure. Feeley noted the backlash from the judiciary, based on what was perceived as interference with the principle of 'judicial independence' and a 'violation of the theory of the separation of powers' (ibid.: 164) between the executive and the judiciary. The separation of powers between the executive government and the independent judiciary is a central principle of democratic governance. Feeley also noted the opposition to the introduction of timing rules by defence lawyers. This related to the argument that time is often needed for defence counsel to mount credible evidence on behalf of accused defendants. However, it was also noted that defence counsel can benefit from delay in terms of financial remuneration for casework based on lengthy time input. Feeley highlighted the defence counsel argument against this with their interpretation that the speedy trial rules pressed for early guilty pleas (ibid.: 175). In this regard, Feeley cites one defence spokesperson who labelled it the 'Speedy Conviction Act' (ibid.: 165).

In line with the recent renewed interests around criminal court efficiencies, both from a monetary cost saving perspective and a timeliness of justice perspective, the CPR 2014 stipulate how cases in the magistrates' courts and Crown Courts should be 'actively managed' by a court officer so that they achieve the least number of appearances in court as possible. In English legislation the CPR were first established under the Courts Act 2003[1] and lay out the duty of the courts and criminal court actors in the preparation of criminal cases for hearing. In addition to the issue of timeliness, this includes an obligation to adhere to the overriding procedural justice aim of dealing with cases 'justly'. Stipulations supporting this objective refer to the criminal justice system goals of acquitting the innocent and convicting the guilty and recognising the fundamental rights of the defendant in line with Article 6 of the European Convention on Human Rights. This deals with the right to a fair trial and having cases dealt with efficiently and expeditiously. The Rules refer specifically to discouraging delay and dealing with as many aspects of the case as possible on the same occasion to avoid unnecessary hearings. The Rules stipulate giving direction and where appropriate nominating a court officer for directing what must be done in case preparation, by whom and when, in particular by the early setting of a timetable for case progression.

From the interviews carried out with serving magistrates as a part of this research, it was evident that respondents recognised the importance of achieving swift, speedy justice and efficient case management. Some magistrates said that courtroom case management had become more demanding in the recent period and when contrasted to their previous role functions:

> The Chairmen in particular of the bench are expected to manage the case management; they are expected to manage decisions of adjournments, numbers of witnesses, set directions. That is quite different to the work we did before, and it is quite detailed as well.
>
> (Male, aged 53, 12 years' service)

If we take the criticisms made by Feeley (1983) regarding the speedy trial rules where defendant's cases can be rushed to trial and completion within a specified time frame, possibly without all the components in place, then disadvantages are apparent with this directed, timed approach. Some magistrates expressed concern with the pressure in pushing forward cases when they are not fully prepared or where the defendant is not entirely aware of what is going on. For instance, the availability of important, potentially exonerating evidence that needs to be relied upon could be missing. One magistrate commented on these risks specifically with the directive of seeking the defendant's plea at the first court hearing when sometimes the necessary paperwork is not yet in order:

they haven't got enough information to proceed or the CCTV isn't quite ready, or they haven't been able to track down certain witnesses. And under the European Convention of Human Rights everybody has the right to a fair trial, and yet if the paperwork hasn't been finalised, then the attitude is 'oh well, we'll go ahead anyway'. So in a way I believe that a person isn't being treated fairly. It's too rushed as it were. I know we cannot delay justice, but then again I feel as though with making a plea on the first hearing, it could actually hinder a person's right to a fair trial.

(Female, aged 59, 20 years' service)

In pursuing speedy justice initiatives and quicker case progression, it was noted that particular types of defendants, especially vulnerable defendants who may not be sufficiently aware of the ramifications of the guilty plea or even understand proceedings, are disadvantaged. Sanders and Young (2007) comment that the 'innocent who belong to marginalised populations tend to suffer more from plea bargaining than privileged defendants' (ibid.: 433). In addition, there might be a need to seek a mental health assessment before passing judgement as this magistrate comments:

I think it's important both for the person that's committed the crime and for the victims of the crime, for that to come to justice speedily, so I think speedy justice is good, but it's got to be justice.... If a case for example needs a report, perhaps you suspect that somebody has mental health problems or something like that, then there is pressure to try and get an outcome to the case, whereas to me it's important.... If this person has got mental health problems, let's find out what they are. Did it impact on the offence and should it impact on the sentence?... You've probably heard it from my colleagues there's an awful lot of people in prison that have got mental health problems that really ought to be in some kind of mental support units. So I think speedy justice has got to be, the underlined word has got to be 'justice' and if you can do it speedily then all the better.

(Male, aged 62, 12 years' service)

It was also noted under these speedy justice alterations that pressures not to adjourn cases except when absolutely necessary mean some defendants are able to 'walk away' without the case against them being presented. This was referred to in situations where the prosecution service has not received the necessary police evidence to support the accusation against the person. In such cases magistrates are obliged to discharge the case from court. They referred to this as a flaw in the way some people 'get off' within the swifter case management processes being promoted.

Guilty pleas

Linked to the speedy justice initiatives and aims to streamline and remove delays from the court process is the enhanced encouragement of 'early guilty pleas' (Leveson, 2015a). Extracting timely guilty pleas from defendants is seen as an important contribution in reducing many of the time-consuming aspects of contested cases from the system. System efficiency of this type is what Packer (1968) had in mind in his conception of the criminal justice system. He described 'two separate value systems that compete for priority in the operation of the criminal process' (ibid.: 153). The 'crime control model' is at one end ('conveyor belt'), emphasising the need for the efficient control of crime, the processing of criminal activity, limiting legal technicalities and encouraging guilty pleas. The 'due process model' is at the other end, which emphasises the rights of suspects within the prosecution process (the 'obstacle course').

The earliest point at which someone accused of a criminal offence can indicate their acceptance of guilt is at the point of police arrest, and over the years different ways to extract these in a more timely fashion have been introduced. In both the magistrates' courts and the Crown Courts the rate of guilty pleas is high, with around 65 per cent to 70 per cent of all cases being resolved through guilty pleas at some point in the proceedings. The figure is in the region of 90 per cent if motoring offences are included.

Several commentators write on the particularity of common-law systems in which the formal entry of guilty or not guilty pleas is embedded and which greatly facilitates the system in terms of relieving administrative pressures (Cheng, 2013; Roach Anleu and Mack, 2009; Baldwin and McConville, 1977; Bottoms and McClean, 1976). Cheng (2013), writing on lower criminal court operation in Hong Kong, notes the reliance of common-law justice systems on high rates of guilty pleas like those of the UK, US, Canada, New Zealand, Australia and Hong Kong. Moreover, Cheng finds it is the early resolution to a case that is found to encourage admissions of guilt and guilty plea entries. He notes from his research that 'overall defendants plead guilty to terminate as quickly as possible "the punishment" of being caught up in the criminal justice system' (ibid.: 257). Worthy of mention here is Feeley's (1992) criminal court research, published under the evocative tile of *The Process is the Punishment*. This specifically emphasises the lengthy, indefinite and doubtless stressful route to case conclusion through the criminal court process. Many commentators argue the system's pressures to plead guilty undermine due process (Ashworth and Redmayne, 2010; Ericson and Baranek, 1982). Cheng (2013) and Ashworth and Redmayne (2010) comment that, within this process of incentivising and achieving high rates of guilty pleas, the prosecution is not required to put its evidence to the test. Bottoms and McClean's research (1976) on the decision-making of criminal defendants in the lower courts in Sheffield in the 1970s included the decision on how to plead as one of the crucial decision points. But they reported from their sample that a significant proportion pleaded guilty because they were in fact guilty.

Similar findings are revealed in criminal court statistics from other jurisdictions, reflecting both the willingness of defendants to accept guilt, but acknowledging even in disputed cases that the system is weighted towards encouraging defendants to waive rights of contest and bring forth guilty pleas (Pen, 2015). In the English justice system there is massive encouragement for defendants to plead guilty, and to do so at the earliest point in the process, since it is officially incentivised through the 'sentence discount principle'. This was enacted in the Criminal Justice Act 2003, where a reduction in sentence for early guilty pleas was established in statute. Ashworth and Redmayne (2010) illustrate this – 'In E&W the law provides a strong incentive to plead guilty, in a provision that now appears in s144 of the Criminal Justice Act 2003' (ibid.: 291). The system is actually designed to encourage a high rate of guilty pleas.

In a similar way it was acknowledged by the magistrates interviewed that the speedy justice initiatives are problematic for people with vulnerabilities, such as those who have mental health issues or learning difficulties, requesting pleas to be entered at first hearing was also mentioned as troublesome:

> we do have the occasional person who's got mental health issues and people with learning difficulties. We do get people like that in adult court and … I think they are just pushed into it and they are told what to do whether they like it or not. They need the help and the guidance more than people like you and I. We can actually think for ourselves and we're confident enough to be able to say no I'm pleading not guilty to this, because you know that you weren't there and it wasn't you. But there might be some people who are at a disadvantage who feel that they're being coerced into pleading guilty.
>
> (Female, aged 59, 20 years' service)

In looking to other jurisdictions similarly going through processes of modernisation and efficiency savings within the lower courts, comparable streamlining efforts can be seen. For example, in New Zealand the 2011 Criminal Procedure Act (CPA) made several procedural alterations, such as restricting defendants' rights to the lengthier and more costly trial by jury. This move is intended to exclude cases in which the sentence would be less than two years in prison and to allocate these to a 'judge-only trial'. The CPA also introduced elements of administrative justice in the way guilty pleas to low-level criminal offences punishable by monetary penalties can be filed by post or email.[2] Such shortcuts, which essentially remove the time and hassle incurred in having to turn up at court, could provide inducements for people to plead guilty for the same reason that Cheng (2013), Baldwin and McConville (1977) and numerous other writers note defendants do: to get the case over and done with. The offences mostly included in this administrative category in New Zealand are driving offences,[3] but also public disorder criminal activity in 'offensive and disorderly behaviour' and 'fighting in public' charges. A concern is that progressively more serious cases will come to be resolved in this administrative way. This development mirrors the way certain offences in European jurisdictions are categorised as administration offences and are processed out of court as a paper-based exercise rather than being adjudicated through the courts (Jehle and Wade, 2006). As such, if the person pleads guilty the case is disposed of administratively. Shifts mirroring this streamlined office-based criminal court case processing are emerging in the English criminal justice system.

Criminal court closure and amalgamation

Another feature of the modernisation project being directed at lower criminal court operation is the widespread closure and amalgamation of courthouses across the country. Matching the promised reform of public services as laid out in the 2010 Conservative Party manifesto, along the lines of cultivating 'higher productivity' and the efficient use and management of resources, the closure of a number of courthouses across cities and towns of England and Wales can be identified as a feature. The Courts Estate Rationalisation Programme (CERP), as it was officially titled, began in July 2009, when 286 magistrates' courts across England and Wales existed. In June 2015, the number of lower-tier courthouses stood at 195, 91 fewer than were in operation in 2009.[4] The court service divides its estate into seven regions – Midlands, North West, North East, South East, South West, London and Wales. Table 2.1 illustrates the regions by number of court closures. An additional 90 courthouses were earmarked for decommission in June 2015 and a further 86 were identified in February 2016. The Midlands and South East regions have seen the largest number of court closures, with 18 going between 2009 and 2015 in each of these areas; 10 lower-tier magistrates' courts have closed in London.

In 2010, not long after the UK Conservative Party gained shared political power, the then Justice Secretary, Kenneth Clark, justified the court closure programme in a written statement with the claim that 'providing access to justice does not necessarily mean providing a courthouse in every town or city' (BBC News, 2012). This view has been reinforced in subsequent announcements in February 2016 of more impending court closures.

Table 2.1 Magistrates' courts closed since July 2009

Region	Number closed since 2009
Midlands	18
North West	8
North East	12
South East	18
South West	14
London	10
Wales	12
Total closed since 2009	92

Source: Ministry of Justice (2015) Figures obtained from freedom of information (FOI) request.

Consultations carried out by the executive branch of the criminal courts – Her Majesty's Courts and Tribunal Service (HMCTS) – prior to the closures and amalgamations were designed to consider the impact that the closures would have on court users. Local transport links and the costs of travelling to the closest courthouse were also considered (Senior Presiding Judge, 2010). In reacting to concerns that the principle of the 'access to justice' could be compromised, it was said that courthouses would remain geographically positioned so as to enable '95 percent of citizens to reach their required court within an hour by car' (ibid.: 2). In rural parts of England and Wales, where people reside far from towns and metropolitan centres and with limited public transport links, the closure of local courthouses can greatly inhibit access to justice in the form of getting to a courthouse with ease. On magistrate reflected on this:

> Access to justice is important and if you take that away from people, you are taking away from them their basic right. The further they are from the centre of justice, the less likely they are to get justice.
>
> (Male, aged 68, 37 years' service)

The magistrates interviewed in this research commented on access to justice as an important principle and drew attention to the significance of having the chance to appear and the case heard in open court in person. The logistical and negative impact that court closures have was frequently pointed out, particularly for defendants who are unemployed and on supplementary benefits. The magistrates in one research area were contending with the recent closure of two local courthouses and they commented on the ramifications for accused defendants who now had to endure long and expensive train and bus journeys to reach the closest court:

> I think like all services, services should be accessible, accessible both for victims of crime, but for those who are being charged as well. They deserve a fair crack of the whip. Again whether you are a victim or a defendant if you live in Bushton[5] and you have to get to Ripon and you are on benefits then that becomes a major problem for you. You are talking about a two hour journey plus the cost.... A lot of our clients unfortunately come from, are unemployed people, people who are on benefits they can't afford cars and transport to Ripon, so local justice I think is a big problem.
>
> (Male, aged 68 years, 10 years' service)

Critics have argued against the widespread closure of courthouses on a number of fronts, in particular the way that local justice is being removed (Morgan, 2013). Donoghue (2014a), in her article on reforms to the role of magistrates, discussed local justice as a key characterisation of the magistracy. Having knowledge of the local community in which magistrates dispense justice is underlined. When court work is consolidated into a smaller number of operating areas in urban towns and cities the meaning of local justice disappears.

One solution emerging for defendants, witnesses and family members facing difficulties in getting to court in line with the widespread court closures going on[6] is the introduction of virtual court facilities, which have opened up in some parts of the country. The Ministry of Justice consultation document (2015a) laying out the proposals for further court closures across England and Wales noted the use of virtual, digitised mechanisms. The proposals made for the way justice can be alternatively delivered via digitised systems, and out in community settings, such as in local libraries, are attempts to plug the gaps left by the large-scale closure of courthouses across the country. The courthouse closures and property sell-offs are promoted as enabling enhanced financial investment in digitised systems and electronic technology for use within modern court delivery.

The amalgamation and closure of courthouses across England and Wales are occurring as a part of a court rationalisation project aimed at reducing the running costs of court buildings at a time of fiscal austerity. This is together with taking advantage of advances in communications technology and the broad reach and delivery capabilities that live video link systems provide. Different terms are used in reference to the video link technologies being used in court proceedings. I use the terms 'live links' and 'video links' interchangeably. It is likely the advances with live link technology in courtroom proceedings will function as a replacement for the lost courtroom provision resulting from the widespread courthouse closures.

Courtroom digitisation and virtual courts[7]

Another development occurring within the lower criminal courts, which fits neatly within notions of modernisation and managerial justice processes, is the increasing use of digitised systems and video link technology in court proceedings. The use of video link technology within court processes is being advanced in a number of jurisdictions and in a range of ways, which include witnesses and defendants giving evidence from remote locations (Rowden *et al.*, 2013), links from prisons to courts where prisoners' bail or remand hearings are conducted (Plotnikoff and Woolfson, 1999) and courtroom connections made across international borders (Fabri and Contini, 2001; Young, 2011; Gray, 2004). The use of prison live link technology has been in place for some years in the UK, so that defendants remanded in custody can be produced for bail hearings from within the prison rather than being transported in person to court. However, the various technological advances that are becoming embedded in criminal court operations in the UK in the current period are radical additions and generate the need for fuller discussion (cf. Mulcahy, 2008, 2011).

Advances in the area of digitised court methods in the UK take the form of trial evidence being given in criminal court trials over live link by the police and by vulnerable witnesses, which for both groups is found to produce enormous benefits. This is in terms of the time savings for the police in their line of duty and the greater willingness of witnesses to give evidence at trial, especially for those who may otherwise feel intimidated or fearful of appearing in person.

A less publicly commented upon development in methods of court digitisation is the emergence of virtual courts that have come into use across some areas of the English criminal justice system. Defendants appear via a live video link from a holding police station to a magistrates' courtroom for the first hearing plea entry, bail and remand decisions and, in some cases, the plea and sentencing decision in the one hearing. The main benefits of this innovation relate to time and efficiency savings, allowing straightforward, guilty plea cases to be resolved in a matter of minutes and court time not being blocked up with various person appearances. This has been in place within the English system since 2009,[8] when the 'UK Virtual Court' pilot model was first tested. The model has since been taken up across some police and prosecution areas and with the level of enthusiasm for streamlined and digitised courtroom methods of delivery they could shape the way of the future for summary justice lower court hearings (Leveson, 2015a; Ministry of Justice, 2014b). As with the other highlighted alterations occurring to lower court justice discussed in this chapter, serious questions about due process can be raised with these digitised virtual court innovations.

So far, virtual courts operate in a limited number of areas and none of the magistrates interviewed in this research was working within courthouses using these methods. But key informants involved with these virtual court developments were interviewed and courtroom operation was observed in Kent in the early stages of my research with magistrates hearing from defendants and their legal representatives over live video links.

These technological developments clearly match UK government policy interests in advancing efficiency through courtroom modernisation and the use of digitised systems. The 2010 Conservative Party election manifesto had a central theme of 'modern Britain' and mentioned the deployment of new technology in offender management and specifically its facilitation in bringing 'persistent offenders to justice more quickly' (The Conservative Party, 2015: 60). Moreover, the Leveson Report (2015a), covering a review of efficiency in the criminal courts, stated in its terms of reference that it was focusing on areas of the criminal court system where 'better use could be made of technological and other advances' (ibid.: 7).

Aligned to this digitised direction of travel, the main thrust of the 2015 Criminal Justice Management conference hosted on behalf of the UK government was the integration of modern technology into criminal justice and court work. The concentration of international computer technology and software companies exhibiting and marketing digital file share systems and platforms was noted. Further, the various 'high-tech' products and 'Apps' designed to enhance information transfer between criminal justice agencies were indicative of the conviction that enhanced digitisation can serve for future modernised public service delivery.

A keynote address by the Chief Executive Officer (CEO) of Her Majesty's Courts and Tribunal Service (HMCTS), Natalie Ceeney, set out at the conference her conception of a 'new streamlined summary justice'. Her speech stressed the issues of cost burdens and resource waste that could be eliminated by pressing ahead with virtual live link court facilities, mentioning specifically time savings to the police in giving evidence in court via online transmission. The further intention to remove waste was emphasised in the wish to eliminate transporting remanded prisoners to court for what was referred to as 'five minute bail hearings'.

The main arguments in favour of video link technology in courtroom proceedings are the time and cost savings they achieve, since they speed up the rate at which cases progress through the system and remove some of the logistical issues and discomfort that comes with transporting prisoners from police stations and prisons to courtrooms for remand and trial hearings. They are said to facilitate giving evidence at trial for vulnerable or intimidated witnesses, who might otherwise be put off or be fearful of coming into contact with their crime perpetrator. Indeed, Mulcahy (2008, 2011) draws attention to the research evidence supporting the value of live links for some victims. She notes that respondents said the facility meant the difference between them not appearing and appearing. She cites research suggesting 33 per cent of witnesses using 'special measures' said they would not have been willing to give evidence without live link and that the police, Crown Prosecution Service and court staff view live links as effective or very effective (ibid.: 165). Satisfaction has also been found among crime victims at the swift pace at which offenders can be punished following their committing the crime (Terry *et al.*, 2010: 27). Video link facilities are also seen as removing prisoner escape risks, which occasionally occur with prison-to-court transportation (Rowden *et al.*, 2013).

However, serious due process concerns also emerge in regard to advanced digitisation in courtroom work. Experiences coming from the audience at the Criminal Justice Management conference highlighted what might be teething problems with the implementation of technology in courtroom proceedings. One serving magistrate recounted being involved in a pilot initiative which she interpreted as unsuccessful because of the adjournments caused through live link connection malfunctions. Also noted in these discussions was the impact of the current staff shortages in English prisons. It was commented that prisoners are dependent on stretched prison officers' goodwill to engage in producing prisoners over the links. Moreover, a complaint about the perception of waste caused through transporting prisoners to court for five-minute bail hearings came from a defence lawyer in the audience at the conference. She pointed out the importance of bail hearings, stating that the five minutes appearing in court in person can be the difference between a person's liberty and custody.

The empirical research base has not yet mapped onto the operation of virtual courts as they are advanced in the UK, and it is not apparent that the model is replicated in other jurisdictions. Given the radical alteration that virtual courts introduce into criminal court operation, research is needed with court users. Research is in particular needed with defendants who experience this style of court hearing to gauge their perceptions of fairness, and whether there are elements within the process that undermine due process and produce injustice (cf. Rowden, 2013: 102).

In some police force areas there is enthusiasm for the time and efficiency savings virtual courts provide in bringing cases to justice more swiftly. Kent has operated virtual courts since 2010 and other police force areas have followed suit. Hertfordshire has four police stations equipped to produce people held in police custody before the courts, and in 2015 Norfolk and Suffolk opened a 'Police Investigation Centre' (PIC),[9] which in design is similarly equipped to proceed in this way. A key informant interviewed for this research, Detective Inspector Bob Platt, a police specialist and consultant in virtual court practice, is in favour of their potential for swift case processing and time savings but identifies stress points and the different risks that have emerged. Specifically mentioned were the greater responsibility and risk that have come to the police. This is in the overnight staffing of the police custody suites, which on a busy weekend night might contain upwards of 20 arrested people, some whom may be unwell and who are held in police custody until being produced over live link when the court opens on Monday morning. In discussing advancements in the courts, Bob Platt says:

> we're talking about a virtual court and not the other sort of use of video, because obviously we now extensively use video for witnesses as in police officers and vulnerable witnesses. That was always going to be beneficial, but the virtual court side of it comes at a cost to police forces because we have to get additional staff than we'd normally have in a custody suite. We also have to keep the prisoners longer than we would normally like.
>
> (Detective Inspector Bob Platt, 2015)

The longer time period arrestees spend in police custody when using the virtual court approach was alluded to in an H. M. Inspectorate of Prisons report following an inspection of Hertfordshire's police custody suites (H. M. Inspectorate of Prisons and H. M. Inspectorate of Constabulary, 2015) The report mentioned that the 'virtual courts' were operated by dedicated court officers but that staff reported there was 'still difficulty getting detainees accepted by the remand court later than 1 pm or 2 pm' (ibid.: 11).

Previous figures provided by the Hertfordshire virtual court area as a part of this research give a partial picture of its operation, recording that between April 2013 and April 2014 a total of 576 police arrests were put through their virtual 'remand courts'. The most typical offence category was 'breach of court order/ bail', followed by 'theft' offences. It was not possible to get a more nuanced picture from these figures, but the police professionals working within the Hertfordshire police custody suites who engaged in discussion with me in relation to these courts believed that the defendants found appearing from the police custody suite to be a more positive and 'less daunting' experience than being transported in prison vehicles and waiting in shared court custody cells. This was said to be particularly so for women. But the different police prisoner care and welfare responsibilities placed on the police were noted, with it being suggested there was a variation in police officer mindsets, personality types and 'empathy'.

Research is needed with defendants who experience this style of court hearing to gauge their perceptions of fairness.

An early evaluation of the UK Virtual Court pilot produced mixed results (Terry *et al.*, 2010). The study aimed to determine whether virtual courts were more efficient in terms of time and cost savings and how they measured on dimensions of fairness in criminal justice process. The evaluation analysed case throughput in the virtual court pilot area, which included two magistrates' courts and 15 police stations, with case processing compared in a London area operating a traditional court style. The virtual court model was found to quicken the average time from police charge to first hearing. The number of failures to appear in court for first hearings was also lessened, with 1 per cent recorded compared to 5 per cent in the traditional court area (ibid.: iv). Other results were less favourable, with slightly higher rates of guilty pleas recorded among defendants appearing in the virtual courts against the comparator area. A lower proportion of defendants was legally represented in the virtual court sample, at just over half (54 per cent) that of the traditional court (68 per cent), and guilty pleas were higher among people who were not legally represented. Prison custody as a sentence outcome was also slightly higher for people appearing in the virtual court compared to those appearing in a traditional courtroom, and levels of sentencing people to community penalties were lower when dispensed from the virtual court.

Moreover, reservations about virtual courts were also raised in the interviews with criminal justice practitioners involved in the virtual court pilot. Interviews with legal defence practitioners, magistrates, district judges and prosecutors were completed as a part of the evaluation. The fact that defendants were physically separated at a police station made it harder for defence and prosecution advocates to communicate before and during hearings. Legal defence professionals claimed defendants would be encouraged to plead guilty and refuse legal representation to speed up the case, and might see the police as part of the prosecution, rather than as an institutional body making an accusation which the defendant has the right of challenge. Here it was suggested that police stations are not 'sufficiently neutral' spaces and that defendants might be predisposed to plead guilty in this context (ibid.: 21). The magistrates and judges interviewed found that the short time slots which cases were allocated for hearing created a form of 'hasty justice' and that some types of case, such as complex bail applications, were not considered suitable for virtual court hearings. They also thought that the court had difficulty imposing authority remotely and that defendants took the process less seriously than they would if they appeared in court in person (ibid.: 22).

Around the same time as the UK Virtual Court pilot was being conducted, the Law Society of England and Wales expressed its disapproval with this style of court innovation, mainly in relation to the disadvantages to accused defendants and their procedural rights. It was argued that interactions between defendants and their legal advisors would be weakened by virtual connections and that the privacy of legal advice conversations would be compromised. Put simply, the importance of meeting and discussing with defendants in person was removed

(Terry *et al.*, 2010; Ridout, 2010; Atkinson, 2012; Dean, 2010; Rowden, 2013). In 2012, Richard Atkinson, then chair of the Law Society's Criminal Law Committee, stated that it 'frequently means defendants don't meet their lawyer before the court decides upon their case'. He went on to contend that 'some defendants are sent to prison without ever having seen their lawyer in person'. Atkinson also highlighted case complexity and argued that, in addition to the issue of guilt or innocence, the mental elements of the case need to be considered. He stressed that the transmission of delicate and personal information in a way that a defendant may not feel comfortable revealing to a lawyer they had only met over a video link while sitting in a room at police station was a problem.

Certain safeguards are in place with the operation of virtual courts in that legal restrictions lay out who is not suitable for inclusion in virtual court dispositions (Law Society, 2012). These include people defined as vulnerable, who require the support of an 'appropriate adult' and who have not had face-to-face guidance from a legal advocate, those aged under 18, those with language difficulties and who require an interpreter, those in need of immediate medical treatment (see Office for Criminal Justice Reform, 2010: 10). However, the government is committed to progress with the use of these courts, as is apparent in the amendment to earlier legislation made through the Coroners and Justice Act 2009, making it law that a person does not have the right to refuse to appear via video link from a police station following charge (Terry *et al.*, 2010), with the exception of those defined as not suitable. Thus, those arrested in a virtual court police force area can have their case started and finished at a police station – the arrest and charge laid and the sentence dispensed to the person over live video link from within the space of policy custody. It needs to be acknowledged that the due process protections that defendants are entitled to during stages of police arrest occur within the non-neutral space of a police station, while a person is in police custody and under the control of a custody sergeant. It fundamentally moves away from the principle that defendants should have the case heard against them in an open impartial court (cf. Ridout, 2010).

Mulcahy (2008, 2011) draws attention to advances in courtroom technology and live link proceedings. She believes that if technological advances and remote virtual appearances are the way of the future in criminal court administration then definitions of due process need rethinking, particularly to the principle of 'open justice'. In her wider study on legal architecture and legal geography and the way courthouses and courtrooms can be seen as a physical expression of our relationship with justice ideals, she calls for further debate on the implications of virtual proceedings, specifically relating to the giving of evidence. She notes that there are signs that courtroom sessions in which opposing parties gather together in each other's physical presence could become a thing of the past and that our 'prime site of adversarial legal practice is in danger of being dematerialised' (2008: 465). She also highlights how the power and symbolism of legal proceedings are being compromised, as is the meaning of the 'day in court'. Here, she is referring to the way that an individual appearing over remote live link will be unaffected by the influence of the court (ibid.: 173).

In the new digitally mediated environments being envisaged, and slowly realised by policy makers and 'techno-evangelicals', the character and content of legal discourse are being transformed. Encounters within the courtroom are in danger of becoming sanitised as participation in the trial becomes akin to a fleeting televisual encounter.

(Mulcahy, 2008: 465)

The human experience aspects of live link technology in the way they save prisoner journey to court time, while at the same time eliminating the risk of a prisoner losing his/her cell space and coping with relocation to a different cell, cell mate or even prison, are laudable. These are true features of prison-to-court appearances and indeed the criminal defence lawyer interviewed in my research said his clients requested to be produced over live link for these reasons. He explains the type of situation in which a client would prefer to stay in prison and appear over live video link as typically when a defendant is exercising their right to a second bail application but expect this to be rejected and the remand in custody status retained; to avoid prison relocation he explains how they 'hedge their bets' and prefer to appear over live link:

if I'm not going to get bail, I'd rather stay here.... I'll make the bail ap [application] but do it on a video link, if I don't get it that's fine, I'd rather be here rather than be produced, come all the way there, you don't get bail and then I get carted off somewhere else.

(Criminal defence lawyer)

In expressing his views more generally about virtual courts and their expansion across police areas, he considered them useful and legitimate in straightforward guilty plea cases for the cost and logistical court savings. Plus, he emphasised the personal discomfort of the prison van and being moved around in handcuffs:

Let's just say black and white [cases], clear cut shop lifting that the defendant is not even questioning.... Then it's certainly not a saving to be knocked at, preventing the logistics of that individual being brought from the police station to the court, being held in custody at court and then eventually being given a disposal that results in their release ... it may as well be dealt with by a virtual court. It is probably better for the defendant not to be put in one of those wagons which are quite tight and narrow and be carried over, being moved around in handcuffs from one place to another.

(Criminal defence lawyer)

However, he also set out the problems experienced in virtual court connections, with the loss of quality in communication and conveying information from paper documents being impaired, as well as the difficulties faced with the tight fixed time slots. Highlighting these deficiencies in material and visceral experience is important because this subtle weakening in the strength of the legal advice brought about through video links can be the difference between a defendant's ability to mount an effective defence and not:

> If it's a bit more complex, it gets harder and when we're dealing with clients on video link, it is much harder because you have slots, so you are under time pressure and one of the things you can't do on video link is 'have a look at that, see what it says here' and that sort of stuff can often make a huge difference because when I'm reading something the attention span will only go so far. Also with video links you tend to have to wait for each other, you know I finish saying something, I don't know whether that's necessarily, but usually I find it hard to listen to somebody on a video when I'm speaking.
>
> (Criminal defence lawyer)

The positive features of live link technology focus on the humane element in the way that they can greatly relieve the pains of prisoner transportation and travelling in hot, cramped and sweaty prison vans. Moreover, there are advantages with virtual courts in reducing delays between arrest and sentence, and it can be that this cuts the uncertainty that lingers over a person in unresolved cases. But reservations and criticisms also emerge in how live links and virtual courts challenge procedural due process and interpretations of fair hearings (Ward, 2015; Mulcahy, 2011; Ridout, 2010).

It is important to consider these areas of concern regarding virtual courts, because of the issues at stake: admission of guilt even to a low-level charge leads to a criminal record with life-changing implications. Moreover, bail and remand decisions determining whether a person spends the time between charge and trial at liberty in the community or on remand in prison are key justice issues. As yet, we have been unable to scrutinise whether these are more likely case outcomes in virtual court hearings, but it is evident that research is needed that looks more comprehensively into these procedural prosecution matters and the experience of court users. Mulcahy (2008, 2011) cites Rowden's (2009) 'Gateways to Justice' research, funded by the Australian Research Council, as one of the few studies that have included the experience of users of remote video link technology. Rowden (2013) examines an earlier claim by the Ministry of Justice in the UK that there will be 'no loss of quality' for a defendant experiencing a virtual court hearing compared to a traditional one. From this Rowden inferred that there is an assumption 'that videoconferencing technology is benign and neutral and can be easily inserted into existing conditions and used without significantly altering the nature of the experience' (ibid.: 102). She expresses doubt about whether the people appearing in court in this virtual way would agree.

These arguments are important to this book's narrative since they point to issues of procedural rights and principles of 'open justice' becoming weakened within virtual court styles of delivery. The experiences and perceptions of users in relation to fairness are important to gauge, and certain categories of 'vulnerable' defendants, young people and non-English-speaking defendants need special attention for their probable unsuitability in virtual court hearings. Also, the increase in people staying overnight in police custody and what that means to them requires addressing. Are these low-level offenders who would normally be bailed following arrest rather than being detained overnight in custody? These issues need full and careful consideration as virtual courts advance and expand more widely so that adequate protections are in place and to ensure that injustices do not occur with this remote, more detached courtroom experience.

The empirical research carried out with magistrates provided some sense of mood change in relation to moving to electronic methods of operation with enthusiasm among some for some changes but not for others. Since the operation of virtual courts in the style described above has been rolled out so far just in a few areas, the magistrates interviewed were not sitting in bench areas where these virtual courtroom advances are unfolding. As such, they were not able to share insights or views on this form of justice delivery. However, their working environment with regard to electronic and digitised methods of administration was altering at a pace, requiring proficiency in accessing web-based training tutorials, judicial email communications etc. and they provided some views on the introduction of digitised and electronic transformations within their work role.

Changes to legal aid provision

Another area in which major alterations are being made to summary justice, which is impacting on criminal court work, is the funding cuts to the criminal legal aid budgets and the restrictions that these have imposed on eligibility for representation. The magistrates' interviews mentioned this as having a significant bearing on their criminal court work, with an increase in the number of unrepresented defendants. The following comment by one of the London magistrates notes the extra time generated with defendants trying to defend themselves is particularly problematic for those who don't speak English or who are unable to understand the legal process:

> Unrepresented defendants have become much more frequent since the legal aid change. Well obviously, because it set the boundary at which you can get it higher, so more people are unrepresented ... and it just takes forever. Particularly ones where you are having to go through an interpreter and not everyone is bright enough to understand the intricacies of it.
>
> (Female, aged 58, three years' service)

There is a history in the UK of legal aid entitlement modifications in efforts to reduce the cost of criminal legal aid (Sanders *et al.*, 2010). Legal aid generally is estimated to cost approximately £2.2 billion per year. Just under £1 billion funds the criminal legal aid bill. The latest eligibility alteration came in the Legal Aid, Sentencing and Punishment of Offenders Act 2013. It was stated by the then Justice Secretary, Chris Grayling, in defence of the funding cuts that England and Wales has one of the most expensive criminal legal aid bills in the world.

Within these funding reductions, there has also been a suggestion that charges towards legal representation will be introduced at the level of Crown Court cases, where an accused defendant found guilty will be required to pay towards the costs of their legal defence. Proponents of legal aid have argued that this is a fundamental attack on the freedoms of the UK and that it is necessary for defendants to be protected against the strong power of the state and equally able to compete with the prosecution's case, funded on behalf of the state. This relates to the principle of 'equality of arms' and is considered an important due process protection. Various writers note changes occurring to legal aid entitlement across different countries raising issues of disadvantage to accused defendants (Smith, 2013; Sommerlad, 2004, 2008; Edwards, 2011).

Swingeing changes have been made to criminal legal aid provision in England and Wales in the recent time period (Ministry of Justice 2013b), which are also evident in other common-law jurisdictions. There are two tests in granting state-funded legal advice to an accused defendant. This is the 'means test' and the 'merits test'. The means test sets an earnings threshold, above which a person has to pay their own legal costs. The threshold has been reducing over the years and a person with not especially substantial earnings comes within the income bracket that requires self-funding.

There is also the merits test, otherwise referred to as the 'interests of justice' test. Even if a person is under the earnings threshold, the merits test has to be passed and a person will only be legal aid represented if the offence they are charged with is punishable by a prison sentence. This excludes a lot of people who appear in the lower criminal courts accused of an offence but have reasonable mitigation and want to fight the accusation against them, or at least present the reasons for the incident occurring. However, with these funding restrictions on who is granted legal aid, it is the case that some people simply plead guilty in a sense of defeat without exercising the right to challenge, for cost reasons. There is always the free duty solicitor at court, who can provide brief advice on the day if a person needs assistance. However, from the magistrates' reports, duty solicitors, especially in large city courts, experience large numbers queuing up for their services.

A package of legal aid reforms has come forth under the current Conservative government. Fixed fee payments for providing legal aid work have been introduced. Fixed fee payments relate to the way a legal defence firm will be paid a fixed amount for a case, rather than by the length of the case. Some argue that the legal profession has an interest in cases being delayed and adjourned because of payments made on the length of time it takes to process a case. Legal defence firms argue it is not economically viable for them to continue doing court defence work under fixed fee rulings. Opting out of this work by the legal defence fraternity is potentially worrying because it could leave a skeleton of low-paid solicitors who are possibly the least qualified to defend people accused of criminal wrongdoing in prosecuted court cases.

Competitive tendering processes have also been brought into state-funded legal aid work. The current Conservative government had radical plans to significantly reduce the number of contracts awarded so that legal aid work was concentrated into a smaller number of firms than previously. There was intense opposition to these plans and, for the first time in legal history, in 2014 solicitors and barristers walked out on strike. In early 2016, following the legal challenges mounted, the government retracted the plans. The outcome of the competitive tendering alterations would have meant defendants are limited in the choice of legal firms which represent them, which is considered important in terms of who defendants know and feel comfortable with, especially in regard to foreign language and interpretation issues. The competitive tendering set-up and lower fixed price fees were argued as forcing companies to take on more clients so that individual lawyers would have large caseloads and less time to spend on case preparation (Ministry of Justice, 2013b).

Similar changes have occurred in New Zealand, reducing the number of contracts awarded to private legal defence firms to cover legal aid. This brought the overall total of this work provided by the New Zealand government's Public Defence System (PDS) to 50 per cent (Sharpe, 2014). A representative from the New Zealand Law Society claimed that the move was a disincentive for private lawyers to specialise in criminal defence work and over the longer term would reduce the depth of experience and quality at the private bar. The lack of independence of government-salaried lawyers is also raised. In some ways, the UK change would establish a public defence service in the style that exists in New Zealand and the criticisms are that these agencies or individuals effectively work for the state, so their defence of accused defendants and providing a robust defence to a person against state prosecution is a contradiction in terms. The competitive tendering process firms have to go through to win the contracts has driven down the fees, with the firms bidding with the cheapest contracts likely to win the contracts.

The civil liberties campaigning group Liberty responded to the government's proposals to transform criminal legal aid and the competitive tendering for this work, arguing that they demonstrated a disregard for the administration of justice and contravened the democratic principle of the right to a fair trial under Article 6 of the European Convention on Human Rights (Liberty, 2013). They specifically refer to the creation of a declining quality of legal aid provision through the competitive tendering set-up, in which legal aid firms had to win contracts to qualify to provide state-funded criminal legal advice and assistance.

This chapter has put forward some of the main alterations occurring to lower court summary justice in the English criminal justice system, which fit with the modernisation project currently going on, such as speedy justice initiatives and active case management, encouragements within the system for the entry of early guilty pleas, the rationalisation of the court estate and the consequent closure and amalgamation of courthouses, and the increasing developments in digitisation and the use of live link technology in criminal court proceedings. It has linked these changes to what is referred to as managerial or technocratic justice, an unfolding style in which business management approaches and principles are brought into the running of the criminal courts and the processing of cases within them (Corcoran, 2014; O'Malley, 2008; Bohm, 2006; Raine, 2000, 2005; Raine and Willson, 1993, 1995). Similar alterations of streamlining and the enhanced use of technology are occurring across other jurisdictions similarly impacted by neo-liberalist economic policies, where rigorous drives for efficiency and streamlining are taking place.

Questions have been raised about whether the modernising and rationalising alterations maintains the position of fair and equal justice at the heart of democratic society. Criminal court reforms have been unfolding for some years under processes of rationalisation and economic efficiency strategies, and what we have seen in the recent past has provoked opposition in respect to the UK's reputation for fair justice.

This chapter has presented a summary of some key changes occurring to summary justice within the lower criminal courts under the broad rubric of delivering public services in tune with a changing world and in the modern era. The focus now moves to centre on the magistrates' courts in action and the experiences of magistrates, judges and other criminal justice professionals.

Notes

1 The first Criminal Procedure Rules came out in 2005 and have frequently been amended by statutory instrument according to criminal justice policy requirements.
2 Adhering to the principle of open justice the offence allegations and responses of guilt or non-guilt are read out in open court, but the charge to which defendants respond is put to them by post or electronically on a 'plea by notice' form.
3 Examples of offences dealt with in this category are 'Driving While Forbidden' and 'Careless Use of a Motor Vehicle'.
4 Figures were obtained from the Ministry of Justice on a Freedom of Information Act request.
5 Fictional names have been given to towns and courthouses mentioned by the magistrates to avoid identifying the region.
6 The Ministry of Justice consultation document (2015a) laying out the proposals for further court closures across England and Wales notes the use of virtual, digitised mechanisms.
7 An earlier version of this section on virtual courts was published as Ward, J. (2015) Transforming Summary Justice through Police-led Prosecution and Virtual Courts – Is 'Procedural Due Process' Being Undermined? *British Journal of Criminology*, 55, 2, 341–358. I would like to thank the *British Journal of Criminology* and Oxford University Press for their kind permission to reproduce the text.
8 A pre-pilot prototype was tested over 12 weeks in 2007.
9 The purpose built police custody suites that sit alongside virtual court operation have facilities to accommodate 20 prisoners in overnight police custody.

3 The magistrates' courts, magistrates and lay justice

The previous chapter has laid out alterations occurring to summary justice in the lower criminal courts that have largely evolved through managerial processes of reform, but have also coalesced around running modern public services that are responsive to the diverse make-up and demands of contemporary society. The purpose of this chapter is to bring to the fore operations within the lower-tier magistrates' courts, and the powers and procedures at work within them.

This chapter gives an overview of the magistrates' courts, the high volume and broad range of criminal cases they process, the breadth of decision-making powers magistrates hold, the sentencing options at their disposal and the role they are tasked with in appropriately sentencing offenders. It emphasises the historic function of the magistrates' courts as summary justice courts and the need to take an interest in justice administration within this context (McBarnet, 1981b). It draws upon observation material extracted from time spent within London magistrates' courts and provides textual detail on the working environment and atmosphere within the court setting. It is useful to make reference back to the earlier point that the English justice system is unique in its use of volunteer lay magistrates in dispensing criminal court justice.

The magistrates' courts are located at the lower tier of the criminal court hierarchical structure and are typically assessed to deal with 95 per cent of all criminal court work. This is because most prosecuted crime is categorised as being less serious in nature and falling within the lower court jurisdiction. The magistrates' courts are also courts of 'first appearance', meaning that all cases, even the most serious ones destined for hearing in the higher Crown Courts, begin proceedings in these courts before 'committal' upwards. Magistrates perform a wide range of legal decision-making roles, including granting the police warrants to search private homes, awarding utility companies rights of access, making bail and remand decisions, sentencing convicted defendants through an assortment of penalties, from monetary fines at the lower end of the scale to up to between six and 12 months in prison custody,[1] or two years if passing judgement in the youth courts (Davies *et al.*, 2015).

Due to the high volume of work passing through the lower courts, Sanders *et al.* (2010) refer to them as 'the workhorse of the system' (ibid.: 500). They add to that by drawing on McBarnet's (1981a, 1981b) argument in her study of summary justice in the magistrates' courts. McBarnet writes that, with the jurisdiction of these courts dealing with minor, less serious criminal matters that they are typically constructed as processing 'trivial' matters. With this, she argues that less public attention is attracted to them and that 'two tiers of justice' have been created. Sanders *et al.* (2010) pick up on the notion of triviality to state that the legal decisions and powers of punishment held within the remit of the magistrates' courts are of 'far-reaching importance'. In this regard Sanders *et al.* (2010) argue that:

> the signals given off by magistrates' courts are that they deal with trivial matters in which the issues are straightforward, defendants willingly accept their guilt and the consequences for defendants of conviction are slight. In truth, however magistrates are responsible for decisions of far-reaching importance.
>
> (Ibid.: 447)

Many studies have used the criminal courts as sites of observation and bring to life case proceedings, the rituals of drama and social control played out within them and the experiences of defendants, witnesses and victims in the criminal court process. These are too numerous to refer to here but they include Carlen's (1974) research from the 1970s based in London's 'Metropolitan Magistrates' Courts', taking account of courtroom ritual and how 'justice' is arrived at in this space. There is Rock's (1991, 1993) ethnography based in London's Wood Green Crown Court, focusing on prosecution witnesses and the way that 'conflict' plays out within the trial process. There is the courtroom observation work of Adler (1987) and Lees (2002) on rape trials using High Court rape trials to appraise the treatment of female rape victims in the court procedure. Feeley's research from a courthouse in Connecticut in the USA referred to the 'courthouse workgroup' as the group of criminal justice agents operating in tandem to adjudicate on the substantive law. More recent court observation research has emerged from Australia in the extensive study carried out on the lower magistrates' courts[2] by Roach Anleu and Mack (2005, 2007a, 2007b, 2013, 2014). They analyse the work of these courts within different themes including the intricate management of daily court lists, the magistrates' interpretations of their court work within notions of 'therapeutic jurisprudence' (2007b) and being motivated by the role in achieving social change. Also from Australia there is the observation work of Travers (2007) carried out within the youth courts. There are studies involving observations in the Crown Courts as trials overseen by judges and juries (Jacobson *et al.*, 2015; Shute *et al.*, 2005; Hood, 1979, 1992) and various observation studies of case processing, bail and remand and sentencing decisions in the high-volume lower criminal courts (Herbert, 2004; Hucklesbury, 1997; Tarling, 1979, 2006; Hood, 1979), among many others.

Criminal court observations are a rich research technique noted for the nuance and depth they enable in understanding cases (Roach Anleu *et al.*, 2015). Baldwin (2008) writes on the value of courtroom observation as a method, but adds that there are limitations in using the approach on its own. He stresses that courtroom observation provides only a partial view of events surrounding a case (ibid.: 375), but that they are nonetheless a useful way to capture the real-life nature of criminal case deposition. Courtroom observations are insightful for the detail they provide on individual defendants' offending, the circumstances behind police arrest, for example through routine 'beat patrol', accusations by the public, romantic partners and employers, defendants' acceptance of guilt or not and for a general appreciation of summary justice in action. For the purposes of my research, courtroom observation enabled a view into the workings of the lower criminal courts within these modernising and streamlining times of speedy justice, tighter case management, court amalgamations and legal aid restrictions and of lay magistrates performing in their courtroom role.

Magistrates' court justice

Summary justice in the lower-tier magistrates' courts is organised such that cases are heard by a panel of three part-time volunteer lay magistrates or a legally qualified judge sitting on his or her own. In the English justice system, judges are titled district judges (DJs) and deputy district judges (DDJs). Daily court lists are allocated between lay magistrate benches and the courts run by professional judges. The courtroom sessions run by lay magistrates comprise more or less the same case types as those run by judges. However, judges are allotted the longer, more complex cases due to the practicality of their full-time employment compared to the more occasional part-time sitting of lay magistrates. Differential case allocation between magistrates and professional judges is a recurring theme within court business, with serving magistrates pushing for parity in caseload allocation. This is to ensure that they retain their professional competence in the breadth of courtroom administration tasks and to guarantee a mixture of case complexity for the purposes of satisfaction with their voluntary court role (Green, 2014).

A 'justices' clerk' is active in both court set-ups. Their professional training establishes them as the legal advisor to the lay magistrate benches. The clerk advises on points of law in adjudication, but is not involved in decision-making on guilt or non-guilt, or on the penalties and sentences dispensed. Various alterations to the role of the justices' clerk have occurred within the bureaucratic streamlining processes over the years, with some voices of contention arguing that it is leading to a gradual erosion of 'independence' as the job is drawn more closely into the operations of the civil service and the managerial demands of the government's executive. Hanson (2004), a journalist writing on behalf of the justices' clerks at a time of change to their status, wrote of concerns among them regarding the 'dilution' of their historically independent judicial status.

Magistrate appointment is open to the general public, but applicants must be aged between 18 and 65 years and be able to demonstrate various attributes of integrity and local standing, being of 'good character', sound temperament and maturity. Recruitment is based on levels of need across the court service, but also in endeavours to achieve balanced benches and diversity across the magistracy in terms of age, ethnicity and professional class background. On successful passage through the selection and appointment process, magistrates are 'sworn in' by the Senior Presiding Judge and serve on behalf of the judiciary as lay volunteer members.

Youth courts

The youth courts are also located with the lower court jurisdiction. They deal with criminal prosecutions of 10- to 17-year-olds and are presided over by specially trained magistrates and single sitting professional judges. To qualify for practice in the youth courts, a magistrate must have at least four years' experience and be specially trained in youth issues, taking life stage and life-course development, psychosocial maturity and welfare needs into consideration. Several of the magistrates interviewed were serving as youth court magistrates. There is some shift occurring within the English justice system in respect to the management and rehabilitation of young offenders, with a substantial drop in the number of under 18 year olds sentenced to prison custody since 2010 (Prison Reform Trust, 2015: 44). This can be linked back to the Conservative Party's penal policy and the wish to rely less on the use of prison custody as a form of criminal penalty. Powers of sentencing are greater in the youth courts, with sentencers able to impose prison terms of up to two years. In commenting on magistrates' powers of punishment, Sanders *et al.* (2010) emphasise the strengthened role and responsibility when it comes to the youth courts, in some regard exposing the English legal system as peculiar in the extent of power and influence that is located within the youth jurisdiction.

Magistrates' court caseloads

Criminal court case management is in a period of high activity in terms of enhancing efficiency and removing what are considered time-intensive cases from the courts. Alongside the transformations occurring to court business, in 2015 motoring cases were consigned to administration-style hearings in designated traffic courts which can be dealt with by a single sitting magistrate, rather than as a bench of three in the way they ordinarily were. The Criminal Justice and Courts Act, introduced in April 2015, brought in changes that allow lay justices to sit alone in dispensing other low-level uncontested cases, as well as performing court judging work outside the courtroom setting. Such moves intend to rectify the high numbers of motoring offences clogging up magistrates' court time, but also pave the way for more court administration to be adjudicated by magistrates sitting alone (Ministry of Justice, 2012).

Indeed, as mentioned in the introductory chapter, successive alterations have been made to criminal court case processing over the years that have led to a growing number of cases being moved to the lower courts from the higher-tier Crown Courts (Cammiss and Stride, 2008). Offences are categorised into three types – 'indictable', 'triable either way' and 'summary' offences – and determine whether they are heard in the magistrates' courts or the higher Crown Courts. Over time a greater range of offences has been categorised within the midway 'triable either way' category, open to hearing in either the higher or lower courts. A defendant retains the right in contested triable either way cases to elect for trial by jury, but it is suggested that it takes a knowledgeable and pushy defendant to exercise this right within committal negotiations. Bottoms and McClean (1976) note the unlikelihood of some defendants in knowing their rights to request a summary trial. This shifting allocation of criminal cases is a trend observable in other common-law countries, such as Australia (cf. Pen, 2015) and New Zealand, and can similarly be mapped onto cost and efficiency savings, since it is more costly to dispense with cases in the higher courts than in the swifter-moving lower courts (Sanders *et al.*, 2010). The alterations to case allocation are also for the purposes of reducing time delay and ambitions to cut the time between arrest and conviction or acquittal, as desired by the speedy justice initiatives. An interactive tool on the 'Open Justice' website (www.open.justice.gov.uk) collates the 2015 Ministry of Justice criminal court case statistics and reports that the average length of time for a case to reach completion from the point of arrest in the Crown Courts is 51 weeks, compared to 22 weeks in the magistrates' courts. However, the figures conceal large differences because early guilty plea cases dealt with in the lower magistrates' courts will record a considerably shorter time frame than contested cases (Ministry of Justice, 2013d: 41).

The great volume of cases dealt with in the magistrates' courts each year and between 2010 and 2014 is documented in Table 3.1. The table shows the total number of criminal cases brought before the courts with cases separated into those dispensed in the Crown Courts as indictable offences and those in the magistrates' courts as summary offences. Motoring offences make up nearly half of all the summary offences and include driving without a licence or insurance, speeding and dangerous driving. Removing motoring offences from the total, the number of cases heard in the magistrates' courts remains at over half a million cases per year (*n*=566,000).

The figures in Table 3.1 show a decrease in criminal court case volume over the years since 2010. This relates to the higher Crown Courts and the magistrates'

Table 3.1 Defendants proceeded against at the magistrates' courts 2010–2014 (thousands)

Year*	Total defendants entering the criminal courts	Total indictable offences*	Total summary offences in the magistrates' courts	Summary offences (non-motoring)	Total summary motoring offences
2010	1,653.2	438.0	1,215.2	607.1	608.1
2011	1,580.0	424.0	1,156.1	606.5	549.6
2012	1,484.6	377.0	1,107.7	581.9	525.8
2013	1,441.3	370.6	1,070.7	546.1	524.7
2014	1,467.8	354.9	1,112.9	566.2	546.7

Source: Ministry of Justice (2015d) Criminal Justice Statistics Overview Table – Excel Spreadsheet.
Note
* The separate years are recorded as between January 2014 and December 2014.

courts and is progressive over time. The decrease in court case volume is variously interpreted and explained, with the growth in the use of out-of-court penalties in the form of fixed penalty notices and police cautions mainly identified. However, the number of cases dispensed with in this way has also decreased (see Table 3.4).

Cases dealt with in the magistrates' courts are highly individual but typically include anti-social and public nuisance activity, drug possession, domestic violence, drink driving, theft from retail stores and harassment cases. The official published statistics recording the vast and varied range of offences processed through the criminal courts categorise offences into broad bands, for example 'theft offences', 'drug offences', 'violence against the person' and 'miscellaneous crimes against society'. (Ministry of Justice, 2015c). As such, the more nuanced differences between criminal cases are difficult to discern. Nonetheless, as illustrated in Table 3.2, in the year 2014 'theft offences' were the most typical in the magistrates' courts, followed by, in descending order, 'drug offences', the catch-all category of 'miscellaneous crimes against society', 'public order offences' and 'violence against the person' (Ministry of Justice, 2015c).

Over time, offence re-categorisation had led to the magistrates' courts dealing with a substantial number of cases that can be interpreted as serious offences, in addition to high-volume routine crimes. Table 3.2 shows the numbers of defendants sentenced in the magistrates' courts within the different offence categories between the years 2009 and 2014. It illustrates a high number of 'violence against the person' cases and a rising number of 'sexual offences', although the raw figures deny a more detailed understanding of these trends. This finding can be linked to the earlier point made in connection to McBarnet's (1981) arguments stating that the perception of 'triviality' that surrounds the work of the magistrates' courts is indeed a misrepresentation.

Penalties in the magistrates' courts

Fines in the form of monetary penalties are the most common sentence dispensed in the magistrates' courts. Community penalties follow, involving a vast array of conditions and restrictions, such as electronically monitored home curfews, alcohol sobriety orders, mental health treatment orders, drugs treatment and unpaid work in the community. (Davies *et al.*, 2015). A smaller, but significant number of penalties in the magistrates' courts are defendants sentenced to time in prison. Table 3.3 illustrates the distribution of penalties dispensed from within the magistrates' courts between the years 2010 and 2014 and shows that in 2014 prison sentences were given to nearly 13,000 people. Absolute discharge is the least likely sentence decision made in these courts, with fewer than 2,000 prosecutions being discharged. I have argued elsewhere that judicial-led acquittal with the decision of absolute discharge could be exercised more in these courts, especially in 'trivial' matters that are not in the public interest (Ward, 2013). The table similarly shows the decline in cases coming before the magistrates' courts, which is evident from the total numbers sentenced over the five-year period from 2010 to 2014.

Table 3.2 Number of offenders sentenced at magistrates' courts 2009–2014 – year ending 31 December (thousands)

Offence group	2009	2010	2011	2012	2013	2014
Violence against the person	12,942	13,422	12,362	10,585	10,004	11,026
Sexual offences	1,131	1,360	1,381	1,347	1,438	1,527
Robbery	2,865	2,848	3,127	2,628	1,870	1,310
Theft Offences	110,912	119,293	118,968	108,003	104,622	100,158
Criminal damage and arson	5,672	5,484	4,902	4,206	3,084	1,605
Drug offences	43,003	46,395	45,686	42,549	40,924	35,925
Possession of weapons	10,728	9,056	8,522	7,111	6,651	6,571
Public order offences	10,187	11,801	11,370	10,749	11,203	11,844
Miscellaneous crimes against society	31,016	33,203	31,044	26,768	23,262	20,462
Fraud Offences	10,014	10,266	9,549	7,654	7,694	9,036

Source: Ministry of Justice – Justice Statistics Analytical Services[1] (2015d)

Note
1 Ministry of Justice (2015) excel data file provided by Justice Statistics Analytical Services 'Criminal Justice System Statistics Publication: Sentencing: Pivot Table Analytical Tool for England and Wales'.

Table 3.3 Offenders sentenced for summary offences (excluding motoring) by sentence disposal 2010–2014 (thousands)

	2010	2011	2012	2013	2014
Total sentenced*	493,652	494,300	470,241	436,446	458,633
Immediate custody	14,643	15,161	13,953	12,318	12,936
Suspended sentence	9,560	9,510	9,007	9,551	10,382
Community penalty	64,723	60,846	53,799	46,080	44,067
Fine	344,911	352,968	343,355	321,396	345,046
Absolute discharge	2,917	2,730	2,600	2,384	1,923
Conditional discharge	44,627	42,378	38,997	36,201	35,390
Compensation	4,706	3,919	3,724	4,520	3,264
Otherwise dealt with	7,574	6,788	4,806	3,996	5,625

Source: Ministry of Justice (2015d) Criminal Justice Statistics Courts Proceedings excel files.

Note
* The figures include TEW offences that have been heard in the magistrates' courts.

Guilty pleas are more frequent in the lower-tier courts. Excluding motoring offences from the calculations, between April 2012 and March 2013 68 per cent of cases in the magistrates' courts had a guilty plea entered (Crown Prosecution Service, 2014). When motoring offences are included in the overall calculation the rate climbs to around 90 per cent.

Declining business in the magistrates' courts

Despite the large volume of criminal court work located in the magistrates' courts, overall business has been declining. Moreover, this is considered to be contributing to a perception of diminishing importance relating to lower court work, a sentiment in part confirmed in my interviews with magistrates. The reducing business is variously explained and includes the growth in out-of-court penalties in the form of penalty notices for disorder (PNDs), cannabis warnings and diversionary cautions. Penalty notices for disorder were introduced under the Criminal Justice and Police Act 2001 and were rolled out nationally from 2003/04 (Sanders *et al.*, 2010). Out-of-court penalties are those concluded by the police at the street level through 'on-the-spot' fines or through police diversionary measures. In the lead-up to the legislation that introduced these, it was argued by policy makers that it was not necessary for some less serious criminal behaviour to come before the courts. However, there has been much criticism with this style of justice (Ashworth, 2013; Padfield *et al.*, 2012), and in particular the fact that some more serious and violent offences are dealt with as out-of-court cautions. Although out-of-court penalties continue to be recorded in significant numbers and are altering criminal court volume, the use of them has decreased since the peak period in 2007 (Robson, 2014; Ministry of Justice, 2013c).

Table 3.4 records the number of out-of-court penalties dispensed and highlights the high quantity of PNDs given out following introduction of the legislation. It also shows the significant decline in their use since the high point in 2007 in reaction to the criticism with this style of prosecution. The most typical offence for which the higher level PNDs are dispensed is 'drunk and disorderly' behaviour and 'theft under £100' (Ministry of Justice, 2015c).

There is indeed greater encouragement for diverting certain groups of offenders from criminal prosecution, particularly young offenders (Carlile, 2014) and people with mental disorders or and drug and alcohol problems who commit minor low-level crime (Ministry of Justice, 2010; Department of Health, 2009). To what extent this is being operationalised with the latter group is not known, but it is reported that more young offenders are being diverted from criminal prosecution. Overall the magistrates' courts are operating against a general decline in the number of criminal prosecutions, with their workload and daily work experience impacted as a result.

The declining workload in the magistrates' courts is also influenced by an overall decrease in police recorded crime. Although police crime figures are not generally considered a reliable picture of real crime trends because much crime goes unreported and the new forms of digital and internet crimes are found to be difficult to detect. Decreases in crime levels in the UK, USA and elsewhere have been recorded across most offence types since the 1990s (Van Dijk *et al.*, 2012). These include murder, violent crime and theft and property crimes. Explanations for this so-called 'crime drop' are many and varied, but it aligns with the steady and significant decline recorded since the 1990s (Matthews, 2014). Some explanations for the downward trend, as summarised by Marlow (2014), are the lesser return in value for stolen goods, design inventions making thefts of cars with alarms and trackers more difficult than in previous periods, shifts in drug markets, specifically the decline of the 1980s crack cocaine market and its association with violent crime, changed forms of youth socialising involving more at-home engagement in virtual and online worlds and a generally civilising society.

There remains some disagreement on whether crime rates in the UK have indeed gone down, or whether other factors have a bearing on the figures. Some commentators are sceptical, presenting the suggested fall in crime to be associated with flawed police recording (H. M. Inspectorate of Constabulary, 2014). There has also been a substantial reduction in police numbers in England and Wales since 2010 (College of Policing, 2015), connected to the financial downturn and imposed austerity measures, and as a result it is expected that the total numbers of people arrested will alter correspondingly. Sir Bernard Hogan-Howe, the chief of the Metropolitan Police Service (MPS) at the time of writing, stated that swingeing cuts to police budgets, anticipated in line with reduced public-sector funding, will have consequences for front-line policing (Dodd, 2015; Hogan-Howe, 2014).

Observations in the magistrates' courts

Statistics on the types of crime dispensed with in the lower courts are illuminating in terms of case volume and typicality of offence, but observations made in

Table 3.4 Number of out-of-court penalties and cautions issued (thousands)

Offence category	2005	2006	2007	2008	2009	2010	2011	2012	2013	2014
Higher-tier PND offences £90	141,522	195,036	200,754	170,112	164,985	136,542	123,530	103,163	81,525	63,365
Lower-tier PND offences £60	4,959	6,161	6,790	6,052	5,408	4,227	4,000	3,042	2,743	2,049
Total PNDs	146,481	201,197	207,544	176,164	170,393	140,769	127,530	106,205	84,268	65,414

Source: Ministry of Justice (2015d) Criminal Justice Statistics Courts Proceedings excel files.

Note
* PNDs include 16-year-olds and older.

courtroom settings bring criminal prosecution into sharp focus for its bearing on certain social groups. Moreover, the tight interplay between the different courtroom actors is revealing. Feeley (1992), from his study carried out in a court in Connecticut in the USA, refers to the 'courthouse workgroup'. This is the working group of state prosecutors, legal defence advocates, judges, ushers and legal clerks notable for their collective performance in processing defendants and within due procedures. The courthouse workgroup is a useful concept to apply to my courtroom observations. The important nature and high responsibility that magistrates carry in their role as legal decision-makers is central in this chapter. Roach Anleu and Mack (2005) have carried out a substantial amount of research on the lower magistrates' courts of Australia, including observations of proceedings, and portray the courtroom as 'a dramatic and symbolic location where law and society interact' (ibid.: 595). This is a useful visualisation to hold on to as we move to the following section, which lays out the courtroom action as I observed it.

To provide a backdrop to the reflections and evaluations given by the magistrates interviewed and as presented in the following chapters, the forthcoming section gives a detailed description of a London magistrates' court on a busy Monday morning in January 2015. Further description is given from observations of proceedings overseen by a judge sitting alone later on in 2015. These illuminate the breadth of cases that come before the lower courts, the typicality of defendants' circumstances, and the penalties handed out to them. They highlight the sometimes miserable existence that defendants' lives are located within, alongside the frequently revealed complex health and social care needs they have. Other researchers similarly point to the lower criminal courts as dealing with high numbers of defendants saddled with social and economic hardship (Roach Anleu and Mack, 2007: 183).

Inner London magistrates' courts are busy, bustling places and this is more so with the court closures that have been occurring across London since 2011. Local court closures have squeezed the volume of business into a smaller number of courts, with the result that they are congested, hectic places. This is especially so on a Monday morning following the weekend and Saturday night arrests, when those in police custody over the weekend are produced. The London magistrates' court where the following observations were made sits within a court bench area covering four neighbouring local borough councils serving a population of around a million people. The court operates 12 courtrooms five days a week, plus some on Saturdays. The courtrooms range in function from 'remand courts' processing upwards of 20 'first appearance' cases, those set up with video link systems to hear bail applications and plea entries from defendants on remand in prison custody, 'traffic courts', courts set aside for contested cases in summary trials and dedicated youth courts for 10- to 17-year-olds. This last category is off limits for public viewing.

The doors of the courthouse open to the public at 9 a.m. with formal proceedings beginning at 10 a.m. The first hour before official business sees the building fill up with large numbers of people. These include accused defendants summonsed to attend, friend and family supporters, legal defence, prosecution service staff, court administration staff, and uniformed police arriving to hand over photo evidence or give testimony in person. The crowds gathering in the waiting areas are clearly distinguishable as the accused and their support networks and those working in the criminal justice industry. Dark-suited lawyers arrive with bulging briefcases and wheeled travel bags ready to seek out clients they are scheduled to represent. Some defendants are anxious-looking, bewildered by what seems an unknown system. Others appear worn to the routine, seemingly having experienced it before. Some are clearly affected by poverty, ill-health and the ravages of drug and alcohol dependence and some have made their best efforts to dress formally for the occasion. Some are in and out catching a last-minute cigarette before heading upstairs to the courtroom to await their turn among the many other people appearing today.

Apprehensive-looking defendants arrive and are processed through the airport like security, following requirements to place mobile phones, keys, bottles of perfume and hand sanitiser in plastic trays before proceeding through the metal detector arch. Like other public buildings in cities and towns across the globe, courts are operating on heightened security concerns, with systems stepped up to detect the possible disguise of weapons and lethal fluids. Security staff, commanding in their black-and-white uniforms, heavy shoes and serious expressions, scrutinise people and possessions as they enter the building.

The day's lists of appearances are pinned to the wall in the main concourse waiting area. They are long, computer-generated lists divided by courtroom and prosecuting authority. There are the long lists prepared by the Metropolitan Police Service (MPS) and the many being prosecuted by the Driver and Vehicle Licensing Authority (DVLA) as motoring offences. A large orange sign directs people to locate their name on the list and consequent courtroom number.

I take the steps to the building's first floor, where the separate courts are located. Three have the paper lists pinned to the outside wall. More than 20 names are listed on each. One appears to be a high-volume traffic court with the DVLA ready to process a string of motoring offenders. I avoid that one, choosing another that looks to promise a busy morning's business and will include people held in police custody over the weekend. For all of these cases to be completed, swift processing will be required. Roach Anleu and Mack (2007), in their research on the lower-tier criminal courts in Australia, refer to the necessary efficient management of progressing through the court list as 'judgecraft', with careful decisions and negotiation at play to minimise delays and move through the lists as swiftly and fairly as possible.

I take a seat in the small public gallery partitioned off with glass panelling at the rear of the room. The court is in full view and audibility. I'm accompanied in the public gallery by awaiting defendants and their husbands, wives, partners, friends and drinking partners. A notice on the wall dictates gallery behaviour – 'no talking, no smoking, no drinking, no eating, no caps/hats, no mobile phones, no children under 14 or infant in arms'. The 'no talking' rule is not closely observed.

It is 10 a.m. and business gets under way. In line with the longstanding tradition of respect, the court and public gallery are called to rise with the command of 'all stand please' voiced by the usher as the three magistrates enter and take their place on the bench. The courtroom today is managed by a bench of magistrates: two women and a man. They are white and look to be aged in their mid-fifties. Today's chair is one of the women. She is the voice of the bench and will deliver the case-by-case magistrate decisions. The magistrates are assisted by a justices clerk, also a white woman seemingly aged in her fifties. Computers, laptops and tablet devices are positioned on workstations ready to retrieve case information, access booking systems and set forthcoming trial dates. A current development occurring within courtroom operation is the digitisation of case file and communication systems. The high piles of cardboard folders, seen previously, containing police arrest and prosecution details are now replaced by hand-held and laptop devices holding electronic casefiles and notes of each defendant. The different defence lawyers scheduled to represent summonsed clients rush in and out checking the day's list for where on it their clients appear. They're trying to work out what time within the morning's proceedings they are needed to stand up commanding knowledge of their client's offence and plea and any mitigating and personal circumstances that can be put forward to lessen the penalty, or retain liberty if bail and remand decisions are in the mix. Legal aid defence lawyers typically carry large caseloads, it sometimes being said they have little time to fully familiarise themselves with defendants' cases.

Once in full swing the courtroom operates its formal proceedings within a sea of noise and disruption, as defence lawyers, duty probation officers, defendants and their family members meander in and out of the public gallery preparing to take the dock. Defendants wait patiently, but sometimes impatiently for their turn to arrive. Delays push back what was thought would be a morning's appearance over to the afternoon, with evident inconvenience displayed. Some will have taken time off work to appear or arranged childcare in their absence. Hearings can be put back if a defendant needs the assistance of a language interpreter or the services of the duty solicitor, as well as through sheer caseload volume. Interpreters and duty solicitors are spread thinly between defendants.

Eleven cases are dealt with within the three hours of the morning's operations before the magistrates rise for a break at 1 p.m. It is difficult to summarise the morning's cases for typicality. They involve drugs possession, domestic violence, drink driving, vehicle theft and other sundry cases. They include younger and older men and women, local London people, recent migrants and people on prescribed medication; three are noted as having mental health issues. None is presented as in secure employment.

Supporting the high rate of guilty pleas entered in the magistrates' courts, seven of the 11 defendants in the dock this morning plead guilty to the accusation, two plead not guilty and the case against one man is withdrawn because no prosecution notes are available. He is told he is 'free to go'. One enters a 'no plea', demanding his case is sent to the Crown Court.

Table 3.5 summarises the morning's proceedings. The defendants are mostly aged in their thirties, two are 21-year-olds, and two are in their forties. They are of mixed ethnicities and nationalities. Just two are women, both of whose cases

Table 3.5 Observed cases proceeded against in a London magistrates' court

Socio-demographics	Offence and plea	Mitigating the sentence	Penalty dispensed
1. F, aged 30s, white[1]	Charge – drink driving Plea – guilty	Single parent with two daughters aged seven and 14	Disqualified from driving for 12 months, total fine £235 to be paid at a rate of £20 per week, attend driving course
2. M, aged 21, white	Charge – assault on girlfriend Plea – not guilty, sent to trial		Bailed with conditions – 'no contact with witnesses' but then retracted
3. M, aged 32, white	Charge – criminal damage Plea – guilty	Homeless with mental health problems	Sent to prison to await sentencing. Sentencing delayed to follow a probation report
4. M, aged 30s, Asian	Charge – withdrawn – 'free to go'		
5. M, aged 30s, white	Charge – receiving stolen motorbike Plea – guilty		Bailed for sentencing. Sentencing delayed to follow probation report in three weeks' time. Noted as 'all options open including custody' and/or going to Crown Court for sentencing. Unconditional bail
6. M, aged 30s, Asian	Charge – beating girlfriend Plea – not guilty, denies facts		Summary trial set for five weeks' time
7. M, aged 22, white	Charge – possession of three bags of herbal cannabis Plea – guilty		Twelve-month conditional discharge

8. F, aged 30, white Eastern European	Charge – driving under the influence Plea – guilty	Four children including six-month-old baby twins, depression, on medication	Seventeen months' disqualification, £230 fine and ordered to reapply for licence once the disqualification is spent
9. M, aged 21, black	Charge – taking brother's car Plea – guilty		Eight penalty points £896 fine
10. M, aged 46, white	Charge – 369.9 grams of cannabis in hydroponic plant form Plea – no plea entered		Trial date set for Crown Court in 15 days' time – unconditional bail
11. M, age 47, black	Charge – possession of 2.23 grams of mephedrone Plea – guilty	On prescribed medication	Fine: total £145
12. M	Due to be produced over live link from prison- not produced		

Note
1 The ethnicity of the defendants was recorded based on appearance and as such amount to broad and rudimentary categorising.

are drink driving. Those who admit guilt have their cases variously decided. Some are fined, disqualified from driving and ordered onto an alcohol driving awareness course there and then. Fines given out range in amount from £145 to £896 and, reflecting the mainly unemployed status of those receiving them, incremental benefit deductions and payments are granted. Pre-sentence assessments from the probation service are ordered and a man with mental health issues is detained in prison custody to await assessment and sentencing. This is the most surprising decision of the morning since it is noted he is mentally imbalanced and the criminal damage he caused is obviously a result of his mental condition. This case brings to life the very real issue of inadequate diversionary mental health provision and facilities at the different stages of the criminal justice system, at the levels of policing, prosecution and court administration. Bail conditions are being set in the contested cases. Problems emerge in the two cases of alleged 'assault on a girlfriend', with the accused persons being informed that they must not have contact with the witness. Both illuminate the problems with domestic violence cases, with the 21-year-old continuing to be in a partner relationship with the victim despite the prosecution against him going ahead. The condition of 'no contact' with her as the witness is retracted. The other man similarly accused is going to lose contact with his nine-year-old daughter until the case is resolved.

Some defendants are visibly relieved as they leave the courtroom with what might have been an unexpected outcome, or just thankful that the day in court is over. For others, this is less so, with the enormity of the error etched on their faces. This was an emotional morning in court for its illumination of the impact the penalties imposed are likely to have on the lives of defendants and their ability to function in the way they are used, for instance the already-depressed mother losing her driving licence for 18 months when she has four small children to get to and from school and hospital appointments to keep for her unwell six-month-old twins, on top of the elderly mother she looks after.

The following section describes in more detail some of the cases I observed from this morning's hearings. This draws out the individual nuances, legal technicalities and real-life circumstances as revealed through the accounts given by the prosecution, legal defence representatives and one defendant's interjections. The adversarial justice system minimises these as far as possible, funnelling defence and justification accounts through the words of the legal representatives. Some defendants though, make themselves heard loud and clear.

The case of Ms Jackson

The first defendant of the morning is a white woman aged in her late thirties. She is charged with drink driving. Once confirming her name and address, the case against her is read out, followed by the request for a plea. Like most other defendants in court this morning and in general, she pleads guilty. It is read out by the prosecution that Ms Jackson had been out with friends when she consumed two glasses of wine before getting into her car to drive home. The police had seen her get into the car and followed before pulling her over for questioning. She admitted to consuming alcohol, with the reading read out as 58 micrograms of alcohol. The legal limit is 35 micrograms per 100 millilitres of breath.

Ms Jackson is represented by a young Asian female solicitor, who offers details about the case and about Ms Jackson. Since Ms Jackson has pleaded guilty to the charge, the facts read out are for the purposes of mitigating the sentence (Easton and Piper, 2012). It is noted by the defence that Ms Jackson 'pleaded guilty at the earliest opportunity' to the arresting officers at the scene. Compliance with the justice process in this way usually attracts a reduction in the sentence imposed and this is where the 'sentence discount principle' of up to a third reduction in penalty becomes evident (Ashworth and Redmayne, 2010). The defence offers that Ms Jackson is a trainee hairdresser and is required to attend a specified number of training hours per week to qualify. She is a single parent with a seven-year-old and a 14-year-old. She is reported to be 'of good character', with her only previous court appearance many years earlier. It is stated that Ms Jackson showed remorse for the incident. The magistrates confer among themselves and return a sentence of disqualification from driving for 12 months and compulsory attendance on a drink driving course, which needs to be completed within the next seven months. The penalties they have given demonstrate strict adherence to the Sentencing Guidelines. Ms Jackson is also ordered to pay a total fine of £235, but accepting her limited means she is granted to pay at a rate of £20 per week. The first payment is due in a week's time. Ms Jackson leaves the courtroom with a pained expression, no doubt contemplating the reorganisation of life in the months ahead with no transport, less money, a driving course to complete, hairdresser training to stick to and children to single-handedly care for, all a heavy burden for a night out with friends.

The slant of the sentence mitigation has a gender emphasis to it, with Ms Jackson's sole childcare and work responsibilities highlighted. Easton and Piper (2012) write about the 'differential impact' of sentencing on certain categories of offender, within which women with children are included. This is for the damaging impact that, specifically, prison has on the mother–child relationship. Although relating mainly to imprisonment, 'motherhood' is argued as a relevant personal mitigating factor for consideration at the court sentencing stage (Minson *et al.*, 2015; Gerry and Harris, 2014).

The case of Mr Miller

Another of the cases I observe during the morning's proceedings is Mr Miller. He is a 32-year-old white man appearing in the dock from police custody, where he has spent some of the weekend following arrest for criminal damage of 'a bed and a television within a property'. Further nuisance was caused at the street level, with Mr. Miller reported as 'attempting to destroy a White Mercedes Sprinter car by opening the car door and damaging the remote locking system', in addition to setting light to some rubbish. The owner of the car was present at the scene. Earlier in the day Mr Miller had demanded £100 from his mother. The structure of the incident as recounted begins to illustrate someone who is 'not of sound mind', rather than a malicious offender acting with conscience. On being asked to confirm his address by the magistrates, Mr Miller responds, 'I'm homeless sort of at the moment, I can't remember.' Mr Miller pleads guilty to the charge.

The duty defence lawyer representing him is a young black woman who from the file notes says 'no mental health issues are recorded', but that she feels certain there is personality disorder and depression; she reads out 'he was under the influence of alcohol and drugs at the time of the offence'. She reports that a previous but unsuccessful Drugs Rehabilitation Requirement (DRR) was given to Mr Miller and his previous recorded offence was 10 months earlier, in 2014.

Mr Miller's case is adjourned for sentencing pending an assessment relating to his mental health status. This is booked to be carried out by the probation service in three weeks' time. In the meantime, despite what is arguably relatively minor criminal damage committed by a mentally disordered person, Mr Miller is remanded to prison custody. It is stated the assessment hearing will be conducted over video link from the prison. This case is striking for a number of reasons. The first is that Mr Miller obviously has mental health needs, which are in all probability the cause of the outburst leading to the criminal damage. It also demonstrates a clear absence in adequate mental health assessment cover both at the police station and within the courts and the availability of suitable provision and accommodation to bail him to. The Sentencing Guidelines, which magistrates are encouraged to rely upon to assist guiding their decisions, are rigidly adhered to. He is reported as having previously offended while on bail and is dealt with as a regular offender rather than as a vulnerable person with special needs. Moreover, he is subjected to the same streamlining mechanisms introduced to deal with prisoners' bail hearings from within the prison in the use of the prison video link technology. In the same way that the virtual court is deemed inappropriate for 'vulnerable' offenders held in police custody as set out in the 'suitability criteria' guidance (Office for Criminal Justice Reform, 2010: 10), the video link assessment should also be deemed unsuitable for a person with Mr Miller's needs. He was held overnight in police custody and was now remanded for at least the next three weeks pending assessment.

This case clearly illustrates the challenges of mental disorder, its interaction within the criminal justice system and the importance of its identification at the different stages in the system, such as at the police station (Peay, 2012), and the need for appropriate support and diversion services to be called upon at these points.

Through the morning's work, 11 cases are completed from the list before the magistrates request to rise for lunch at 1 p.m. They haven't taken a break since the start of proceedings at 10 a.m. The justices' clerk is eagerly tying up unfinished business before an interlude and before the afternoon session gets under way in an hour's time. This includes directing the magistrates to phone through to the London prison from where a man on the morning's list (see case 12 in

Table 3.5) should have been presented over video link. The arrangement hasn't gone ahead and it is mentioned by the court usher that the prison 'can't put him over video link' today. The clerk notes that the defendant has been in prison for three months since October 2014 and 'needs to be produced'. No further details of the case were revealed that morning, but the situation brings into focus the use of video link technology within courtroom proceedings. The growing popularity with video link technology in some police areas was noted in the previous chapter and fits closely with the government's court modernisation project. The issue of glitches in connectivity, though, is a serious concern for the delays generated, and also for the potential for injustices to increase within the system.

It is evident from this morning's glitch, and through further elaborations by magistrates who have experience with the use of court video link technology, that there are weaknesses with the set-up, which when it goes wrong impact negatively on defendants and can call into question issues of due process. The Criminal Justice Management conference revealed examples of scheduled cases not going ahead for hearing, interpreters not being available for non-English-speaking defendants and extra pressures placed upon already-overstretched prison staff. Thus, capacity in coordinating scheduled hearings in overseeing prison-to-court video link connections can be compromised. Enhancing digital systems within criminal courtroom operation is an area of investment committed to by the Conservative government and is progressing apace through the Ministry of Justice-led criminal court modernisation project, but it is evident that teething issues exist. Moreover, as I have already argued, it is essential that due process protections are observed alongside these developments.

The morning's cases proceeded one by one, with little variation in form from the offence being read out to the defendant, the request for the defendant to enter a plea ('how do you plead?'), scanning the online courtroom timetable for available trial dates and times and the magistrates consulting the Sentencing Guidelines to establish the allotted penalty and fine amounts. This is until we arrive at case number 10 (see Table 3.5), who is a white man aged in his forties. He has been waiting in the public gallery along with his partner for much of the morning. He is a weighty man with a scar on his face. He's comfortably dressed in a grey flannel tracksuit. He moves about with a crutch, displaying physical discomfort in his leg. His charge is read out as having had 369.9 grams of cannabis in the form of cultivated plants at his home premises, a fact he does not deny. He enters a plea of guilty to the offence, but as the case proceeds to the sentencing stage he realises a recent change to 'committal hearings' in the magistrates' courts has removed a point in the process he was waiting for. He demands that the case go to the Crown Court – 'I want to go to Crown Court'. But, with the changes introduced in 2014/2015, if the plea is indicated then consideration must be given to whether the gravity of the crime permits retention within the jurisdiction of the lower court or whether it should be transferred upwards to the more powerful Crown Court. Since he has entered his plea as guilty, his case is moving to sentencing.

However, this man is knowledgeable of the process and insists he wants his case to go to the Crown Court. It seems with the display of pain he might want to put forward personal mitigating factors along with the guilty plea, which he appears to want to do with the formality of the higher-tier Crown Court. The clerk tries to explain that since they have a guilty plea there is no room for the case to be committed to Crown Court proceedings. There is a toing and froing of dissatisfaction from him and frustration from the justices' clerk that his past knowledge of committal hearings no longer stands. Eventually his solicitor is instructed to leave the courtroom to explain the detail. It might be deduced that the choice he wants to make connects to the perception that a fairer trial is received in the Crown Court under the instruction of a Queens Counsel judge and trial by jury, as found in Hedderman and Moxon's (1992) study of defendants' mode of trial decisions (cf. Vennard, 1982). On return to the court, the guilty plea is retracted and the justice's clerk obliges by booking the case into the Crown Court to take place in 15 days' time. In the meantime, he is granted unconditional bail. Our eyes connect as he limps out of the courtroom. I'm trying to gauge his mood. He glares, probably wondering who I am and why I've been taking notes in the public gallery all morning.

This is a case that is almost entirely taken over by the justices' clerk, who is forced to draw upon her legal proficiency and expertise given the level of technical knowledge the case requires, including familiarity with the legislative change to committal hearings. It illustrates the magistrates' court lay justice model operating under the legal guidance of the justices' clerk. Indeed, in comparisons made between courtroom working performed by lay justices to that of legally qualified judges it is the legal technicality and competence of lay participants that is sometimes questioned (Malsch, 2009).

Courtroom observations of a district judge

From another morning's ethnographic observations in the same courthouse later on in September 2015, the work of a single sitting judge was observed. The main difference between her operation and that of the lay magistrates was the active case management and paperwork the judge takes responsibility for. She spent the three hours shuffling papers and juggling the 'put backs' decided upon for the purposes of assisting defendants with legal and language interpretation difficulties, and for the prosecution to further consider its case against the 18-year-old woman with psychiatric problems accused of lashing out at a police officer. Here the prosecution was asked to consider whether going ahead was 'in the public interest'. All of this was at the same time as listening to detailed case evidence. Observing benches of lay magistrates similarly in operation, the justices' clerk performs the case management role. The allocation of cases between magistrates and judges is said to be broadly equal, but the sitting judge that day commented on the sometimes complex legal knowledge required, such as today's cases, with one prosecution brought by a regulatory agency, and awareness of mental health law needed.

What was striking from observing the two morning's proceedings was the time and attention given over to each of the defendant's cases, with genuine consideration directed at the personal mitigation put forward by the legal representatives, as well as taking interest in defendants' wider circumstances and ability to achieve the sentence demands (Easton and Piper, 2012).

In critiquing whether the lower courts are operating swift, speedy justice that might be threatening fair justice as I suggest with the arguments made in the previous chapter, from this morning's courtroom observations this could not be supported. There were, however, cases that stood out for the constrained decisions of magistrates in working with the Sentencing Guidelines and the bearing that the uniform application of these has on defendants, especially those with mental health needs. This was also the case for the man accused of beating his partner, the facts of which he strongly disputed, mentioning the abuse he suffered from her. This disagreement would be adjudicated in a summary trial, but in the meantime the bail conditions of not 'contacting the witness/victim' would stop him seeing his nine-year-old daughter until the case is resolved in five weeks' time. On raising a concern with this anomaly caused through the bail conditions, he was instructed to talk to the duty solicitor outside the courtroom. This was clearly distressing for him. In this instance, a difference was noted in the way female defendants were listened to, with an emphasis often placed on their child caring role, yet less consideration was given to this when parenting responsibility was raised from a male defendant's position. Comfort (2007) and others have written about the impact of 'punishment beyond the legal offender'. This usually discusses the effects on children who have an imprisoned parent (Evans, 2015), but it is apparent from this morning's hearings that bail restrictions that forbid contact with victims who are family, such as domestic violence cases, inadvertently impact upon the children in the relationship. This is an issue that requires recognition in this regard.

Magistrates are to a certain extent restricted in their sentencing options. This is due to the introduction of Sentencing Guidelines in 2009, in an attempt to achieve greater consistency in sentencing across courts and across similar offence types. The Sentencing Guidelines manual lists all offence categories, such as 'possession of a Class B drug' and 'theft from a dwelling', with a grid listing the probable mitigating and aggravating factors relating to the offence. These include 'first offence' and 'pleaded guilty at the earliest opportunity' and are the factors guiding the sentencing decision. The Sentencing Guidelines laid out in the manual are characterised as guidelines and 'not tramlines', as a number of magistrates commented in the interviews, leaving room for the application of discretion in individual sentence decisions, which is indeed instructed in the central principle of 'judicial independence'. From observation though, it seems rare for magistrates to deviate from the guidelines (Roberts, 2010, 2011). Rigid adherence to the Sentencing Guidelines fits with the increasing professionalisation of lower court justice and the broader pressures to operationalise sentencing consistently and as efficiently as magistrates' legally qualified colleagues (cf. Herbert, 2004). The newer, more recently recruited magistrates included in my research verbalised the tendency for some longer-serving magistrates to be mildly opposed to the regulations surrounding the application of the guidelines for the lack of discretion they enable. From my court-room observations, and moreover in specific cases, I argue that there should be more deviation from the guidelines when justifiably called for, and that magistrates and judges should have more confidence in using their powers of 'judge-directed acquittals' and sentences of 'absolute discharge' in cases that are deemed not in the public interest (Jehle and Wade, 2006). As illustrated in Table 3.3, of almost 500,000 cases sentenced in 2014, just under 2,000 were decided in this way.

Criminal justice commentators Sanders *et al.* (2010) assess the extent to which magistrates and magistrates' courts embody the principles of 'fairness, efficiency and accountability', as contended by Doran and Glenn (cited in Sanders *et al.*, 2010: 536). These, Sanders and colleagues say, are the principles that underpin justice administration in the Crown Courts in trial by judge and jury, and as many elements as possible should be strived for in the magistrates' courts. In their appraisal they state the 'efficiency principle is implicitly being prioritised over the principles of fairness and accountability' (ibid.: 541), but that fairness was better achieved by lay magistrates than salaried stipendiaries (ibid.: 541). They go on to state that 'It is no exaggeration to say that magistrates' courts are crime control courts overlaid with a thin layer of due process icing' (Sanders *et al.*, 2010: 551).

From my court observations, the statement by Sanders and colleagues is agreed with to some degree. But this relates to the difficulty in some cases to understand why and how they had reached this distance. This is particularly those involving defendants with mental health problems. Questions are raised regarding policing and prosecution decisions, and the earlier diversion decisions are clearly not adequate. As such, my appraisal of magistrates' court justice concurs with notions that the magistrates' courts are crime control courts, but the due process icing is not as thin as Sanders *et al.* (2010) imply. Defendants have time and attention put to their cases that are heard in open court, with options to contest guilt and with legal representation granted, albeit often by duty lawyers dealing with large caseloads and with little time to spare.

It is important to accept that the lower criminal courts are dealing not just with technical law breaking but with complex facts of dispute that carry mitigating and aggravating features. The person has the right to be heard and carefully listened to, especially since the outcomes have far-reaching consequences on the lives of those concerned. Some research studies report the longer time it takes magistrates to process cases and get through their daily lists compared to the operational pace of single sitting judges (Morgan and Russell, 2000; Ipsos MORI, 2011). Policies and guidance are in place urging speedy, swift justice and reducing the number of adjournments in a case, so that the time taken between arrest and conviction or acquittal is shortened. A broad premise put forward by some commentators, however, is that swift justice is not necessarily fair justice (Morgan, 2008), and my argument aligns with this. Due process becomes undermined by objectives of economics and speed.

District judges in the lower courts

In line with the modernisation and streamlining approaches being applied within the lower courts, a shift towards increasing professionalisation is a recurring perception (Morgan, 2013; Cox, 2010; Seago *et al.*, 2000). This is alongside the notion that a growing role is being carved out for full-time salaried judges in dispensing lower criminal court work in the same way that over time other common-law jurisdictions, such as Australia (Douglas and Laster, 1992) and New Zealand (Harkness, 2015, 2009), have moved. These legal systems have replaced an earlier predominant reliance on lay justices with stipendiary professional judges. Morgan (2013), in stating his views on the future of the lay magistracy and the threats they face, emphasises the growing number of salaried judges employed since the turn of the millennium in the English justice system and argues that 'the fact that district judges are replacing magistrates is unarguable' (ibid.: 8).

The government has refuted the claim that salaried judges are being brought in to replace lay magistrates (Green, 2014). Indeed, continuing governments make pledges they are committed to retaining the role of the lay magistracy and that they greatly value the contribution they make to community and local justice (Ministry of Justice, 2012). Despite words to the contrary, there is evidence of an increase in the number of single sitting judges employed within the magistrates' courts. According to official statistics put forward in response to a parliamentary question tabled by Lord Beecham in 2013 (cf. Gibbs and Kirby, 2014: 11) (see Table 3.6), the number of full-time district judges has remained fairly consistent, but there has been a rise in the number of deputy district judges employed. Deputy district judges have the same jurisdiction as full-time stipendiary judges and sit in judgement alone in the way of their full-time colleagues (Courts and Tribunals Judiciary, 2015). Between the years 2006 and 2012, around 140 full-time stipendiary district judges were employed in the magistrates' courts, but the number of deputy district judges increased from 137 to 173 in this same period, with the greatest increase coming in the years since 2011. This can be said to mirror the lower court streamlining and efficiency changes

Table 3.6 Number of district judges and deputy district judges employed in magistrates' courts 2006 to 2012

Year	Number of district judges	Number of deputy district judges
2006	141	137
2007	142	131
2008	137	127
2009	143	142
2010	142	141
2011	149	144
2012	142	173

Source: Hansard (2013) HL Deb 22 May 2013, vol 745, col WA80.

occurring in this recent modernisation period. It can be interpreted as a shift in staffing policy at this level of judicial appointment, with the pool of single sitting judges running courtroom proceedings in the lower magistrates' courts expanding in recent years, in the way Morgan (2013) contends.

It is difficult to get information on the deployment of salaried judges in the magistrates' courts, on where they are located and on the official spread and division of lower court work they are tasked with. Moreover, it is not made public whether they are replacing the work carried out by retiring and resigning magistrates or whether they are being positioned to assist in city-centre high-volume courts of need. The Ipsos MORI (2011) report noted the fluctuating number of judges working in the lower courts over the years and stated that numbers had grown more recently in the provincial areas (ibid.: 82). Gibbs writes extensively on the lay magistracy and reports on the steady decline in magistrate numbers over the last decade and also refers to an ongoing freeze on magistrate recruitment. She links this to shrinking business in the courts, but also asks questions on the role of salaried district judges (Gibbs and Kirby, 2014). Table 3.7 illustrates the fall in magistrate numbers since 2006. A sharp decline is shown in the five years since 2011. The number of magistrates has reduced by 10,000, from just under 30,000 in 2011 to fewer than 19,000 in 2015. This decline in number corresponds with the time period in which salaried qualified judge numbers have increased.

Given the reducing number of serving magistrates in the last few years (Gibbs and Kirby, 2014), together with business in the lower courts also declining and an increase in the number of salaried judges, who process cases at a faster pace, it has to be assumed that more lower court work in English criminal justice system is being carried out by professional legal experts.

Most of the magistrates interviewed were working in courthouses where salaried judges were employed on a fixed, resident basis or were rostered to come in when heavy court workload required. Magistrates in one focus group mentioned the employment of a resident judge in their court within the previous two

Table 3.7 Total magistrate numbers in England and Wales

Total serving magistrates	Numbers
2006	28,865
2007	29,841
2008	29,419
2009	29,270
2010	28,607
2011	29,966
2012	25,170
2013	23,401
2014	21,626
2015	19,634

Sources: Years 2006–2013: data taken from Gibbs (2014b: 8) (source: Judicial Office statistics); years 2014 and 2015: Judicial Office statistics.

years. This was greeted with reservation by some. The sentiments articulated by the magistrates in their working relationship with judicial judges was that they coexisted in the same courthouses with not a lot of professional interaction between them. Some magistrates felt undermined by what they perceived to be a different and higher value placed upon judges than on themselves as lay justices. This was despite seeing themselves as performing the same role and dispensing the same court work with the same level of proficiency as their legally trained colleagues. The two salaried judges interviewed in my research acknowledged the different and faster pace at which they process cases compared to their lay colleagues. They stressed that this was inevitable because they do not confer with others in their court decisions in the way lay magistrates are compelled to do, which results in added time.

Since salaried judges sit in judgement alone and there is an incremental increase in their numbers, this means an increased proportion of criminal court work in the English criminal justice system is being conducted in a way which mirrors the professional justice system in most continental European countries. Indeed, it is argued by Malsch from her research on different European court systems that single sitting judges is a style of justice administration that is contrary to developing an increasing trust in legal systems (cf. Malsch, 2009).

Returning to McBarnet's research (1981) and her summary of the quality of justice administration in the magistrates' courts, she discusses the 'image of triviality' surrounding these courts. This is in their dealing with minor, everyday offences and the supposed relative inconsequence of the penalties dispensed for these. She argues that this has the effect of keeping the public's interest away from the lower courts, which strips away aspects of due process protection in the form of open public justice. McBarnet aligns what she refers to as 'two tiers of justice' to the history of summary justice. She notes how summary justice was a 'statutory creation' brought about in the nineteenth century and that it was specifically established to process the 'high volume of less serious offences, quickly' (ibid.: 188). In quoting the Oxford English Dictionary, McBarnet defines summary justice as 'proceedings in a court of law carried out rapidly by the omission of certain formalities required by the common law' (ibid.: 188). As such, she argues that summary justice is therefore characterised in legal terms 'not by positive attributes but by negative ones: it negates many of the procedures held to be necessary in the traditional ideology of due process' (ibid.: 188). She criticises the dismantling of due process protections, arguing that they are equally necessary for people accused of less serious offences as they are for people charged with higher-tier offences.

This chapter has provided an overview of the lower-tier magistrates' courts as they operate in the English justice system and the quantity and nature of cases that lay magistrates and their fellow district judges' have powers over. It has considered the quality of summary justice and argues that perceptions of trivia surrounding the work of the lower criminal courts are misplaced, especially since over the developing decades summary justice now incorporates judging a greater number of more serious and violent cases and enables magistrates and judges to impose a wide band of restrictive penalties in the form of fines and community-based and custodial penalties. Due process protections are as necessary here as they always have been.

The material presented in this chapter provides a backdrop to the magistrates' interviews drawn upon in the following three chapters, in which they convey their experiences within this shifting criminal court terrain.

Notes

1 Magistrates have a maximum power of imprisonment for six months, but this rises to 12 months for a second concurrent imprisonable offence (Davies *et al.*, 2015).
2 The lower courts in Australia are also called magistrates' courts but they differ to the English magistrates' courts in that 'magistrates' in Australia are professionally qualified in the law.

4 Magistrates, motivations and contributions to justice

The previous chapters have discussed alterations occurring within the lower criminal courts in light of the streamlining and modernising processes being implemented. Courtroom observations illuminate the type of cases and general atmosphere of law adjudication in these courts. In this chapter empirical research with serving magistrates is drawn upon. Lay magistrates are at the centre of criminal court case processing in the English justice system and their experience in this role was a key focus of my research. This chapter first reports on the broad social and professional backgrounds of the magistrates interviewed before discussing their motivations for serving and the contributions they view they make to lay justice.

There is little recent research on the way lay magistrates experience their court working role. This is despite their large number, the volume of cases they preside over and the important legal decision-making powers they preside over. Some research incorporates magistrates as interviewees in explorations of criminal court service delivery (Donoghue, 2014b; Dhami, 2013, 2004; Ipsos MORI, 2011; Morgan and Russell, 2000) and studies have been carried out from within magistrates' courtrooms that analyse dynamics of power between judicial actors and the defendants appearing in them (McBarnet, 1981a, 1981b; Carlen, 1974). There is also a body of research focusing on the social composition of the magistracy. This typically draws attention to the mainly privileged, socio-economic strata that magistrates come from, with issues of community representation raised (Gibbs and Kirby, 2014; Dignan and Wynne, 1997; Burney, 1979; Baldwin, 1976). There is some research on magistrates and ethnicity (Davis and Vennard, 2006). For example, King and May's research (1985) on 'black magistrates' examined levels of involvement among black and Asian members and associated the research to race relations in the administration of justice. They found limitations with the recruitment approach, with it being considered that local black and Asian community groups could be mobilised more effectively to encourage their greater representation in the lay justice role. Grove's (2002) textual account reports from courtroom observations and conversations with fellow magistrates across the country and brings to life the divergent nature of lower court work by region and social and economic history. Grove commented on the ethnic representation among magistrate benches and remarked on the mixed ethnicity in the large city benches he visited in Birmingham and London. There are other studies that have been carried out with serving magistrates that deserve mentioning (Malsch, 2009; Brown, 1991; Parker *et al.*, 1989, among others) but there is less analysis of magistrates' working role from their perspective.

Together with there being limited recent research with serving magistrates on court working experiences, scant evidence emerges to shift the emphasis from measuring magistrates in terms of blunt socio-economic variables. There is little that moves us beyond the narrative that largely portrays magistrates to be from conservative sections of society, whose lives and lifestyles are distinct from the general public's and whose experiences do not reflect those they sit in judgement over.

Periodically, there are recruitment drives to boost the number of serving magistrates and to shape a more diverse profile of magistrates than has historically, and to some extent consistently existed. The core definition of lay justice as performed by magistrates is that it is local justice dispensed by ordinary members of the community. It is therefore considered important that those who dispense courtroom justice are reflective of society's diverse make-up (Thomas, 2010). Over the years efforts have been made to draw greater representation from ethnic minority communities and younger age groups. Indeed, the issue of 'judicial diversity' and, in part, lack of it is not limited to the lower criminal courts or to discussion of the UK. Similar calls to achieve greater diversity among jurors sitting on jury trials in the Crown Courts have been made (Thomas, 2010), and other jurisdictions centre attention on achieving a greater ethnic and gender mix among judicial members occupying this high-level legal role.

Returning to the issue of the social composition of the magistracy, earlier research by Burney (1979) addressed the social backgrounds of serving magistrates. She studied the profile of magistrates in seven 'bench areas' and situated their high social status within the selection and nomination process of the time. She highlighted that nomination mainly came about through recommendations from other magistrates. In this way, Burney referred to the selection process as too easily turning into 'self-perpetuating oligarchies' of privilege (ibid.: 73). Similarly, Dignan and Wynne's (1997) critique of the magistracy was generated from research carried out across a bench of magistrates in the north Midlands. They also made reference to the restricted social class background among the surveyed magistrates. They pointed to the limited number of local areas the magistrates resided in across the region and the higher property values of the areas when compared to the national average. They mentioned the predominance of professional backgrounds among magistrates, identifying a particular social elite. They asked, given the fact that magistrates come from mainly middle-class and professional career backgrounds, whether it is time to portray the magistracy more realistically. They go further with this argument to suggest questioning what is wanted from the magistracy in terms of its function. One offer they state is that it might be time to consider committing to a 'quasi-professional panel of suitably qualified people' (ibid.: 196). Dignan and Wynne cite other studies conducted among magistrates back in the 1970s and make reference to magistrates' membership within certain organisations such as the Freemasons and Rotary clubs. They similarly state that these revelations help to fuel notions of 'a local self-selecting elite that is highly unrepresentative of the community from which it was drawn' (ibid.: 189). Baldwin's (1976) study of the social class backgrounds of magistrates in the 1970s used the Registrar General's classification. This separates occupational status into 'professional' in the higher working class tier and unskilled occupations in the lower tier. Baldwin found an over-representation among the magistrates he surveyed to be from the professional and managerial class, with the absence of working-class magistrates emphasised within his findings.

Gibbs and Kirby's (2014) research focuses attention on the issue of diversity among magistrates in the current period. They stress that there is a need to strengthen efforts to achieve greater societal representation but assert widening out from the domains of age and ethnicity is needed to account for the varied religious affiliations, social class backgrounds and sexual orientations of community members'. They suggest that the viable future for the magistracy is at risk if it does not represent the make-up of society as a whole.

This chapter picks up on the theme of diversity among the magistracy, but moves away from focusing on their middle-class status to comment on the varied personal and professional backgrounds that magistrates come from. Background information is provided on the magistrates interviewed before critically examining the way they experience this working role and the contributions they consider they make to the system of lay justice. From my research, I develop an argument that diverse and balanced benches are indeed paramount, but it is not the social class backgrounds of magistrates that matters. What matters is that a reasonable understanding of the social ills and disadvantage inherent in society, which overlaps for some into offending pathways, is appreciated and that the administration of justice is executed with confidence in effecting the fair application of justice process and procedure.

The magistrate sample

Thirty-three magistrates were interviewed for my research. This was in the form of three focus group interviews, with six and seven magistrates ($n=20$) in each, and individual one-to-one interviews with a further 13. A short questionnaire collecting socio-demographic information provided an overview of their wider social, professional and personal backgrounds.

The magistrates interviewed were self-selecting, coming forward from requests put out via acting 'chairs' in three 'bench areas'. 'Bench areas' refer to the organisational structure magistrates' courts are managed within, and include several courts within a designated geographic area. Research access was facilitated through the Magistrates' Association, who put me in touch with the acting chairs in the local bench areas. Following communication of the aims and purpose of the research, the chairs compiled the focus group participation to represent serving magistrates across their area and make efforts to include a range of magisterial experiences. The 13 individual interviews were carried out to increase the overall sample size but also to include a sample of newer recruits to the magistracy. Eight of the total magistrates interviewed had joined the service within the previous six years. These more recent recruits were younger than the other magistrates and were analysed as constituting a different group, whose experiences are referred to in more detail in the following chapter. The research was going on at a time when recruitment activity relating to enhancing diversity among the magistracy was ongoing and these magistrates can be seen as a part of this activity.

The self-selection approach obviously raises issues in terms of who comes forward for interview and therefore who has been represented in my research. I sought to include a broad profile of magistrates, but it is likely that certain groups of people came forward and others did not. For instance, it is probable that magistrates who are in full-time employment and who juggle their magisterial duties alongside their work have little extra time for research. One young woman who came forward for the recently recruited booster sample had tried to meet with on a few occasions. She was 30, working full time and had four children. Due to her commitments we eventually gave up trying. Thus, although my sample included a handful of younger magistrates, those working full time were not well represented. Using the bench chairs to compile the focus groups could also have influenced who was included. It was agreed where possible that a diversity of magistrates would be drawn upon to reflect length of service, role responsibility, gender and age and this was achieved in the groups. However, it is possible that the chairs approached certain magistrates to participate through their familiarity with them, friendship or for certain reasons of judicial reputation. As such, the sample may include magistrates of a particular status and it might be influenced in this regard. The magistrates who did participate were from a range of social, professional and personal backgrounds and provided different views and experiences of the role they perform. This gives a unique and under-reported insight into the daily working lives of serving magistrates of the English criminal courts.

The benches from where the magistrates were drawn included a London bench, which by its nature covers a large population of more than one million people across four neighbouring local authorities. Another large English city court covering its city and several surrounding regional towns was involved. The third area was an English county bench, which incorporated a number of smaller-sized cities, neighbouring towns and rural communities. The bench areas were chosen for their different locations and possible variance in the profile of magistrates, the nature of criminal court work they were processing and their experiences of the various transformations occurring to court working practice. It was considered that this might be more pronounced in some areas than in others. It was apparent that some features of criminal court transformation were being felt more intensely in some areas than in others. This was specifically found in relation to the court closures and amalgamations taking place.

The general questions put to the magistrates in both the focus group and individual interviews revolved around the various alterations being made to lower court justice; how these changes interacted with their day-to-day work experience, if at all; their motivations for coming forward to participate in the lay justice role; and the value they consider their contribution brings.

Seventeen of the 33 magistrates interviewed were women and 16 were men, with their ages ranging from 37 to 70 years. Twenty-six were aged over 55. Just three were aged in their forties or younger. This gender balance and older age representation is reflective of the national profile of serving magistrates. In the year up to April 2015, just over half (53 per cent) of the 19,634 magistrates were women, and 59 was recorded as the average age. The average age of London magistrates is slightly lower, at 56 in central and south London (Courts and Tribunals Judiciary, 2015). Common explanations for the older age distribution of magistrates connects to the time required to commit to the role, which is considered restrictive for many working-age people (Davies *et al.*, 2015: 318). This is a situation that was believed among the magistrates to deprive the service of a younger, more diverse cohort of members. Several of the magistrates had joined at a time when employees were encouraged to perform civic duties, with paid leaves of absence built into some working contracts. The public service release system remains a feature of some employers' conditions, but the difficulty for younger-aged working people to take time out from their day job within today's competitive labour market was noted as a barrier to joining.

The challenge of combining full-time employment alongside serving as a magistrate was reflected on by the youngest magistrate. He was aged 37 and was in a full-time salaried job. He had been a magistrate for the previous five years, but recently suspended his services due to demanding work commitments in combination with family responsibilities and young children. His comment reflects on this, but also on the perception that performing as a lay justice is not widely appreciated by employers. In his view, this has a bearing on the composition of the lay magistracy, which is especially pertinent in the current period, when emphasis is placed on the need for a greater diversity among serving magistrates:

> the bench is predominantly relatively wealthy people often who've retired relatively early.... It's very difficult to be a magistrate if you're of working age, and there's very few working age people I know who have to work for a living who are magistrates. There is only one other magistrate that I can think of, that I've ever met at court at least ... who is of comparable age to myself and in a comparable social situation, vis à vis being, having to work full time.... I don't feel in this day and age being a magistrate is appreciated by wider society, certainly not by employers and so it's a liability for me rather than an asset.

> (Male, aged 37, five years' service)

The eldest of the magistrates interviewed was aged 70. She had retired from the bench three months prior to the interview but was included because of her active service at the start of the research. Magistrates retire from service on their seventieth birthday and a few were close to this age. It was evident from conversations with them that their impending retirement from the role was not being greeted with great joy, mainly because they found the work to be hugely satisfying, but they also considered themselves as having a lot to offer in the role. The looming sense of loss that some magistrates communicated regarding their departure was the same that might be expected an able-bodied and -minded person in a professional career feels on reaching retirement age. Moreover, this connects to the general positive features of working life and work–life identity (Ardichvili and Kuchinke, 2009).

The age the magistrates had joined varied, but most had begun service when aged in their forties on finding themselves at a point in life with time to spare and seeking something worthwhile to do with their extra time. The magistrates held different lengths of service. Some had served for many years and some were newer to the role, having been appointed within the previous few years. But the majority of the 33 magistrates had served on the bench for between 10 and 20 years. Five had been in post for over 30 years. This long length of service links to earlier research findings, which similarly reveals that magistrates serve for many years in post (Baldwin, 1976). The magistrates I interviewed related their long length of service to the huge satisfaction they derive from the role.

Along with the different lengths of service among the magistrates, seniority in magisterial duty was held, in addition to more beginner mentored roles being performed. Also, with their range in service lengths, differing experiences in regard to the transformations in court service delivery were communicated. The more recently recruited magistrates had come into the role at a point of court modernisation with nothing previous to hinge their understandings upon.

Given the long lengths of service, most of the magistrates were in lead magisterial positions, for example acting as the bench chair, chairing the training and development committee or chairing in the youth courts. Some mentioned serving in the Crown Court on appeal panels and some were members of the Local Advisory Committee, which is involved in the appointment of new magistrates. These are essentially senior judicial roles that call for a large degree of professional experience and require significant dedication to the court system. The position of bench chair requires at least two years' experience and special training; it entails acting as the lead magistrate on behalf of the bench on a court working day. Indeed, the role of bench chair has been altering alongside the court closures and amalgamations occurring in the recent years. In some regions the chair's responsibilities can involve the oversight and pastoral care of over 300 serving magistrates.

Overall, the magistrates were sitting in court two to four full days per month. Some of the more experienced ones were serving over six days per month. It was apparent that among some magistrates the role had become a form of replacement work for them, with a day-to-day work–life identity shaped through their judicial role. Most were working in the adult courts, but some sat across the different court categories in the youth court and family courts as well. In one of the three research areas, a few magistrates had moved across from the adult courts to work in the family courts, where child protection and care proceedings are administered but also, importantly, where more sitting days were available to them. This connects to the point made in the previous chapter relating to the declining business in the lower-tier magistrates' courts. In wanting to retain a satisfactory level of participation in their magisterial role, some magistrates had moved across to ensure it. In one research area a 'dedicated drug court' (DDC) was operating and two magistrates regularly worked in that court, in which therapeutic problem-solving approaches with drug-dependent offenders were being offered.

Magistrates' social and professional backgrounds

Just a few of the magistrates were in full-time, salaried work tied to an organisation. A number reported working in a 'freelance', self-employed capacity in various job types. In analysing the previous employment, professional and educational backgrounds of the magistrates, a wide range of skilled professions were represented among them. These included working as teachers and in specialist education, nursing, the probation service, engineering, surveying, accountancy, information technology, the civil service and the legal profession. Approximately 10 of the 33 magistrates were from teaching and social work backgrounds. Only one had been employed in a manual occupation, as a van driver. In addition to coming from skilled professional backgrounds, most of the magistrates held tertiary-level qualifications or university degrees. Even the older magistrates had university backgrounds. This is noted because it meant gaining a university education in the 1960s, when university attendance was not a common trajectory, especially for women. In the 1960s, one in 20 young people went to university, compared to the one in two young women and slightly fewer young men who go to university these days (Coughlan, 2010). Thus, similar to the findings of earlier research focusing on the social composition of the magistracy (Dignan and Wynne, 1997; Baldwin, 1976), the group of magistrates interviewed as part of my research came from highly skilled professional and educated backgrounds, indicating a particular status of this group.

However, in reflecting on the profile of the magistrates they sit alongside on the bench, the magistrates noted a broad cross-section of people and emphasised that as the strength of the lay justice model. A number of the magistrates mentioned the different occupations represented among the magistrates on their bench, with bus and taxi drivers, refuse workers and security staff given as examples. Further, they considered that the magistracy is now much more balanced than it had been in the past:

> Twenty years ago no it wasn't. I felt you had magistrates who looked down on defendants, but I think nowadays there are people more like me who are very sympathetic and empathise and understand what some of the defendants are going through and do not look down our noses at the defendants.
>
> (Female, aged 59, 20 years' service)

Aside from the van driver, manual workers were unrepresented in my sample of magistrates. The following comment made by him highlights a perception of exclusivity that he certainly held prior to his appointment. He reflected upon his 'ordinariness' and surprise at being recruited to the role:

> I was a van driver, white van man and I'm out there doing deliveries one day, listening to the local radio station and they had an article from the magistrate's court about the magistrates and how they were looking for 'ordinary people' to sit as magistrates. I thought to myself well I could do that. But I didn't for the life of me think that they meant as ordinary as I am.... I don't think anybody was more shocked than me when I actually got appointed. [Laughs] When I went for my first days training, the first chap I met was a bank manager and I thought well I'm really out of my depth here! [Laughs] But when you're sat with everybody, you are all the same, you are magistrates and there is no level, no class, no nothing,
>
> (Male, aged 62, 16 years' service)

My sample cannot be considered to represent the overall population of serving magistrates, but it is probable that it is reflective in terms of the concentration of magistrates from high professional backgrounds. Although the magistrates considered that they sat alongside a broad cross-section of people, efforts over the decades to modify the composition and achieve greater diversity across the various domains that Gibbs and Kirby (2014) argue is necessary for the lay magistracy's future viability have not vastly altered it. The social status that surrounds the magistracy persists as one of exclusiveness and it can be argued that this contributes to difficulties in attracting a broader cross-section of the community. However, it is the time limitation of most working-age people that is found to be the main barrier to entry.

Motivations for becoming a lay justice

In addition to my research interests being on the wider social and professional backgrounds of lay justices, a key focus was on what motivated them to become involved in volunteering work of this nature. Given the serious judicial work that magistrates perform, and the centrality of that role to the operation of criminal justice, the motivations for why they had become involved in work of this nature and whether principles of justice formed a part of that motivation was of interest to my research.

Volunteering and contributing to society

Different motivational explanations were given by the magistrates for putting themselves forward for this role, but a common reflection was arriving at a point in life with time on their hands and wanting to do something useful with that time. Spare time had come about alongside instances of early retirement, experiencing redundancy later in life and no longer being dependent on salaried work, shifting family responsibilities and being self-employed with the flexibility to take on volunteering. There was an implicit sense that they were lucky to be in this position and along with the privilege of having time to spare replies came within the general theme of wanting to contribute to society. Narratives also came alongside seeing themselves as having much to offer. The majority of the group had long and successful careers in which they held high levels of managerial and organisational responsibility and accrued expert skill and professional know-how. Careful consideration had gone into finding something of interest which matched their previous skilled backgrounds.

The following explanation given by one magistrate on what had led him to apply illustrates his motivation of reaching a privileged point in life with time on his hands and wanting to return something to society:

> What brought me to it? I was made redundant in '96 and I started working for myself which meant that my time was much more flexible. I also thought I've got a damn good life, thank you very much, it's about time I did something to contribute, to give something back. I wanted to do something that was interesting.
>
> (Male, aged 63, 12 years' service)

In addition to being in the advantaged position of having time to spare, motivations for volunteering as a lay justice could be aligned to a particular set of personal politics, with several magistrates mentioning their interest in a sense of community and having a community spirit. Here it was added by a few magistrates they were someone who had always been involved in volunteering mentioning roles that they held now and in the past. Moreover, some located their community spirit as shared among their wider family and household politics. The following comment emphasises one of the London magistrates' commitment to the community and it being behind her motivations for joining:

> I very much believe the community we live in is important and for that end I've always done something that's contributed to that, at school we were encouraged to do that and I've continued that through my life. I got to the stage where I wanted to do something that was more meaningful and I knew one or two people who were magistrates and thought that I would look at that.
>
> (Female, aged 62, 12 years' service)

Similar motivations of giving back and contributing to society were found by Gibbs (2014b) in her research among serving magistrates. She found them to be motivated by 'wanting to give back' to society and having an interest in contributing to 'civic life' (ibid.: 17). Carpenter and Myers (2010), in writing on volunteering and why people volunteer, comment that the 'prominent role of volunteering in the charitable provision of goods and services has helped to motivate a range of theoretical models of prosocial behaviour' (ibid.: 911).

To give an overview of the individual and varied inspirations put forward by the magistrates, the following responses are drawn from seven magistrates who took part in the London focus group. As illustrated, these combine around an attraction to community giving, previous work experience and having an interest in the law.

1   Charity administrator, aged 53, sitting for 12 years, motivated by an 'interest in the law' and enjoyed the administrative side of criminal court procedure.
2   Property manager and ex-chartered surveyor, aged 54, sitting for five years, motivated by strong beliefs in law and order society and wanting to contribute.
3   Previous director of a photography company, aged 58, sitting for 27 years, encouraged while a student and visits to the courts.
4   Worked in publishing and as a family lawyer, aged 65, sitting for 13 years, had time on her hands and appraised her skill base as suitable for the magisterial role.
5   Manager of a hospitality company, aged 62, sitting for 12 years, expressed a belief in the community and contributing, and enjoyed the way 'the role connects with society'.
6   Company director in the arts, aged 65, sitting for 17 years, noted that their aunt was a magistrate and they 'wanted to do some good'.
7   Company chairman, aged 65, sitting for 10 years, 'believed in local justice'.

Motivations for social change

The responses given by the magistrates on what motivated them to join included interests in influencing social change. A few magistrates articulated the view that, if they wanted to go some way towards impacting society, it was necessary to be involved. Alongside the professional competence of the magistrates, they conveyed interests in current social affairs, politics and the general trends of contemporary society. The notion of contributing to social change came over in a few responses, with the disposition of wishing to be a positive and active member of society conveyed. The comment by the following magistrate expresses his sentiment of believing that if he didn't approve of the way things were in society then he needed to get involved:

I wanted to be a positive force within my society. I wasn't prepared to be an armchair critic. If I didn't agree with the way things were going then I had to put my money where my mouth was and do something positively. That's what brought me into the lay visitor, and that's what brought me to apply to be a lay magistrate.

(Male, aged 53, 20 years' service)

One magistrate communicated a more charged interest in social change. This stemmed from his social justice conscience and a belief in an equal and fair society. He held an undergraduate law degree and a postgraduate politics degree, on top of previous work experience as a volunteer Special Police Constable. The law and politics background had given him an understanding of the principles defining democratic society and its translation into criminal justice and legal systems. He expressed a sense of injustice creeping in and articulated his motivation for joining as being linked to, within the rules of the systems, contributing in some part to social change for the good:

> I was quite annoyed about creeping 'administratization', if there's such a word, of the justice system ... for example Fixed Penalty Notices for Disorder rather than going to court.... So I thought you've got to be in it to win it sort of thing. So I thought if I'm part of the system then I can, within the rules of the system, ensure that, as a participant observer if you like, ensure that they're executed properly. And I suppose that's the main reason.
>
> (Male, aged 37, five years' service)

Indeed, the motivation expressed by one magistrate was her strong sense of law and order. Motivations for societal change can also be linked to more conservative views and she said she was encouraged 'by strong feelings of law and order society'. It was not possible to get an elaboration on what she meant by this, but it can be assumed some interests in the lay justice role would connect to interests in dispensing justice for the sake of a solid law-abiding society:

> Two things really I feel very strongly in the rule of law as a principle and I feel that if you hold a view strongly, you should contribute, you're part of it and society is only sustainable if the rule of law is upheld.
>
> (Female, aged 54, five years' service)

Having a sense of contributing to social change was a finding that emerged from Roach Anleu and Mack's research among magistrates in Australia (2007a). Magistrates in the Australian justice system are not lay justices. They hold legal qualifications in their service, but they essentially perform the same role as magistrates in the English court system in the way that they preside over the extensive lower criminal court jurisdiction, and they similarly process large numbers of defendants accused of the lower-range offences frequently connected to drugs, alcohol, poverty and disadvantage. The magistrates in Roach Anleu and Mack's research expressed interests in wanting to positively contribute to court working but also to the lives of the people who populate the courts – 'to make a difference to the operation of the courts and the everyday citizens who use them' (Roach Anleu and Mack, 2007: 188). I will elaborate further on the interface of disadvantage and the criminal courts and the greater need to highlight this imbalance within my arguments calling for the design of more appropriate rehabilitative responses for particular offending types. These discussions are in Chapter 6.

It was in part an unusual finding that few magistrates verbalised the nature of the court work and the lives and predicaments of offenders as being behind their interest in the job. Where these connections were made, they were more likely to come from the magistrates with teaching and social work backgrounds, who demonstrated exposure and understanding of these issues from within their previous work roles. Notions of fairness were bound up with this as communicated by the following magistrate:

> I was in Social Services. I came from a middle-class background and so until I started at the family service unit ... I had never been on the dreadful Titmarsh Estate where it was just absolutely terrible, where people hardly had enough clothes, or food or whatever it was, and husbands were in prison it was really grim.... I felt that there was a lot of unfairness around and somewhere along the line you could do something to try to adjust that. I think that is one of the reasons why I went into social work and one of the things that I feel very strongly about when I am sitting on the bench.
>
> (Female, aged 70, 16 years' service)

Previous professional backgrounds as motivation

Motivations behind becoming a magistrate were located within magistrates' previous employment experiences. As noted, the magistrates had been in previous roles of high professional practice and managerial status and an interest in the lay justice role originated in applying these experiences. These previous experiences included legal backgrounds, in the case of a few magistrates who had worked as solicitors and one as a barrister, and they also overlapped with previous social services and youth work roles and aspects of these that interacted with legal court processes. Several magistrates came from education and secondary school teaching backgrounds. They expressed intersections between the skills acquired in these professional careers and the tasks they performed as lay magistrates, specifically in their work with certain types of people, for instance troubled youngsters, or households experiencing imprisonment. The magistrate just quoted whose previous work was within the probation service and then social services, said that the legal and criminal court aspects of her previous careers and working with families in difficulty were linked to her original interest in becoming a magistrate:

> [I]t was linked to previous work. I'd been a probation officer at the beginning of my social work career.... I enjoyed the legal side of it and the court side of it, the preparation of reports and seeing people before and after court, why they had committed offences, what their sentence meant to them.... I was still dealing with people who quite a lot of them had people serving time in prison as a part of their household because they were in difficulties, so it was always a part of my working life I guess.
>
> (Female, aged 70, 16 years' service)

Similarly, the following magistrate refers to his professional background in mental health nursing and an involvement with employment law in that role as stimulating his interest to join:

> My background is nursing ... mental health nursing in particular and working with families, which is one of the reasons why I'm interested in the family system. I worked for many years with families ... I did a lot of family work, family therapy that sort of thing and then later on I worked for the Royal College of Nursing and I was involved in a lot of, in employment law. And I've always been interested in the law and that was one of the motivations for becoming a magistrate actually.
>
> (Male, aged 68 years, 10 years' service)

Experiences and social benefits of being a magistrate

Most of the magistrates had entered the lay justice position to fill spare time and capacity in their lives and it was evident that it served immense personal benefits for them in being positively engaged in interesting work. Moreover, it is a working role that provides a strong sense of purpose, with recognition and standing associated with the judicial status. Magistrates viewed themselves to be performing an important role, but they experienced the work they do as deeply fulfilling and this was one reason many remained in post for as long as they had. One personal benefit they took from the job was the mental and intellectual challenge it presented. This was in having to exercise capacity in making important and difficult decisions, including bail and remand decisions or taking someone's liberty when sentencing them to prison custody. This London magistrate links the serious decision-making element of the job as central to his interests in it: 'So that's actually the interest and the fact that you are constantly making very serious decisions about people's lives'. In addition, the magistrates enjoyed the team working experience and strong feelings of camaraderie generated from the shared sense of enterprise of arriving at the important decisions they do on people's lives and futures.

Despite expressing pride in the lay justice role, the significant shifts in the organisation and delivery of lower criminal court work across the English justice system were having an impact on their work experiences, the number of sittings they could access and the sense of value they derived from it. The difficulties being experienced and indeed the sense of undermining were voiced by some magistrates:

> I'm very proud and honoured to be a magistrate and I feel very, very upset at the changes, recent changes that have all been driven by finance, no other reason, that are making the job that we do less effective and will become more and more difficult to do in a challenging climate.
>
> (Male, aged 68, 37 years' service)

The high social status derived from serving in a judicial role and its contribution to shaping positive self-expression and identity were not likely to be forthcoming in the magistrates' narratives since these are difficult sentiments to express. However, the social importance gained from the role was apparent. It was implicit in some comments that holding this judicial position provided an important sense of self-identity. This can be linked to the way positive identity is shaped through regular working lives. It was also evident in the conversations with the magistrates who were reaching retirement and the sense of identity loss that could be deduced among them. Ardichvili and Kuchinke (2009), in writing on the meanings of work and working, say that 'work is found to offer useful meaning to life such as providing sources of identity, opportunities for achievement and determining standing within the larger community' (ibid.: 155). Given that many of the magistrates were engaging in their magisterial work role as a supplement to their former working lives, it was obvious it functioned in useful ways to shaping a sense of self-worth, value and a positive self-identity. It could also be interpreted from some narratives the fact they were playing a role within the judicial system was a position of prestige, with one magistrate articulating a sense of importance in being a member of the magistracy. Even though it was said in a jocular way, he referred to it as 'the most exclusive club in Ellerston'.

Contributions to lay justice

In addition to exploring the motivations behind the magistrates becoming involved in criminal court working and their experiences in this role, I was interested in how they interpreted the contribution they make to the system of lay justice. This related to the strength they provide as a collective of lay justices in conducting the majority of lower court work in the English justice system. Therefore my research was interested in how they as a working group embody the values of lay justice. The English criminal justice system has retained a system of lay justice over the centuries and decades, which has been praised by successive governments of all sides. Moreover, there is commitment within the current court modernisation project to continue with the participation of lay justices, with it being referred to as a fine example of 'participatory democracy' (Green, 2014; Ministry of Justice, 2012). England and Wales has held on to a system of lay justice while other common-law jurisdictions that previously operated similar styles, such as New Zealand[1] and Australia, have replaced their reliance on a lay involvement with structures run by legally qualified professionals (Harkness, 2015, 2009; Lowndes, 1999). Despite guarantees made by parliamentarians, it can be argued that the magistracy is at a crossroads in terms of its future role, with reform high on the policy agenda.

The responses by the magistrates regarding their contribution linked to the advantages put forward in the introductory chapter on the value of citizen participation in legal adjudication and a belief in the ideal of lay local justice as dispensed by community members. Responses came along the lines that it represented the principle of being 'judged by your peers', by ordinary members of society who are rooted in the local community and who bring common sense to criminal court adjudication:

> I think the idea of being judged by people who are your peers, who have the same sort of status as you, in law at least, is a very ideal one.
>
> (Male, aged 69, 10 years' service)

Added to this dialogue on the influence they as lay justices make, it was considered that the public was likely to perceive this system with a greater level of confidence than justice administered by a single sitting judge whose working career and life have been steeped in the legal profession, as commented by this magistrate:

> [W]e will, I think have more influence on the perception of how justice is done and on public confidence in the justice system, because lay people like us, I think are perceived more as possibly more in touch than somebody who has just spent his whole life climbing the judicial ladder.
>
> (Female, aged 65, 13 years' service)

In this way it can be said the magistrates saw themselves as symbolising the longstanding principle defining lower court summary justice as lay local justice (Donoghue, 2014a; Bell and Dadamo, 2006; Seago *et al.*, 2000). Dignan and Wynne (1997) make reference to the historic underpinnings of local justice, stating that 'one of the attractions of the lay magistracy has always been its capacity (or at least its potential capacity) to ensure that local conditions may be reflected in the application of criminal justice' (ibid.: 186). They cite a quote by Lord Merrivale in connection to the value of the lay element: 'the justice which matters most in the homes of the people is the justice administered by the magistrates in their midst'. (ibid.: 186).

Indeed, the notion of local and localised justice is a historic principle in the delivery of summary justice and is communicated as a desired attribute within the appointment criteria. The magistracy application documents state the close proximity a magistrate should live from the courthouse they are applying to sit in. This is proof of the endeavour to embed local justice within the design of lower court justice. 'Applicants are expected to be living or working in, or reasonably close to, the area in which they wish to serve'. The document goes on to state that if an applicant is called for interview the person will be able to demonstrate 'good knowledge and understanding of social issues in the local area, in particular the causes and effects of crime' (Judiciary of England and Wales, 2015: 5). Support for retaining local justice is embedded within the visions in the reform policy documents that support seeking a diverse modernised magistracy that is connected with their local communities and services (Green, 2014; Ministry of Justice, 2012).

Several responses by the magistrates communicated points about local understanding and the value they bring from being located within their communities.

They considered their community presence useful and important in understanding what matters to local people and to the particular issues that arise within people's lives, as expressed in the following magistrate's comment:

> [A]s a member of the community, I feel ... I know my community. I feel I know my community because I live in Windle, I can see the concerns and problems that are in Windle community, in the city itself. So there are urban problems that you can come across and you sort of know the area that's around. So that is quite an important role.
>
> (Woman, aged 44, six years' service)

Being from their local communities and having knowledge of existing social issues and an understanding of the difficulties some members face were presented as powerful. This included the victim-type situation of certain defendants who make frequent appearances in the lower courts. One magistrate commented on his familiarity with the drug problems people present with in court as connected to his own insights. From his knowledge of the local drugs market in his home city, he said he has empathy for some people whose lives are tied up among it and who are sometimes unwittingly drawn in. He comments that his knowledge assists within the bounds of justice to arrive at a reasonable decision:

> [T]he number of people that appear before us quite regularly and go through the drugs rehabilitation, are clean and then nine months later, or a year later are back in front of us again and because we've seen them before, we say 'what went wrong?' 'Well the house I live in all the pushers know where I am, or it's in an area where there are a lot of pushers, and as soon as I go back there they give me a few drugs for nothing and I'm hooked again'. So in that sort of circumstance I would understand that because it's a close community and so I might be more lenient.... But it is down to being local and having an understanding of the area.
>
> (Male, aged 63, 12 years' service)

Localised area knowledge was also mentioned as valuable in instances of road traffic cases. This is illustration of the predominance of traffic offence work that comes within the magistrates' jurisdiction. Area knowledge was said to be useful for understanding particular road systems as the cause of disputes. With this local knowledge it was said they are more easily able to assess culpability and driving offence seriousness:

> It is important because sometimes you might be dealing with a case, perhaps a driving, dangerous driving or something like that, and you know the roads that that person has been driving on, and you think ah yes, however serious the case is being put to you, if you know the place you'll understand the seriousness better.
>
> (Male, aged 63, 12 years' service)

There was, however, a different viewpoint held by some magistrates in relation to the value of local justice as it is constructed in regard to the lay magistracy. This was in relation to the conception that a local person is somehow more meaningful to the delivery of justice compared to when it is dispensed by someone who isn't local or doesn't reside in the vicinity of the court they sit in. This is a compelling argument when pitched alongside what has become the working approach in the lower courts in efforts to achieve greater uniformity in sentencing and decision-making. The requirement to operate in accordance with the Sentencing Guidelines is a key feature of magistrates' work. But the Sentencing Guidelines constrain individualised, locally informed sentencing decisions. It is argued that the power of 'judicial discretion' and the tailoring of case-by-case responses to defendants have been weakened with the introduction of the guidelines and that deviation from them requires justification (Ward, 2013). The following comment made by one of the London magistrates illustrates his disagreement with the idea that being local has a bearing on delivering a fairer form of local justice:

> I disagree with John about the locality and the local justice bit, because what we are there to do is to listen to facts, to decide on guilt or innocence and to apply standards set in the Guidelines, as punishment or deterrence or whatever the function the sentence happens to be in that case. So I don't think you need to know or live near the court that you are administering justice in, or need to know much about it.
>
> (Male, aged 58, 27 years' service)

This magistrate is essentially referring to the meaninglessness of local justice as it is held to have a place within court work in the form of applying local understanding. This is because the nature of courtroom decision-making is required to apply 'equal justice' and adhering to the Sentencing Guidelines to achieve this greatly reduces the capacity to apply discretion in individual sentence responses (Roberts, 2010, 2011). Having an appreciation of local social issues and problems, which might explain a person's offending and which can be responded to with common-sense solutions, conflicts with the requirements of the equitable dispensing of justice. The more recently recruited magistrates often mentioned the emphasis that had been placed on them to engage in guided sentencing, which was a core feature of their early magisterial training. The introduction of the Sentencing Guidelines can be argued as further evidence of the changing streamlined justice environment that magistrates' court work is operating within.

In line with the unique contribution to lay local justice that the magistrates consider themselves as making, some were critical of fellow jurists who live far from the constituents they are dealing with in their courtroom work and who therefore have no conception of the social issues and problems some people face in their particular communities. Some critics, though, and indeed some magistrates, argue that it is not about understanding a community or being from the local area that matters in justice administration, because, as alluded to in the previous comment, the job is about interpreting the law and judging the facts on whether someone is guilty or not. This may well be true and it is the nature of the adversarial justice system, but it can be argued that there is space within the work of lower court justices to implement understandings of individual people's current lives and sometimes social lifestyle problems (Roach Anleu and Mack, 2007b). This is certainly the case at the point of sentencing, when personal mitigating factors can be taken into account when deciding upon an appropriate sentence (Easton and Piper, 2012: 196). This is an argument I pick up on again in Chapter 6 in my discussions of social justice in the context of the lower criminal courts.

Baldwin's (1976) earlier work, critiquing the ongoing issue of the narrow social class composition of the magistracy, cited the *Royal Commission on Justices of the Peace* (1948). This set out the necessary attributes of lay magistrates in their involvement in criminal court justice, with the issue of social understanding highlighted. The Commission contended that an understanding of the poor and their difficulties was needed – 'it is essential that there should be many among the justices who know enough of the lives of the poorest people to understand their outlook and their difficulties' (1948, cited in Baldwin, 1976: 171).

It can be argued that the desired quality of a lower court justice in having a social understanding of people's lives shifts the focus from the social class bias attributed to serving magistrates to the more important requirement of having an appreciation of the lives and predicaments of people they sit in judgement over. Social class background and diversity among magistrates is important, but social and cultural awareness, sensitivity and understanding is more so.

Erosion of local justice

The magistrates' reflections on the contributions they make to the administration of justice and the view that the lay influence is unique and helpful included an evaluation that the principle of local justice was being lost alongside the various transformations. This, in particular was connected to the amalgamation and closure of many courts across the English criminal justice system (Ministry of Justice, 2015a). As discussed, there has been widespread and ongoing closure of courthouses since 2011. The courts some magistrates had previously sat in are now closed or earmarked for closure. These closures meant that some magistrates now live far from the courts they serve in, and this was believed to be contributing to a 'loss of local justice'. A magistrate in one research area spoke of regularly being asked to perform court sittings in neighbouring towns located 40 and 80 miles from the city in which he lives and where his local knowledge is founded. These distant courthouses stand within the geographic area of his magisterial tenure, but are a far distance and impinge on him being able to argue that he has a good local knowledge as stipulated in the magistrates' appointment criteria. A situation like this undermines the meaning of local justice in the way it has been interpreted:

The difficulty there is that gradually with closure of courts, there's less local justice ... very often we get emails to say we need a magistrate in Gainstree or Retstone or somewhere like that and I'm happy to go down there, but I don't know the area at all and I possibly don't know the type of people that are down there. I mean it may well be much more of a farming community, much more of a rural community, I've always lived in towns and I'm a town person.... So I think yes local justice is important and it's being lost.

(Male, aged 63, 12 years' service)

The streamlining processes occurring as part of court management restructures have put regional centralisation in place. Moreover, some commentators argue that this hinders any real capacity for meaningful responses to localised crime issues and relevant community-based reactions (Donoghue, 2014a; Gibbs, 2013). Court business across England and Wales is centrally managed by the court service and is organised into seven regions – London, the Midlands, the North East, the North West, the South East, the South West and Wales. Within these seven regions, there is further organisation into 'local justice areas' (LJAs). In 2016 there were 105 local justice areas. This is a reduction from the 118 in 2015 and a significant reduction since 2005, when they numbered 254.[2] Magistrates are assigned to a local justice area and these include several courts across an area and, in rural areas, this means more sparsely located courts. Magistrates can be asked to sit in any of the courthouses located within their local bench area. It is through this creation of fewer but larger local justice areas that the concept of local justice becomes lost. It contradicts governmental ambition for magistrates to be driving criminal justice innovation in their local communities, referred to at the beginning of this book.

Shared decision-making, common sense and peer judgements

Further responses put forward by the magistrates relating to the question on how they make a specific contribution to lay justice were not directly associated to dimensions of lay influence but to the style of adjudication they preside over. Working as a bench of three – or on occasion two – people engaged in shared and joint decision-making on whether a defendant is guilty or not and arriving at an appropriate penalty was considered a strength of the lay justice system. Here, magistrates argued in favour of their different background experiences and views, which they brought to their decisions. This was strongly pitched alongside the working model of professional judges operating in the lower courts, who in contrast sit alone in judgement in their criminal case adjudication:

[W]e've been well trained working as a team, it's a definite strength of the system. It's also the personal experiences that the three sitting together have because it could be own family experiences of people you know of, or in some cases it's technical knowledge because someone might come from a medical profession or teaching, where they can say actually 'I understand the circumstances in which you can have that'.... And it's putting all that together in the melting pot which I think makes it work, which a district judge wouldn't do.

(Male, aged 62, seven years' service)

Indeed, it is the balance achieved through combined and shared knowledge of magistrates' bench working that Baldwin (1976) refers to in the following statement on the purpose of the lay magistracy: 'the very *raison d'etre* of the magistracy rests on the principle that justice can be administered by groups of laymen whose idiosyncrasies and prejudices will be neutralised and absorbed in deliberations with others from different backgrounds' (ibid.: 174). However, Baldwin was pointing out the persistence of magistrates being from professional social class backgrounds and that prejudices will therefore not be neutralised.

A number of the magistrates expressed strong and negative views on the role of judges sitting alone as they operate in the magistrates' courts. This came from the feeling that sole legal decision-making was wrong in principle. But it was also from a belief that such decisions were better made as a group. It was frequently stated by the magistrates they would not like to be making potentially life-changing decisions of guilt or non-guilt and of suitable sentences on their own, in the way that salaried judges do. It was often put that the fact they made decisions as three people was a safeguard and reassurance to them that they had arrived at the right decision, with it difficult to appraise if the task was performed alone.

[I]t's the principle that one person can be judge and jury and make decisions from one person's perspective, I think that's wrong. It's the only tribunal in the country where it happens.... I think that principle is wrong.

(Male, aged 68, 37 years' service)

All of the magistrates sat in courthouses where, in addition to themselves, district judges were rostered to sit and who similarly presided over the busy remand courts, youth courts and summary trials, and who held the same range of decision-making and sentencing powers as magistrates.

It was interesting that the magistrates held such strong views about sitting in judgement alone, since, at the crossroads we are at in relation to transforming summary justice, ideas for lay magistrates to sit alone in certain low-level uncontested cases are indeed being advanced. This has been enabled through amendments to the Criminal Justice and Courts Act 2015. Magistrates did not refer to this change in their work responsibilities, nor was it something they were opposed to, but plans for their expanded role may have sharpened their views on single sitting judges' decision-making.

Some of the magistrates saw the fact that they were not qualified in the law as an important feature and strength of lay justice, with the value attributed to their contribution as being rooted in their local community background rather than within a legal profession versed in the technicalities of the law:

I think if we went round and looked at our CVs of when we first came on [the bench], you would find that all of us were very involved in our communities ... they've come straight through the system ... law school and may not do anything in the community at all ... if you come the other route, you come because you're clever, you've obviously passed all the qualifications and we're not like that and I think that's our strength, the fact that we have got lots of knowledge of lots of different things.

(Female, aged 66, 30 years' service)

Another contribution set out by the magistrates in what they in particular bring to the justice process was the belief they communicated with defendants in a way that is understandable to them by speaking in laymen's language. As mentioned in the following comment, this was also seen as important since it functioned to provide the defendant with a sense of fairness in the process. This can also be linked to the literature critiquing lay participation in legal decision-making (Malsch, 2009), which emphasises that it brings comprehensibility to legal terminology and the benefits this has for defendants' understanding of the process, as this magistrate notes:

[W]ith us we put it in simple English so that they can understand what's happening and explain what the proceedings are and even if somebody is waiting for the paperwork to be done, I say to them this might take some time, we haven't forgotten about you.... So we keep them informed and it's dealing with them at their level, so that they understand ... they come out thinking yes we've been treated fairly. And it's justice being dealt with by your peers, as opposed to somebody who feels that they're superior to that person.

(Female, aged 59, 20 years' service)

Emotionality within the job

On top of eliciting views from the magistrates on their experiences of performing in a criminal court justice role, and the privilege they derive from it, I was interested in how they coped with the emotional side of the work required of them. Roach Anleu and Mack (2005), from their research in the lower-tier Australian criminal courts, examined magistrates' experiences of 'emotional labour'. They relate the concept of emotional labour to the management of emotions within the courtroom that arise from the disposition and reaction of defendants and witnesses. In addition, it related to how the display of emotions is managed by magistrates in generating a sense of fairness, impartiality, neutrality and public confidence in the system. Roach Anleu and Mack also take emotional labour as required in dealing with the human, personal element of the job and the nature of the decisions they make – 'the affective engagement with people in the court' (ibid.: 612). They highlight the context to this, stating that in presiding over the lower court jurisdiction magistrates 'must make decisions in cases where the criminal offending or the civil dispute often reflects a larger picture of inequality and social disadvantage which inevitably invokes emotions and feelings' (ibid.: 612).

The emotional labour in terms of the 'affect' on the magistrates with the type of work they do was something I was interested to understand. Some of the magistrates articulated the occasional heavy emotional demands experienced through the type of cases they see in court, and the difficult decisions they have to take within the role. Particularly emotional and difficult decisions related to work in the family courts and the judgements relating to the removal of children from parental care in some cases. Fellow magistrates were praising of their colleagues who worked in the family courts, with some drawing a line and saying that this was 'work they couldn't do'. The heightened level of emotionality that decisions like this drew illustrated the removal of someone's child was the most severe decision they make, even if it was for the eventual good they were bringing about:

> I think the ones that always stick with you is family courts … I don't think anyone can't be affected by families. I mean particularly having a family of my own. I can't imagine anything worse than taking somebody's children off them. But on the other hand, I think the good bit about family work is you can actually make a significant difference … you wouldn't do it if you didn't think it was for the better, to some very young lives.
>
> (Female, aged 69, 30 years' service)

Decisions of sending someone to prison and ordering 'the destruction of a dog' were also mentioned as 'heart-wrenching' judgements that they sometimes had to make. In relation to adult and youth court work, sending someone to prison, especially on the first occasion they had been faced with this, was mentioned. Also, in this discussion of the emotional side of magisterial work, they spoke in terms of certain cases that had stuck with them for their intensity. These mostly related to incidents of imposing prison custody on women, especially women with children, and sending a young person to prison. However, the magistrates had devised strategies for these moments of discomfort in sentencing, rationalising the situation and being convinced it had been the right thing to do. It was also justified by the way the person's criminality had led the magistrates to take the difficult decision. Moreover, and of fundamental importance, is that the decision had been arrived at as a group of three, with each of them checking that they were making the right ruling. These responses relate to the 'emotional distance' and 'depersonalisation' strategies that Roach Anleu and Mack (2005) applied to the way that the magistrates they interviewed coped with the difficult emotional elements of their job.

> It was a real emotional day for me and I took that home with me and I didn't like it one little bit. But whenever I've sent somebody to prison, I've always done it knowing that I've done the right thing. If I wasn't convinced of that

I think I would have to resign from the bench. But there are emotions involved, and it is a very emotional job at times and you have to detach yourself to a certain degree.

(Male, aged 68, 37 years' service)

In this chapter the recurring issue of magistrates' social class background has been raised. It seems that little has altered over the years to change the concentration of magistrates being located primarily in professional occupational backgrounds, despite efforts to broaden the composition over the years. Although the judicial statistics do not record social class background, the overall profile of magistrates shows their older age and small numbers from ethnic minority backgrounds. Given the small number of magistrates included in my research, my sample cannot be considered representative, but it can be assumed that it was broadly reflective. The magistrates were almost exclusively from professional and managerial class backgrounds.

Gibbs and Kirby's (2014) argument is that having diverse benches of magistrates dispensing justice in the courts is ideal across the range of social characteristics to reflect the make-up of contemporary society, but my argument is what is more important is that those who are serving in this role are doing so for the right reasons of dispensing fair justice and doing so with the courage to apply common-sense judgements within the technicalities of the law. This will be drawn upon again in the following chapter because the increasing demands of the job and the proficiency required to do it are highlighted and this invariably impacts on who is recruited into the role. It has to be added though that almost a third of my sample came from school teacher and social work backgrounds. If my sample is broadly reflective of the overall profile of magistrates, then I argue that the magistrate population will include a sizeable proportion of people who bring social understanding, care and empathy from these professional backgrounds, which will bring a special contribution to the ideals of criminal justice.

There are other professions that involve making legal decisions and passing judgement over the lives of marginalised people with substantial powers of discretion that are performed by professional people of middle-class status. These include prison parole boards, psychiatrists and social workers. These do not attract attention based on social class in the same way magistrates do. It can therefore be questioned why magistrates attract the level of focus they do when it is not their performance as judicial actors that is analysed in this scrutiny.

This chapter has also illustrated the principle of local justice, which is held to be the strength of lay justice system and the way court justice is dispensed by local people who have an understanding of social issues and problems in their local areas, with it implied that this has relevance for court practice and decisions. This suggests that there is some degree of flexibility in responding to individual defendants within the courtroom based on an understanding of local social, economic and material conditions. Individualised justice is a principle of criminal justice, but this is increasingly in conflict with the equitable administration of justice and the principle of like cases being treated alike. Sentencing

Guidelines have been introduced into lower criminal court decision-making to achieve greater consistency in sentencing outcomes in courts across the country, and the pressure to apply these uniform decisions hampers judicial discretion and 'individualised justice' and indeed contradicts the principle of local justice.

This chapter has also raised important considerations on the lay bench style of adjudication performed by three magistrates and its strength when compared to judges sitting alone, who make powerful judging and sentencing decisions on their own. The magistrates interviewed were strong in their opposition to this style of justice. Moreover, it is important to consider these views and reservation when reminded of the weight of the legal decisions that get made by a single sitting judge, such as sending a person to prison and imposing bail, possibly with a raft of restrictive conditions in the form of curfews, residence orders, exclusion orders, etc. I acknowledge the professional competence of legally qualified judges in their court role and the legitimacy of their judgements, but the magistrates' strong opposition to this growing style of unchecked judging is defensible. It locates the argument within the discourses surrounding professional justice and the lesser confidence from within some domains in justice dispensed by professionals versed in the law (Malsch, 2009). However, we can also assume, as I will argue in the following chapter, that with the long lengths of bench practice magistrates attain they effectively themselves become lay legal professionals, but with the strength of judging in panels of three.

Notes

1 New Zealand still retains lay involvement in lower court justice
2 These figures were obtained from HMCTS in April 2016.

5 Magistrates' courts, modernisation and the future

Magistrates' experiences of working as lay justices, what motivates them to volunteer in work of this nature, the contribution they make to the justice system and the value they gain from serving in a judicial role were explored in the previous chapter. This chapter continues to draw on evidence from the magistrates' interviews and examines the way that the various court alterations that are taking place are impacting on their court working lives, and how they are contending with these. As such, it reports on magistrates' experiences of working within the lower courts of the English justice system at a time of restructure and within the modernised styles of delivery that are being operationalised in progressing to the future.

Broadly, the chapter conceptualises the courtroom changes within the construct of increasing professionalisation, which I argue is evident in lower court justice and at this time of reform (Cox, 2010; Seago *et al.*, 2000; Davies, 2005). It applies themes of workplace restructure, changing court cultures and the professionalisation of magistrates' court justice. It is within this chapter that a distinction between the experiences of the more recently recruited magistrates and magistrates who have served for longer periods comes through.

Seeing that the notion of professionalisation is a key concept applied in this chapter, it is necessary to define precisely what is meant by this. This is important because the literature on the English justice system sometimes refers to the legally qualified district judges and deputy district judges who work in the lower courts and their increased numbers over the decades as indication of professionalisation within the lower court jurisdiction (Seago *et al.*, 2000). My reference in this chapter is slightly different. It relates to the greater emphasis within lower criminal court work on the managerialist approaches and efficient forms of operation that have been introduced, for example the speedy justice initiatives, swift case processing, directed case management procedures and the tight adherence to the Sentencing Guidelines. Magistrates are under pressure to demonstrate competences in these areas of modern courtroom delivery.

It was evident that my research was going on at a time when there was activity within the judiciary in relation to recruiting across a more diverse pool of potential applicants and to encouraging younger recruits to join (Green, 2014).

I was keen to include a sample of recently recruited magistrates in my research. The three focus groups all included magistrates who had joined within the previous six years and a sub-sample of newer recruits was shaped within the individual interviews. Eight of the 33 magistrates had joined within the previous six years. They were younger in age, aged in their forties and early fifties, than the other participating magistrates. I was interested in whether they had different experiences within the lay magistrate role.

Along with the transformations occurring to lower court summary justice, the magistrates interviewed were facing changed ways of working, with shifting expectations upon them. These related to economic efficiency savings in the form of courthouse closures and amalgamations, digitised methods of working and the introduction of tighter case management procedures to quicken the pace that criminal cases progress through the system. The court business rationalisations fit within the modernisation of public services project that began under the Liberal Democrat/Conservative coalition government in power between 2010 and 2015, which have continued in unrelenting fashion under the single governing Conservative Party (The Conservative Party, 2015; Ministry of Justice, 2015a; Leveson, 2015a). This is bearing down on the lower courts in a significant way in endeavours to move the courts into twenty-first-century styles of operation and as cost savings come into practice.

A part of my research was interested in how court business reconfigurations were impacting on magistrates' daily working experiences, but also on their satisfaction within the job. Given that the magistrate role is a voluntary one, aside from nominal expense payments for training days and single days' losses of earnings, it might be expected that greater and increasing demands on them in the form of mastering new knowledge, competences and skills could have an influence on their willingness to continue in the position. Indeed, some writings highlight how serving magistrates in this period of adjustment have felt undermined by the various changes occurring to their profession (Fassenfelt, 2013; Morgan, 2013) and it is suggested that some have left the role sooner than they otherwise would have done.

A lively, albeit renewed commentary from a range of quarters was going on at the same time as my research on the need to increase diversity among the magistracy (Green, 2014; Gibbs and Kirby, 2014). Recruiting younger members is seen as a priority from within government ministerial circles, by the Magistrates' Association and by magistrates themselves. Indeed, along with the various alterations occurring, the magistracy can be considered as at a crossroads in terms of its future owing to its ageing demographic and the impending retirement of many members. It is argued that recruitment needs to be bolstered if the criminal justice system is to continue with its reliance on lay magistrates (Chambers *et al.*, 2014). However, the current crossroads is also owing to emergent ideas about delivering efficient summary justice within modernised processes, as well as ideas for making better use of magistrates' connections within their local communities. Recruitment strategies over the last decade and, especially, recently have been proactive at drawing in younger members (Davies *et al.*, 2015).

Alongside the general interest among the magistrates in politics and current affairs, the reverberations from criminal justice policy announcements on future reforms was something they were acutely conscious of. Moreover, this was to a degree undermining some magistrates' sense of purpose and added to feelings of disenfranchisement. It was also probable that the particular focus of my research on lower court transformations made the participating magistrates reflect more on their current status than they otherwise would. But it was the case that the managerial restructuring going on from within the command of Her Majesty's Courts and Tribunal Service was impacting on their working mood. The sense of uncertainty and urge from above to modernise and operate differently came out in the magistrates' narratives. Here the younger and more recently recruited magistrates referred to their training as managerial in content and style, which for all intents and purposes positioned them as a new breed of magistrates different to the older longer-serving ones, recruited in some cases many years earlier.

Changing court culture

What emerged from the interviews with the magistrates was that court reforms in the form of local court closures and bench amalgamations across the court estate were impacting on the established working cultures of magistrate benches. Besides this, these were communicated as affecting the sense of cohesion and belonging that magistrates garner through their magisterial volunteering role. Court closures and bench amalgamations were a theme emerging from the interviews. This was particularly the case for longer-serving magistrates, who expressed feeling the effects more intensely than magistrates who had served for a shorter period. The newer magistrates were only familiar with this revised model of work practice.

Alongside the limited research on magistrates' experiences in their judicial role, there is no reference to them as a distinct working group with an established occupational culture and work identity. There is an extensive US literature on the presence of 'legal cultures' specific to the courts and the influence they can have on court-based decision-making (see for example Church, 1985). There are various studies from the UK that have theorised local bench cultures and court sentencing patterns (Rumgay, 1995). For instance, the work of Hucklesbury (1997) explored local bench culture and how it can influence bail decisions and variation in bail. Bell and Dadamo (2006) referred to magistrates' court justice as 'justice by geography', implying that justice is dispensed differently according to established entrenched bench cultures, which differ across locations. But there is no research that explores the magistracy as an occupational culture. Mawby and Worrall's (2013) research on the probation service in the UK is useful here for the theme of 'occupational culture' that they incorporate into their analysis. In contextualising their work on shifting identities within the probation service in light of the managerialism models being introduced they define occupational culture, stating that, 'at its broadest, the culture of an occupation or an organisation can be described as the values shared by individuals that manifest themselves in the practices of members of that occupation or organisation' (ibid.: 5). They draw on the management and organisational behaviour literature and cite Schein (2010), who refers to organisational culture 'as applicable to all kinds of government, public, private and voluntary organisations' (ibid.: 5).

My research revealed both the existence of established court cultures and a work identity among some groups of magistrates, in much the same way as these become entrenched in other work environments (Ardichvili and Kuchinke, 2009). However, these appeared to be undergoing some disconnection through the various and ongoing court closures, including the courts the magistrates worked in. Given the widespread closure of courts across the English justice system, the effect was being felt by most magistrates interviewed in my research.

The amalgamated court bench areas that have come about as a consequence of the closures have resulted in bench areas doubling in size in terms of active magistrate numbers. In the case of the London bench area where the research was conducted, the numbers increased from an average of 100 serving magistrates in that bench area to over 300 following the merger in 2011. Court closures and amalgamations have therefore meant that some magistrates are now sitting in a different court to the one that they always had during their service as a magistrate, and they are now part of a large merged bench rather than a small, more localised one where established ways of working and a close familiarity had been built up.

There was some divergence in the magistrate responses relating to the altered court cultures emerging out of this restructuring. Some of the longer-serving magistrates indicated heartfelt sorrow with the disruption, and what they expressed felt like a disappearing collegial spirit and difficulty in getting used to the changes. This was when compared to magistrates joining in the more recent period. The following comment made by a London-based magistrate whose local court had closed refers to now being part of a large merged bench, a period of settling in to a different set of practices to those to which they as a bench of magistrates were accustomed, and the departure of some fellow magistrates who had decided not to continue on in the role:

> [S]trictly speaking I sit on the South Stanley bench which is a construct which has existed for not quite 3 years as a result of the merging of Hamber, Doxton, and Edger benches. The merger took some time to implement and bought its own stresses and strains because each of the benches had its own culture, its own set of practices. It was uncomfortable for the first year or so it is fair to say while people settled down. There were a lot of very good magistrates who decided they weren't prepared to sit on a mega bench of 400.
>
> (Male, aged 65, 10 years' service)

Returning to the previous chapter, the sense of camaraderie that magistrates said they experienced through their court work and the shared sense of purpose they enjoy, it was apparent that for some this was being disrupted through the scale and nature of the court changes.

In reflecting on the court closures and amalgamations that were taking place and the break-up of local court cultures, the more recently recruited magistrates tended to view the situation differently. One magistrate, in post for just three years, discussed the disruption of familiarity and the established court culture as a good thing. In her view the programme of courthouse closures that had taken place in her bench area had ruptured an established clique that she considered existed in one local court. She saw this as a positive shift because she believed that delivering justice in the way magistrates are expected to is not about comfortable friendship relationships, saying, 'it's not meant to be your real life'. She went onto question whether friendship cliques on the bench might have a bearing on the legal decision-making that magistrates are tasked with. She considered that there might be a lesser proclivity to present an opposing view in bench decision-making from the other two magistrates if you are close friends with them. She referred to a group who regularly sat on the bench together and who also frequently dined together and the influence that a cosy relationship like this might have:

> Edger bench was quite small and also they had day benches which meant you only sat on a Tuesday, so you only ever sat with the same 20 or 30 people ... I would say that of the three benches, the Edger people found it the hardest.... I mean the Friday bench still have dinners together, and I can't help but think there would be a greater inclination to agree for the sake of it. Like if you were three friends together and one of you had a different opinion you'd just kind of supress it wouldn't you?... Or you can imagine it becoming more of a social situation and less of a professional situation.
>
> (Female, aged 58, three years' service)

In this way, the large benches generated as a result of the court closures were having the effect of disrupting local court cultures and reorienting magistrate working. The magistrate just speaking went on to express the way the established court culture and sense of cohesion of the Edger bench was being 'mourned' in light of the now large, more anonymous benches that had been created.

Magistrates recruited to the role in the more recent time period were less inclined to express negative sentiments relating to serving on large benches populated by 300 and more magistrates and sitting with magistrates not known to them. This altered way of working in the form of large and ever changing benches was the only style they knew in their magisterial role. In this way, the newer magistrates stood aside from the feelings of nostalgia and occupational reorientation that was apparent among the longer-serving more established magistrates. The following comment by one of the recently recruited magistrates relays the type of views she heard expressed by longer-serving magistrates in relation to the restructured court working experience.

> I have had a number of older, longer serving magistrates say to me it's not what it used to be and they're quite disenchanted. Some of them are think-ing of stepping down maybe earlier than they would have done because they feel they have much less freedom, much less discretion than they used to. It's become very formulaic, the benches are so big now that there isn't the same sense of collegiality there was. They say the training has got better and they say that newly trained magistrates are much more up to speed than they were when they started.... But that's pretty much the only positive thing they have to say about the changes.
>
> (Female, aged 54, two years' service)

In some ways therefore the alterations occurring to magistrates' court operations can be interpreted as amounting to a radical occupational culture change, and with that was forcing a process of resocialisation among magistrate working groups. Another feature of magistrates' court work that was having a bearing on their sense of purpose and professional identity was the decline in court business being experienced in some areas. This was summarised in Chapter 3 with the lower case volumes coming before the magistrates' courts highlighted. For some of the magistrates this was a real feature of their court working environment at this time.

Magistrate work identity

A strong sense was given by the magistrates that the bigger structural issue of crime prosecution and growth in the use of out-of-court penalties and diversion-ary approaches, which is resulting in fewer cases coming before the courts, threatened their position as active magistrates. This was in the way that the declining volume of business has an effect on the number of sitting days that magistrates have access to. The trend appeared to be felt more acutely in the regional areas than in London and the city-centre courts. The magistrates had strong views that the criminal justice approach of what they saw as essentially the police acting as 'judge and jury' in the way that is legitimated through out-of-court justice (Slapper, 2010). Criticisms have been put forward more gener-ally in the way some serious and violent offences have escaped prosecution, when evidence suggests that they should have come before the courts for adjudi-cation (Fassenfelt, 2012; Travis, 2013). Indeed, in some locations it was having a bearing on the frequency at which magistrates could get sitting days and perform their duties and, importantly to them, retain the competences they are judged upon as lay arbiters of the law (Davies, 2005). The magistrates working in courts outside London expressed these views with more emotion than those working in city-centre courts. This is revealed in the following quote by a magistrate serving in the English County Court area. Though magistrates working in London courts spoke of the way that their colleagues and magistrate friends in other parts of the country were being affected by the trend:

> Out-of-court disposal ... I don't think there's any doubt that it's changed the way the magistrates' courts are working. I started 11 years ago as a magistrate after I retired, and at that time in Dunchester we had two main days. We had a Monday and a Wednesday and that's when all new cases or repeat cases came back to court to be dealt with. There were two courts sitting on both those days. Now there's only one main day and that's a Wednesday and a lot of that is dealing with things like probation reports.... The amount of business has decreased quite significantly within Dunchester and a lot of that is down to out-of-court disposals.
>
> (Male, aged 68 years, 10 years' service)

Utilising their spare time by working as a lay justice meant a lot to the magistrates, with it apparent that they devoted a lot of time and commitment to the role, as well as the wider requirements upon them to perform it with the utmost professional competence. Equally it was evident that the position provided them with a sense of purpose and work cultural belonging, self-identity, and, to some extent, status in the same way that regular salaried professional occupations are found to fulfil (Ardichvili and Kuchinke, 2009). In part, the changed operations that were leading to decreases in the number of sitting days available appeared to be undermining the professional identity they derived from their work as a serving magistrate. However, the magistrates had put strategies in place to counter this by moving over from sitting in the adult criminal courts to also serving in the youth and/or family courts, where more work was available.

There is a body of literature on social identities as constructed within the world of work, and which acknowledges the impact occupational restructures and reconfigured employment positions have on the 'work identities' of those affected. Although this work mainly focuses on the education and health employment sectors, the themes of disenfranchisement that this literature addresses (Ardichvili and Kuchinke, 2009) are relevant to my study of magistrates. The themes of occupational culture at this time of court restructure could be applied to the magistrates' narratives. These themes link in the way some magistrates appeared to be experiencing ruptures to their social and professional identity as serving magistrates.

Professionalising justice

Indeed, the accounts of the magistrates in regard to their working experiences illustrated that they were operating within an increasingly professionalised court work environment, which was altering at quite a pace from what they were used to. The changing processes were particularly commented on by the longer-serving magistrates when compared with the more recently recruited ones. According to the newer magistrates, the early initial training in preparation for their magisterial courtroom duties incorporated a business-style introduction to the job, plus a certain corporate language socialising them into the position as lay legal professionals within the judiciary.

Despite there not being a great deal of recent research on lay magistrates, or on them as a working group with an established work culture and identity, a recurring theme within commentary on the lower courts is the increasing professionalisation of lower court justice. My reference to this connects to the streamlining and efficient case processing and bureaucratic demands brought into lower court operational practice. Davies (2005) has written about professionalisation as it applies to the magistracy in a way that can be connected to my analysis. He referred to the formalisation of processes concerning magistrates' skill acquisition, performance and competence. He says over time this moved from an informal approach with magistrates encouraged to undertake refresher training to keep up with changes in the law and procedure, to the introduction of compulsory training. The 'Judicial Studies Board' was established as the official body with authority over the design and content of magistrate training. Davies discussed professionalisation in reference to the Magistrates' New Training Initiative (MNTI) introduced in 1999. This formalised the training, appraisal and mentoring system of serving magistrates and which continues to exist today. Since this professional training system came in at the time the New Labour government was introducing business models of management across the public services, including the police, the probation service, etc., it is reasonable to link these training developments to the trend in managerial justice, which has progressively been introduced across all public services and the criminal courts.

The interviews with the magistrates provided a lot of material on the way it can be interpreted that they, through court changes, are going through enhanced processes of professionalisation. Magistrates' reflections in this regard went back some years and indeed to the introduction of the appraisal system at the end of the 1990s as just mentioned.

One of the London magistrates remembered the point at which appraisals had first been brought into the system and how some fellow magistrates were deeply unhappy with the development at that time. She noted the discomfort with it, particularly as magistrates emphasised their status as volunteers, a position which in their view exempts them from formal occupational performance reviews:

> They were not happy about the fact that somebody was reporting on their performance. What they said was that they were actually volunteers, they had come into the job, they were doing it in their own time, they thought they were perfectly competent. The main emphasis I think was really that they were volunteers, that they had given a lot to the bench, and here was somebody coming along with a tick box and saying 'oh you might not have done that, so well we might have to look at that' and obviously the worst scenario would be that 'oh we've done your appraisal and actually it has not been particularly good'. And it then has to go to the Bench Training

Committee, so it was the whole thing about being appraised ... and person-
ally I thought that was a fair amount of arrogance, but I could see from their
point of view. They hadn't come into do that, and therefore it was quite
shock when that was being offered. Other people accepted it, thought it was
a good thing and went along with it and that was fine.

(Female, aged 70, 16 years' service)

It is evident from her comments that there was division among the magistrates at
the time, with some comfortable with the revised requirements while others were
not. She links those who were more accepting of the new performance measures
to familiarity with appraisals within the regular workplace environment. Others
were not happy with the introduction and, as she says, even left the magisterial
role over it. This articulated division regarding magistrates' acceptance of
professional management processes is returned to later in this chapter.

[T]he appraisal system I think was good. I do remember that quite a number
of the magistrates who had been there for quite a long time felt very frus-
trated and quite angry about the appraisal system and in fact I do remember
one or two members of our bench who actually left and said they were not
prepared to be appraised and they hadn't been appraised before. Those were
very often people who had probably not worked and they found it very
difficult.

(Female, aged 70, 16 years' service)

Moving forward some years from the introduction of the appraisal system in the
1990s to the current period, similar upset was being felt with the requirements
being introduced alongside unfolding modernising processes. Modifications to
the magistrate working role, such as tighter case management responsibilities,
the expected efficient case processing and pressures to move swiftly through
daily court lists (cf. Mack and Roach Anleu, 2007), as well as the consistent
application of the Sentencing Guidelines, were pervasive in the magistrates'
responses. The challenges that they and their colleagues have faced in accomplishing these new working approaches were reflected upon, which included
mentioning the disillusionment of some. However, a sense of pride was also
expressed in rising to the new challenges.

Many of the magistrates welcomed the changes being made to lower court
justice, but it was also stated that what is required of them these days in the form
of high competence needs to be more widely acknowledged. It was considered
by some that the senior directors of the judiciary were not fully appreciative of
the extent of the technical work being performed by lay magistrates in their role
as justices. Here it was reflected that the weight placed on magistrates' court
justice is on the lay element and magistrates as representatives of the community, and that no longer mirrors the work. As such, it was considered that
there is a misrepresentation in the way the magistrate role is communicated to the
wider public and to potential new recruits too. One of the London magistrates

reflected on what he saw as a contradiction, with the emphasis placed on the attributes of lay magistrates as community representatives when it is high-level professional competence that is required, especially in this fast-paced changing arena of lower court justice. His comment illustrates a belief that the nature of the work has fundamentally 'moved on' from its main strength being local community justice:

[A]ll the time we hear that we are meant to be representative of the community. I am sorry that has moved on, you can't just be a member of the community anymore and do all the things we have to do, that has moved on … if you look at the Sentencing Guidelines, look at the new guidelines we have now, I mean it's a minefield working your way through this.

(Male, aged 53, 12 years' service)

There was a feeling among some magistrates that the discourse needed to move on from what the earlier essential prerequisites were to become a lay magistrate. It was pointed out that the necessary qualities, stressing you need to be a 'well-minded' person versed in common sense, should be put to the background to match the reality of the post in the contemporary period. It was stressed that most magistrate activity, but especially that of a chair, requires the capacity to be a skilled professional manager and administrator who is well experienced in legal and criminal procedure in addition to the other required attributes. The following magistrate, with 20 years' experience, expresses this:

Traditionally it's been a case that you'd enter into the magistracy if you were a well-minded person with a good reputation and good common sense, and a judicial capacity, and that was the only requirement really. Where now … [c]ase management is very much that the chairman of the court has to have a very good knowledge of the Criminal Procedure Rules, a very good knowledge of disclosure, a very good knowledge of actually quite a few other things. So we are moving away from where we were, and the court chairman now is a part time professional and the more and more that becomes the case, the better we're getting at managing cases.

(Male, aged 51, 20 years' service)

This was a sentiment similarly held by a magistrate in a different focus group who summarised the range of tasks a bench chair has to manage in a day's courtroom sitting, which are officially recognised and designed into the chairmanship training. As he sets out, the bench chair is responsible for directing proceedings in court on behalf of the three magistrates, on top of handling all the other procedural issues that emerge:

[T]he chair in any of our courts is required to manage the whole court process, to keep advocates in order, admonish them when necessary if they're overstepping the mark, reassure witnesses who have a problem, really to manage every aspect of the court process and that is now formally part of the chairmanship training.

(Male, aged 65, 10 years' service)

For those who spoke out on the topic of the increasing managerial processes within lower court justice administration, and essentially what is a shifting job description for serving magistrates, the alterations were welcomed, with it being agreed that they ushered in much-needed improvements. For instance, actively reducing the time delays occurring to individual cases through adjournments and missing documentation, and placing pressure on the police and the prosecution service to submit papers on time and in order, so that cases progress through the system in a timely manner.

With the shift in expectations and demand placed upon magistrates within the modern structure of the job, a partial division could be detected, with some of the more ambitious and aspirational magistrates expressing enjoyment and pride with the heavy requirements of the job. They were keen to present themselves as rising to this challenge. Some magistrates saw the greater requirements on them in terms of case management as a positive and necessary move. This was because it enabled them to retain their high reputation as judicial officers within the modernising lower court system, and were doing what they could to demonstrate that they were equipped to go forth with the future visions. But a division was identified in the way one of the London magistrates expressed his assessment that some of his fellow colleagues were not up to it:

I think that is good, it puts us in a similar position to DJs, I feel very privileged to do it, however there is no doubt some of our colleagues are not fully prepared and trained for it and some of them struggle. So there is a friction between those magistrates that see themselves as being there to administer and those that see themselves as there to perform a form of social duty if you like, and I am not sure that anybody has looked at this very clearly.

(Male, aged 53, 12 years' service)

In some ways, the behaviour of magistrates keen to prove that they can accomplish the newly commanded skills of active case management, as specified by the Criminal Procedure Rules, can be linked to the literature on occupational restructures. This draws out the uncertainties they can bring in employees, but which also see people reconstruct themselves to fit revised job specifications and changing criteria. Some magistrates were positioning themselves to fend off any scepticism that they might not be able to cope with the current case management challenges.

Within discussions of the increased demands being placed on the working role of magistrates, it was thought that the time requirements and more taxing role, particularly for bench chairs, impedes the recruitment of good potential applicants to the position. This was something some magistrates reflected that government should consider more closely in their wish to attract younger professionals into the service:

> [I]t is almost like a job in that there is a higher level of commitment involved, there is a high level of professionalism when we are here, and we have to have the time to be able do that ... and the level of competence has got so much higher ... and I am not sure that is really spelled out in the recruitment.
>
> (Female, aged 54, five years' service)

My research was interested in examining in more detail the way a distinction appeared to have become established among serving magistrates. The newer, more recently recruited magistrates alluded to being socialised into the lay justice role in line with government ambitions for reform and modernisation. This had the effect of making longer-serving magistrates refute notions of not being prepared for the new challenges of doing modern court business, as one magistrate comments in reaction to the current discourse:

> I think we ought to be careful in drawing distinctions between people who have served for a long time and therefore must be stuck in their ways.
>
> (Male, aged 51, 20 years serving)

It was evident from my observations in the magistrates' courts and from my interviews with serving magistrates that the level and extent of responsibility that they hold in the job, the commitment required of them in order to be judged as competent in the role and the judicial authority required in their courtroom performance are high skill requirements. Further, these are skills that affect their sense of working identity, seeing themselves in many ways as lay legal professionals. Out of modesty, the magistrates were reluctant to refer to themselves as highly skilled professionals. But, on being questioned about the specialised and powerful role they occupy as courtroom justices, it was accepted that to some extent they are a special group of volunteers who are recruited for their distinct professional skills and competence. An exchange emerged in the London focus group in this regard. In reflecting on the credentials required to perform as a magistrate they interpreted their position as essentially as lay legal professionals:

> People who sit on a bench have to go through a rigorous selection process and they are chosen on various criteria, I can't think of exactly what the wording is now, but a lot of it is to do with analytical thinking and in that sense I have to say, we are an elite ... I'm not meaning in any other sense, but we are able to think objectively and think judicially.... We have certain skills, we must have, and we have to say this to you straightforwardly, we have certain skills that most of the population don't have. But we are drawn from so many different places in the public world, we are not just you know legally trained, legally focused, tunnel vision legal people.
>
> (Female, aged 65, 13 years' service)

This can be linked to the work of Davies (2005), who argued in his paper that we see incremental steps towards the professionalisation of the lay magistracy. He says that in an 'increasingly complex legal environment it has proven very difficult to maintain a structure and character which is truly lay' (ibid.: 93). He adds: 'what is largely absent from the academic literature is a consideration of whether lay magistrates are still truly amateurs in the criminal process' (ibid.: 94) and whether developments in training have moved on from being 'rudimentary' and 'minimal'. Davies added that when 'coupled with prior experience and the experience gained sitting on the bench have led to the development of elements of professionalism within the lay magistracy' (ibid.: 94). Davies (2005) looks at lay magistrates as 'judicial professionals'. Malsch (2009) also writes on the notion of 'professionality' within lay legal justice participation. She says, 'Lay people who are involved over an extended period of time, thereby acting as a judge in a large number of cases, acquire some type of expertise that resembles that of professional judges' (ibid.: 63).

It is with the fact that magistrates comprise a particular group who predominately come from professional class backgrounds that Dignan and Wynne (1997) contend that it might be time to more accurately portray lay magistrates by committing to, and promoting the lower criminal court system as run by a 'quasi-professional magistracy', rather than accounting for them within notions of community representativeness. This is an important point to take forward in respect to the way the magistracy is being reformed and revised.

Professional judges in the lower courts

In line with my argument that we are seeing a move towards the increasing professionalisation of lower court justice work is the opinion that a role is being carved out for single sitting salaried judges within the lower criminal courts (Morgan, 2013; Cox, 2010; Seago *et al.*, 2000). The growing use of professional judges was a feature of the magistrate discussions with some insecurities verbalised.

Historically, the lower criminal courts of the English justice system have employed salaried legal judges to perform alongside lay magistrates, but these were mainly located in London and metropolitan court areas (Seago *et al.*, 2000). According to official figures the number of salaried judges employed in the lower courts has expanded year on year in the recent period. As already mentioned, most of the magistrates interviewed were working in courthouses where salaried judges were employed on a full-time basis or were rostered in as and when business required. Magistrates in one focus group mentioned the employment of a district judge in their court in the recent years. To some degree this appeared to be fuelling insecurity on magistrates' permanence and future in the lay justice role. Despite there being a recognised need to maintain magistrates' interests in the job by providing them with a broad range of judicial work and distributing equitably across the lay magistrates' and district judges' benches, it was said by the two lower court judges interviewed in my research that there are particularities with some court work that require their qualified legal expertise.

One magistrate disagreed with the view that the employment of more professional judges in the lower courts was a threat. He aligned himself more closely with the legally qualified district judges working in the court he sat in than with his fellow magistrates. This relates to the point developed earlier in relation to magistrates rising to the challenge with the new demands of tighter case management placed upon them and wishing to prove themselves able and competent within this altered terrain. He was critical of the slower, more deliberative style of his magistrate colleagues:

> I am a great supporter of DJs. I have learnt so much from them and work a great with them and where I fundamentally disagree is this, you can on one day have a bench of one chairman who can barely be able to cope with eight cases and they will have to adjourn everything over to other days, or a DJ will have to come in and complete the list. The next day you will get a totally different bench and they will get through all the work by 4 o'clock. That is the problem there is inconsistency between benches and inconsistencies between magistrates … same problem of training and what magistrates think they are there to do. I will be quite blunt to say I feel I am there to get through a list, that is what I am there to do. Other people feel they are there to spend a lot more time listening and everything as I don't. I am there to get through work.
>
> (Male, aged 53, 12 years' service)

Governmental commentary refutes the idea that salaried district judges are being brought into replace lay magistrates (Green, 2014), but there is evidence of change here. Continuing governments make pledges they are committed to the lay magistracy and greatly value the contribution they make to community and local justice (Ministry of Justice, 2012; Morgan, 2013), but the official figures point to increased numbers of salaried judges working in the lower courts, as set out in Chapter 3, particularly since 2006.

In reflecting on the contribution of lay magistrates to the efficient and professionalised justice system they are operating within, an interview with a district judge of one court supported the view that a professional magistracy has developed. This was in the way that she viewed the continued commitment to the role by some magistrates, resulting in a core of highly experienced competent lay justices and, moreover, that this was fundamental to the efficient and shared running of that court's operation:

> We might have a big number [of magistrates] on the list, but we do see the same … and they really get accustomed to how things work and they get very able, a real hard core of them, get very able and no they are not going to go anywhere, they're here to stay and a good thing too.
>
> (District judge)

Problems with the modernising court system

On top of the magistrates articulating they were rising to the challenge with the new requirements and expectations placed upon them to fit in with the directives of efficient and tighter case management, there were also criticisms. This was particularly of the internal administrative support structures they were working with, to the point that some expressed felt impaired in demonstrating that they were effective participants within the lay justice role. Here, it was accepted that the court service, much like other publicly funded services, including the criminal justice agencies they work closely with such as the prosecution service, the police, legal aid services and language interpretation services, were all faced with substantial budgetary cuts which were having an effect on well-functioning systems. An example mentioned from one magistrate's experience was the way that important information, in some regard crucial to the job, did not flow onto them. For instance, changes to legislation that were necessary for magistrates to know about in their judging role were not passed on. Thus, it could be seen that there were ruptures in lines of communication in the way that information and learning and training were not filtering down to them in their part-time, lay justice role. This left some with the opinion that they were on the periphery of central business and this caused an overall level of dissatisfaction among a few.

The issue of magistrates being excluded from important knowledge transfer was commented on by one magistrate who was previously employed as a mental health nurse. He talked about the online self-training set-up they were expected to engage with. In his experience this amounted to being deskilled. The comment he makes about the lack of training offered to magistrates to keep up to date with the changing nature of their work set them at a disadvantage in maintaining competences necessary to the job:

> I think for me one of the major changes has been the lack of training over the last two years. There's been major changes in the magistrates' courts, there's been major changes in the sentencing structures and Sentencing Guidelines and all sorts of things like that. We've not been trained in them. We are expected as I said to look at a computer and learn that way.... I think the lack of training and that again is cost driven, that is one of the things that's actually affecting the magistrates is the dilution of training in my view. That's why I ended up feeling deskilled in the adult court, too many changes coming through too quick and not getting trained on them.
>
> (Male, 69 years, 10 years' service)

Therefore, there was a strong feeling among some magistrates that the expectations upon them of high judicial competence and professionalism were in some regard undermined by the crumbling and inadequate administrative structures that should keep them included, involved and up to date. A number of the magistrates came from managerial and professional business backgrounds and from these experiences viewed the operational structures they were working with needed improving. An example put forward by one of the newer London magistrates was his discussion of the modern world of work, where evaluation is a key feature of forward planning and resource allocation. In his view, the appraisal of the decisions magistrates make was missing and was something he expected would help in learning important lessons. He reflected that, remarkably, the outcomes of magistrates' sentencing and bail decisions do not filter back to them, which he considered to be a flawed part of the system when pitched against the way good business operates in the commercial world and in other organisations. He was employed as a freelance information technology specialist and had experience of this in his salaried professional role:

> [N]ormally if you make decisions about something in any aspect of life you're looking for some feedback on how your decisions went – were they good decisions, were they bad decisions ... did you make the right decision, how can you improve your decision making process? When you're a magistrate you ... don't have that feedback process ... we are making decisions all the time. We are making decisions on whether people are guilty or innocent, we are making decisions on how to sentence people and also we're making decisions on bail which are very often the hardest decisions about whether you remand somebody on bail, or remand them in custody, pending a trial or sentencing. So you are making all these decisions and you have no feedback whatsoever about whether you made the [right] decision.... I think it would enable us to learn more from our mistakes because inevitably we're going to make mistakes and to have that feedback would then sort of cement our decision making process and make it more resilient.
>
> (Male, aged 46, four years' service)

The issue of the potential for magistrates to be engaged more usefully in court outcomes and monitoring and comparing re-offending rates to help identify good practice and share with other courts is addressed in more detail in the following chapter. However, it is an important consideration when viewing the lower courts as moving towards efficient, modernised models of public services. In the speech delivered by Green (2014) on ambitions for reform to the magistracy he made reference to harnessing 'the traditional idea of public service to modern engagement with communities'. He noted that he wanted magistrates to have a role in cutting re-offending and that court outcomes should be an important part of magistrates' jobs. Ideas drawn from the world of professional work were possibly what Green (2014) was implying when he stressed that he was keen to make full use of and apply magistrates' existing professional expertise to the role.

New and diverse recruits to the magistracy

As already mentioned, the research was going on at a time when there was commentary from a range of quarters on the need to improve the diversity of the magistracy. Through the magistrates' views, it was evident that recruitment strategies have been proactive in drawing in younger members. The newer magistrates gave the impression that the ambitions for reform to lower court justice were a feature of their recruitment and training. Moreover, it seemed that their participation was encouraged based on them being a new breed of younger magistrates who symbolised a break from the past image of the magistracy as older in age and from narrow social class backgrounds. In some ways exemplifying the more modern magistracy the government is interested in shaping, the Magistrates' Association is making attempts to convey this image. The Magistrates' Association has embraced criticism of magisterial membership and has redesigned and re-imaged its public profile. It emphasises the diverse range of characters who serve as volunteer magistrates. This updated message by the Magistrates' Association must also be seen as demonstrating the capacity of serving lay magistrates to administer the law within the English justice system at this time of court transformation (Hughes, 2015), which is permeating government discourse on court management at every level (Ministry of Justice, 2014b; Ministry of Justice, 2013a).

The following comment was made by one of the recently recruited magistrates, who remembered the style of training her cohort had received, which she considered different from the training of the more established magistrates. Moreover, it seems that the training they were given accentuated the professional and managerial context of court work and which the judiciary and court service is attempting to achieve. This can be linked back to what is in essence an occupational restructure relating to the lower courts and the work role resocialisation of magistrates. She had been serving in the smaller English city court for six years and refers to the training in terms of how to deal with 'clients' and 'customers' within the courtroom. This is indicative of the business managerialist model being implemented:

> I think our year, very recently have been trained in the new way ... so we are trained very thoroughly, we are trained in the new way ... we are very well trained in modern thinking in how to deal with clients, customers and other agencies that work within the criminal justice system and we follow guidelines ... we are trained to focus on sentencing guidelines and to work within the team, there's three of you.... So sort of team working philosophy.... So I think that's probably been the way that we're working and perhaps there are maybe more older magistrates ... who can just think off the top of their head, have their own views ... whereas I think our year are much more, the more modern, younger.
>
> (Female, 44 years, six years' service)

Younger recruits to the magistracy are seen as important for its future viability (Gibbs and Kirby, 2014), but it was also stressed that longer-serving members had acquired a wealth of important experience that cannot be lost. Besides this, experience is essential in a role of this nature, where the skill and expertise developed over time are immeasurable. The current shifting terrain and concerted efforts to bring younger people into the magistracy drew mutual respect across magistrates, with older members considering it of great value to have younger people represented on the bench. Further, the younger, more recently recruited magistrates were conscious of the rich experience that longer-serving magistrates brought. Moreover, the learning and mentoring from older, experienced magistrates was respected. It was also considered important to see a mix of magistrates on the bench from the viewpoint of defendants, for the perception that their personal experience is being judged with a balanced level of understanding:

> I think it's nice for a defendant to also see a younger person up there sitting on the bench of three, because if they see a group of people in their 60's and 70's, their impression is oh my goodness, here we go. We've got a bunch of fuddy duddy's who have no idea of what's happening and what I'm going through and what I'm experiencing. That is their first impression of us. So if we have three people who are a mixture of young as well as middle aged, as well as over 60's then at least the person in the dock won't be making judgements on the three elderly people that they see up there.
>
> (Female, aged 59, 20 years' service)

Even though it was considered vital to have younger people represented as a part of the magistracy, the attention on youth and young magistrates was thought of as problematic due to the potential risk of losing important knowledge and skills if older magistrates were to be replaced by younger cohorts. This was in part voiced in response to the *Future Courts* report (Chambers *et al.*, 2014), published by the Policy Exchange shortly before my fieldwork interviews were carried out. In putting forward ideas for a longer-term vision of the lower courts, the report suggested fixed 10-year tenures for serving volunteer magistrates. The magistrates interviewed were aware of this report and one magistrate commented on his sitting period, which was then 10 years. He said that he was still acquiring new knowledge central to his justice administration role, and as a result he considered the ideas senseless:

> I'm ten years [serving] now and I still feel new, even though I've felt deskilled, I still feel I'm new to it, I still feel there's so much I don't know about being a magistrate, and to say to me right you have to go and we'll put somebody younger in. You need both, we need more young people there's no doubt about that, but how you free them up to get the time to do it I don't know....
>
> I've seen so many good people in Fielding having to leave at 70 and all the experience they've got and the good judgements they've got, you've seen it sitting beside them ... and you think why does he or she have to go? But you do need more young people and it's how you get that balance. They're talking about some limited term magistracy now aren't they? I think that's just so stupid.
>
> (Male, 69 years, 10 years' service)

The discourse going on within the court service relating to the competence, efficiency and modernising priorities of lower court justice administration was unsettling what was originally a greater cohesion among magistrate working groups. The interchange between policy actors' messages, which partially downplay the significance of lower court work, and the role of magistrates was felt. This was compounded by the reporting that there is declining business in the lower courts. Voices from within the London focus group, were keen to emphasise the court work that they were engaged in was different in volume and case complexity than in other less metropolitan parts of the country.

The interviews with the magistrates provided a lot of material on the way it can be interpreted enhanced processes of professionalisation are being introduced. These reflections went back some years prior to the introduction of the appraisal system at the end of the 1990s and the culture change that this brought about. The more recent modifications to the working role, such as the case management responsibilities, the efficient processing and competence in 'getting through the list', as well as the consistent application of the Sentencing Guidelines, were present in their narratives. The challenges they and their colleagues had faced in accomplishing these new working approaches were reflected upon, including mention of disillusionment among some, but they also expressed their pride in rising to the challenge.

> [T]here's been a lot of changes in the last four years. But when I was first trained, things like case management were stressed, adherence to the Sentencing Guidelines, all the sort of formalities, working as a team, the framework, the competent framework, all these things were all stressed from day one. So that was four years ago, but you do get a lot of magistrates who were trained before then and sometimes significantly before then who are, I'm not going to say resistant, but I think they would prefer things to be done in the old way.... I've encountered magistrates who resent having to use the Sentencing Guidelines and would feel happier using more discretion in terms of how they go about sentences.... But it's a lot harder these days to use your discretion in terms of how you apply the guidelines. So yeah from my point of view I've always been a magistrate within the new era if you like where everything is quite strictly prescribed. But you do, you hear about the old times from the older magistrates and how things used to be and how good everything was back then and how terrible it is now and this sort of thing.
>
> (Male, aged 46, four years' service)

This chapter has continued with an exploration of magistrates' experiences in their role as volunteer criminal court justices, and has focused on their involvement during a changing environment of tighter administration, budgetary and staffing cuts to major criminal justice agencies, which have impacted in all sorts of ways on their workplace practice and sense of feeling included. From the magistrates' stories it is clear that they are operating within challenging conditions as a direct result of the financial austerity measures imposed on the criminal courts. Alongside various alterations being made to aspects of summary justice, the future role of magistrates is under discussion. Support for the valuable contribution they make to the system of lay justice is expressed, and ideas are put forward to utilise the individual professional skill sets more (Chambers *et al.*, 2014; Green, 2014).

It is useful at this point to return to Dignan and Wynne's (1997) work on the magistracy. Their critique is on the social composition of the magistracy. A point made by Dignan and Wynne is that there is no clear agreement on which of the competing purposes the existing lay justice system is supposed to serve. Donoghue (2014a) also raises this point in her paper on reforms to the lay magistracy. She sets out that, in order to argue strongly for a continued and valued role for the lay magistracy, it is necessary to articulate its precise value. As mentioned earlier, she argues that, given the significance of lay justice to the English legal system, the absence of a sound conceptual basis for magistrates' participation limits the cohesiveness of arguments favouring its retention (ibid.: 932).

My argument links to Dignan and Wynne's suggestion relating to a quasi-professional panel of magistrates and what is currently going on with the increasing professionalisation of lower court justice. Dignan and Wynne put forward three contending arguments in favour of having a lay justice system and set out a backdrop calling for a 'quasi-professional panel of suitably qualified people'. They say in essence that this is what the system is comprised of but that it is not communicated in that way.

It is my argument that, with the changes going on and the tighter bureaucratic demands being drawn into courtroom practice, we are increasingly moving towards a professionalised magistracy with members who are competent in the administration of law. This is crystallised in the experiences provided by the more recently recruited magistrates, whose training is evidently designed to socialise them into managerial styles of performance. With this and along with the fact that magistrates serve in the role for many years, building up tight legal and law administration experience, they can be defined as lay legal professionals.

6 Social justice meets criminal justice

Magistrates' working experiences, alongside the various alterations and modernising processes being implemented within the lower criminal courts, have been the focus of discussion in the previous two chapters. This chapter moves to take a slightly different direction. It returns to the theme introduced in Chapter 3 on the prevalence of social and economic marginalisation among courtroom defendants and emphasises that the lower-tier magistrates' courts are mainly processing people whose lives and lifestyles are enmeshed within complex and tangled situations of disadvantage, who quite often have health and other treatment needs, such as drug and alcohol addiction and mental disorder, to which offending is sometimes attributed. Other criminal justice commentators highlight this as a feature of lower criminal court working, with questions relating to 'equal justice' asked in connection to it (Kramer, 2000; Heffernan and Kleinig, 2000; Hudson, 2000).

Together with the central role that magistrates play in sentencing and dispensing penalties, and the fact that a high proportion of defendants in the lower courts have social, economic and health disadvantages, an interest in how magistrates locate crime and criminality in wider society emerged within my research. In this regard, in this chapter I am interested in the social justice elements of criminal justice (Heffernan, 2000) and how these can be theorised within the work of the lower-tier magistrates' courts. It continues to draw on the research interviews and experiences of magistrates in their working role and examines how social justice conceptions and values are present within magistrates' views and outlooks. It draws significantly on themes of rehabilitative sentencing, 'sentencer supervision' and specialist problem-solving court approaches.

If we take at its most basic that social justice is the equal and fair distribution of resources, as argued by Barry (2005) and Heffernan (2000), themes of social justice can be applied to lower courtroom work and come out from the magistrates' narratives in relation to the sentencing role they perform. At the heart of this chapter's analysis, therefore, is the interconnectedness of social justice and criminal justice, which can be applied to the interplay of rehabilitation, sentencing and offender management as dispensed within the lower court arena.

Alongside the connections that can be made to social justice, this chapter discusses the way that traditional styles of courtroom justice are being appraised and whether the alternative dispute resolution approaches emerging in the form of specialist problem-solving courts, and taking reconciliation beyond courtroom settings into community locations have mileage for the future. 'Specialist courts' modelled on problem-solving approaches are becoming established in the English criminal justice system and discussions are ongoing about magistrates' role in delivering these court models (Centre for Justice Innovation, 2015; Carlile, 2014; Ward, 2014). It emerged through the research that some magistrates are at the centre of social justice innovations that are forward-thinking in design and are uniquely based on their specialised courtroom knowledge of disadvantage among the lives of the people they encounter, such as drug and alcohol dependence, absent parenting and early independence, as well as their awareness of the gaps that exist within social welfare and health provision to help people address these life issues.

One particular example was a group of youth court magistrates in one focus group, who were involved in a problem-solving court approach with young offenders (see Ward and Warkel, 2015). Another was the work of a magistrate who set up a supported hostel for young men coming out of prison with no secure accommodation to move to on release. These examples are discussed further later in this chapter, but my argument is that social justice meets criminal justice within magistrates' court work, and more recognition and utility can be drawn from this in different ways in moving forwards in criminal court and justice reform, and with the central inclusion of suitably qualified magistrates.

With this chapter contributing to theorisations of social justice and the interconnection with criminal justice, it is necessary to return to the overview of social justice as provided in the introductory chapter. Heffernan (2000) connects these two concepts and asks complex questions relating to ideals of social justice as the fair and equal distribution of resources and opportunities (Barry, 2005), or indeed the unequal distribution and the resulting poverty and economic deprivation for some people. He builds within his arguments whether we can justifiably contemplate social deprivation as a defence or excuse within the administration of law. Heffernan draws on Bazelon's (1976) suggestion for the legitimated defence of 'rotten social background' in the knowledge of the dire and blameless circumstances some accused defendants live in and which link to some offending pathways.

This chapter moves to engage with the magistrates' interviews before returning to expand on my theory that the lower criminal courts can be defined as a space in which social justice is embedded within lower criminal court practice.

Social lifestyle issues and links to offending

Along with the central element of magistrates' court work deciding on appropriate penalties for diverse offender types, how the magistrates viewed crime and criminality in society was of interest to my study. In line with this, the onus they placed upon the broader structures of society for some of the 'situational' lifestyle problems they are exposed to in criminal case processing was relevant. Roach Anleu and Mack (2005), in their research on the lower criminal courts in Australia, suggest that courts are in many ways a marker of governmental social and economic policies, with the impact of these exhibited in the predicaments of many defendants. They contend that the radical social and economic changes occurring in modern society over the last few decades, such as increases in income inequality, shifts in employment relationships from secure full-time positions to casual part-time ones, retrenchment in welfare provision and public service privatisation, among others, combine to exacerbate social problems of unemployment, drug addiction, mental illness and welfare dependency that are seen in the courtroom. They state:

> Daily, lower courts confront the human consequences of broader changes in socio-economic conditions and government policies.... These courts are not just dealing with technical arguments but with many people who have ended up in contact with the criminal justice system as a result – perhaps not directly – of the failure of other (for example, welfare, education, employment and mental health) systems.

> (Ibid.: 591)

The relationship between social and economic deprivation, poverty and exclusion in criminal offending is not a causal one, yet there is evidence to support the fact that living with certain conditions correlates closely with some crime pathways (Porteous *et al.*, 2015; Porteous, 2015; Carlile, 2014; Prison Reform Trust, 2015; Social Exclusion Unit, 2002; Young, 1999). A sharp focus in the early years of the New Labour government was on tackling social exclusion in efforts to address the high crime rates in the UK; research emerged identifying specific 'risk factors' locating people as more or less vulnerable to entering into crime. These factors included living among deprived neighbourhoods, with unemployment, homelessness and drug and alcohol misuse, and growing up in state care. The many studies conducted among so-called 'vulnerable groups' note overlaps with offending. Farrington *et al.*'s (2012) prospective longitudinal survey on 'delinquency' and 'risk factor paradigm' research has become noted for illustrating links between life circumstances and offending. Porteous *et al.* (2015) argued, from their research on specialist support services for young people who offend, that very often they have been victims of abuse and violence during their childhood and growing up years. As such, young offenders themselves often need to be considered as victims. A report by Carlile (2014) acknowledged that many young people who offend have experienced problems relating to care and nurture in their growing up lives.

When probed on the subject of defendants with lifestyle problems and their high prevalence among lower court populations, some magistrates expressed sympathy towards certain issues, such as drug and alcohol misuse or mental health disturbance. They voiced unease with the way that the law criminalises people suffering from these problems, which some articulated would be more appropriately dealt with elsewhere. There was also a sense of futility at the way that criminal prosecution leads on to the retributive sentencing of law breaking, rather than providing better opportunities for assigning appropriate rehabilitation, care and treatment or diverting from prosecution earlier in the court process. Thus, magistrates expressed some frustration with the lack of alternative solutions available to them in dispensing penalties. One of the district judges interviewed, whose judicial work also involved prison arbitration, mentioned the frequency of mental illness among women appearing in court and who were in prison, which she considered called for better more relevant responses:

> I think the biggest issue with the cause of crime, well cause of people being in court, particularly for women is mental illness and that is very difficult. Some of these people shouldn't be in court, or certainly they shouldn't be in prison, they should be elsewhere. I notice that when I go and visit the prisons, some of the prisoners that I see are completely out of place, in the women's prisons.
>
> (District judge)

Similar sentiments were expressed by one of the more recently recruited magistrates. She referred to the low-level, petty shoplifting cases committed by defendants with drug and alcohol problems. In her view these are more social care issues than criminal offender ones. Her comment reveals the perception that little else can be done within the current legal set-up, and the pointlessness of the available options when taking into account the plight of homelessness, poverty and sometimes mental health problems present among these people. Her comment acknowledges the needs of shopkeepers who are the victims of retail theft crimes, which obligates magistrates to address offender culpability and dispense court penalties accordingly:

> [T]here are some clients that we see who are perpetual shoplifters … because of a drug habit, usually a drug or alcohol habit and you do wonder why they need to be pushed through this sausage factory of a magistrates' court. … you don't know what to do, you can't fine them because they've got no money, you can't curfew them because sometimes they've got no home, they are homeless. So what can you do to try and stop them, and then probation will say 'well we can put them on this course' and sometimes they will continue with this course … and sometimes they won't. But then you bring in the … is it a crime issue? It becomes a social care issue because there might be mental health concerns there as well. So you think perhaps there should be a medical mental health team effort, more than a criminal, a crime effort because all you're doing is … you're just perpetuating their crime because they are just shoplifting and shoplifting and shoplifting. But then you have pressure from the shops saying well our stock is going, you've got to punish them because they are nicking from us.
>
> (Female, aged 44 years, six years' service)

It was clear from the magistrates' comments relating to their courtroom experiences, as well as through my courtroom observations, that the ambition for diverting certain offender groups, such as low-level offenders with mental health issues, or drug and alcohol complications, from criminal prosecution into care and welfare services have not materialised in the way envisioned. The government policy document *Breaking the Cycle: Effective Punishment, Rehabilitation and Sentencing of Offenders* (Ministry of Justice, 2010), as well as recommendations put forward in the Bradley Report (Department of Health, 2009), sets out wishes for effective diversion, but it is evident that this is not occurring with the pace and comprehensiveness hoped for (Durcan *et al.*, 2014).

Poverty was not mentioned by the magistrates and judges in the discussions connecting lifestyle circumstances to criminal activity, but economic disadvantage among the people they see in court was commented upon. These points emerged alongside discussing the problems with the increasing number of court closures and the way that they see some people facing great difficulty in funding the transport costs to get to court. One magistrate gave an example of poverty and crime from her court working experience. She referred to the particular scenario of magistrates' courts having jurisdiction over the non-payment of television licences. She expressed regret with the mandated sentencing that accompanies this, the misplacement of television licence non-payment as a criminal offence and not having suitable solutions in the form of more useful penalties for those convicted of these offences:

> [W]e find that people on limited income, let's say for argument's sake, 'the poorer members of society', they cannot afford a television licence ... if they haven't got a television licence that is seen as a crime, so they are being criminalised for being poor ... they appear before magistrates, a person from the TV Licensing Authority will be there giving out the facts about this person not having a television licence and they are fined ... and if they don't pay the fine, then they are brought back to the Magistrates' Court and they have to explain why they haven't been paying their fine.
>
> (Female, aged 59, 20 years' service)

According to official statistics, television licence fee evasion is the offence category for which the fines dispensed are least likely to be paid. From the figures collated in 2012 within the year following penalty allocation, just over 30 per cent of the fines were paid in full. When controlled for by gender, women are most likely to be charged with television licence offences (Ministry of Justice, 2015b). It cannot be verified from the figures whether household poverty is explanatory in this, but it might be deduced that non-payment of television licence fees and unpaid fine penalties are associated with limited household funds and prioritising necessary domestic spending instead.

Hudson (2000) writes on the relationship between poverty and criminal justice and refers to the rigidity of the law and legal definitions in not being able to accommodate the social reality of disadvantage so that the categories of

defence and mitigation can be broadened to take account of personal deprivation. Hudson raises the issue of differential justice and the notion of 'blame-
worthiness' in considerations of poverty. She refers more generally to social
policy developments in the US and in the UK in the two decades before the publication of her essay and assesses this as the period in which penal policy
responses came to be a substitute for social policies. Her essay establishes the
difference in view between sociologists of law from those of legal theorists,
whereby sociologists are concerned with removing the disadvantage the criminal
justice system inflicts that adds 'to the social disadvantage impoverished offenders already suffer' (ibid.: 191). The position of legal theory and the principles of
equal justice in the sense that like cases should be treated alike (ibid.: 192) was
referred to by Hudson as an obstacle. The futility of some court sentencing
imposed on people who are virtually penniless and who have obvious and significant lifestyle problems is brought into sharp focus through courtroom observations and makes clear the need for alterations to address these humanity issues.

It was evident that asking magistrates and judges to provide their understandings of the causes of crime was difficult, since their position as sitting bench
magistrates is one of judicial authority in which they are responsible for handling people accused of crime and passing impartial judgement on guilt or non-
guilt on that offence. The magistrates' responses prioritised the judicial and legal
administration responsibilities they preside over, over and above discussing the
lives of the offenders they interact with. When probed on their views, the judicial position was emphasised, leaving out personal expressions of disadvantage
and pity for individuals' circumstances. Distancing sympathies in respect to
courtroom work is a feature of 'neutral justice' and is a key element of magistrates' sentencing training. Several reminded themselves when faced with my
questions in this regard of the guiding line in court decision-making that
'empathy not sympathy' can be applied. Similarly, there was a separation
between themselves in the judicial role and the consideration of the social and
welfare needs of some defendants. Here it was said the assessment requests magistrates put forward to the probation service prior to making sentencing decisions,
and the probation service's links to social services, are in place to pick up social
care issues. One magistrate communicated this distinction between their roles
when engaging in this discussion, saying, 'this is the judiciary, it is not the job of
the judiciary, so no it's not the job of the magistrates to be social workers.'

It was not surprising the magistrates communicated this view seeing that this
is the formal role they occupy, but it is my argument that more can be made of
the lower criminal courts as an arena in which knowledge is generated on the
deep-rooted social and economic problems embedded in society. More use
should be made of the central position that magistrates and judges occupy in car-
rying this information and in helping to look for solutions. As Roach Anleu and
Mack (2005) stress, courtrooms are where 'law and society interact' (ibid.: 595)
and the insights revealed from within them can be used to activate more compassionate therapeutic responses to less 'blameworthy' offending where it is
needed.

Of the magistrates most likely to voice understandings of the social and economic disadvantages among some defendants and the occasional due process concerns relating to vulnerability were magistrates whose professional backgrounds had been in social care and welfare, and in teaching and specialist education. Their previous work had brought them into contact with socially excluded problem families, vulnerability and intellectual disability, such as young people with Asperger's syndrome or educational learning difficulties, and how crime and offending sometimes entwine with these conditions. This is not to say excusals for law breaking were made, but they understood the complexities of people's lives and acknowledged that the prosecution process is problematic in criminalising people with complicated 'criminogenic' needs.

One magistrate however raised a contradiction with the notion that societal inequality and economic disadvantage link as a potential pathway to offending. He had experienced an opposite situation with a young man in court. He recounted that the lad had grown up with great parental wealth and privilege, and connected this to the high-value criminal damage that the young man had committed. In contrast to it being related to disadvantage, he linked it to parental neglect of childcare responsibilities and absence of adult supervision. What is of interest from this example is inattentive and inadequate parenting, which is frequently blamed within analyses of youth offending and the behaviour of 'feckless' youth. The same lack of parental attention can manifest in different ways and in circumstances of social privilege with the potential for the same offending outcomes.

Some of the magistrates verbalised frustration in their sentencing role with the lack of alternative options available in assigning useful penalties, or even appropriate social welfare provision. Yet also in their judgement was the lack of willingness for financial investment in necessary services. Some magistrates were strong in their views about this, believing that there was a need for greater commitment by the government to the sufficient resourcing of help services that might contribute to improved outcomes for offenders:

> The options that are available to magistrates and I imagine to the judiciary ... they're just ... sticking plasters for a gunshot wound and they're not working and people talk about more prisons, more prisons. We send people to prison, but they come out and they offend again because there is an underlying issue. To really sort them out would require a lot of money, a lot of focus and a lot of interest on behalf of society and a completely changed attitude.
>
> (Male, aged 37, five years' service)

Another long-serving magistrate also reflected disappointingly on this. She was the magistrate who set up the hostel for young men coming out of prison and had witnessed first-hand the lack of will behind longer-term funding of such an essential support project:

[S]adly there isn't the money or the will for long term projects that need a considerable amount of funding.

(Female, aged 69, 30 years' service)

We are in the midst of a period of austerity politics in the UK, with ongoing budget cuts across a whole range of services that are having an influence in harsh and depriving ways on some of the most vulnerable people in society. But it can be argued that the criminal justice system is an expensive institution to be picking up the pieces of underinvestment in necessary support services that could have addressed crime antecedents before we arrived upon them.

Rehabilitative sentencing

Together with the discussion of social and environmental factors and links to crime and criminal prosecution, we can raise the topic of rehabilitative sentencing and the role of magistrates in regard to this. By the nature of the courtroom sentencing role, magistrates are participating in offender rehabilitation pathways. Magistrates are tasked with assigning appropriate penalties to guilty offenders, which frequently requires taking into account various vulnerabilities and health and welfare needs. Following a review of the sentencing framework in the English justice system in the early 2000s amidst concerns of sentencing disparity across the courts (Halliday, 2001), the Criminal Justice Act 2003 laid out adjustments. For the first time in allocating criminal court penalties, magistrates and judges were to be minded of the objectives that the sentence being passed is intending to achieve, such as whether it is for purposes of rehabilitation, denunciation, deterrence or a combination of these (Ashworth and Roberts, 2010). These days, magistrates' sentencing is steered by adhering to the Sentencing Guidelines, which direct their decisions.

Assigning appropriate penalties is a large part of magistrates' work. It involves drawing upon the retributive and deterrent dimensions of sentencing in the form of fines, community penalties and time in prison custody, as well as allocating health and rehabilitative treatment to offenders whose criminality is connected to mental incapacity, drugs and alcohol misuse problems. Moreover, magistrates' court sentencing role can be located within the broader endeavours to reduce re-offending among offender populations.

Magistrates execute this function alongside the expertise of the probation service, who carry out assessments and report back with sentence recommendations. But the magistrates expressed being distanced from a proper engagement with the sentencing process, especially the rehabilitative sentencing processes. One long-experienced magistrate, who had previously worked as a probation officer and also a social worker, conveyed a sense of deficiency with the sentencing role in the lack of information that comes back to them on whether a person succeeds or fails with a sentence that has a rehabilitative component to it, in essence the 'what works' in rehabilitation efforts and with what types of offenders as queried by Martinson (1974). This is the underpinning rationale of evidence-based policy making and is important in criminal justice and offender behaviour programmes design; it is argued that magistrates have a core role to play here with the justice administration role they occupy.

Sentence outcome information was considered vital knowledge that ought to be at the heart of magistrate work, both for principles of effective sentencing and for purposes of job satisfaction. Some of the magistrates conveyed an interest in the situational lives of defendants who come before them, and the longitudinal perspective of rehabilitation outcomes was important to them. The probation officer magistrate expresses this in the following comment:

> [Y]ou put people on a drug rehabilitation course which is a very expensive course and particularly expensive if they go away, what you don't know necessarily is how well that works … you don't often get the figures back…. [O]bviously it takes time to see if something has worked … I think in the old days when I was a probation officer I was quite often called in by the district judges/stipendaries to feedback on somebody. It might have been feeding back over only a short period of time not a length of time, but nobody does that now … you don't know whether what you have done has worked … an overall picture for instance of drug rehabs…. The figures must be there but we don't get much of that feedback.
>
> (Female, aged 70, 16 years' service)

These comments link to the point made in the previous chapter of the way lower criminal court work could be more effectively designed if sentence outcome information were made available. Receiving feedback on sentence and bail outcomes was reflected upon as useful, but missing from current practice. The magistrates making those points, and indeed the wider group of magistrates, define the role they perform as predominately one of decision-making and the preparatory magistrate training focuses on sharpening this skill. The opinion of the former probation officer just quoted is similar to the view of the more recently recruited magistrate that was expressed in the previous chapter. The view was that the system is flawed without a mechanism for court-based decision outcomes to be fed back to the magistrates who are making the sentencing decisions. For instance, sharing information on whether defendants have adhered to the bail conditions set, and, if not, why not? He believed that in other areas of professional practice decision outcomes are passed on, so that good use can be made of the evidence and to assist with future, productive and correct conclusions. To him this was an omission in court work when located against other modern styles of managerial operation.

To illustrate the value of the information in the way he conveyed it, it could be that magistrates remand defendants into custody to await trial, rather than bailing them into the community, due to concerns that they might not 'surrender' to a later court hearing. Yet, if there is evidence to prove that the majority of suspects do turn up and do conform to bail conditions, confidence in its use as opposed to remanding into custody might be assumed. This is a hypothetical scenario and magistrates will invariably argue that bail and remand decisions are based on an appraisal of the individual person and the risks they pose, but it can be seen that a systematic approach to delivering sentence and bail outcomes to sentencers is a useful suggestion. In this time of modernisation and court reform this has a central place. Sentence and bail outcome information no doubt exists within court records, but with lower court justice in the English criminal justice system largely administered by part-time volunteer magistrates in the place of a full-time salaried workforce, the data are not analysed and utilised in courtroom work in the way it could be.

The recommendations these magistrates are making link to the sentencing theories of Easton and Piper (2012). They suggest that sentencing legislation is more closely tied to punishment theory and policy making. They imply that court sentencing would more readily achieve the aims of criminal justice policy if theory, policy and the implementation of legislation were more effectively linked. This is relevant to the bail and remand example provided because the prisoner remand population is high and calls for less use of remanding people into custody before trial are frequently made. Fourteen per cent of the total number of people in English and Welsh prisons are on remand and 70 per cent of those are untried prisoners. Indeed, a significant number of remand prisoners are found not guilty at trial or do not receive a custodial sentence for their offence (Prison Reform Trust, 2015; H. M. Inspectorate of Prisons, 2012). If sentencing practice were more closely tied to policy in regard to this, changes would be seen in the prison population.

Rehabilitative sentencing fits neatly with notions of social justice and the lower courts because it essentially proposes improvements in the way courtroom decisions are made according to the evidence of success or failure. This is invariably of benefit to accused defendants in terms of perceptions of fairness. Rehabilitative sentencing, it can be argued, applies principles of procedural fairness within the court process, as theorised by Tyler (2000). Tyler, in his extensive work on procedural justice within legal domains, including within the different criminal justice contexts such as the police, the courts and prisons, argues that people more willingly accept decisions when they feel they have been made through procedures they interpret as fair, even if they don't agree with the outcome. It can be taken that courtroom decisions based on hard evidence will be assessed as more fair by those receiving them than those devised through a series of grid-guided calculations in the style of the Sentencing Guidelines, although individual case-by-case decisions taking into account personal mitigation will invariably be considered the fairest.

In effect, what these magistrates were requesting was an expanded role in sentencing beyond the limited one they currently perform. This is a theme drawing commentary in some criminal justice circles in the UK and aligns with the emerging interest in models of 'sentencer supervision' or 'sentencer review' (Samuels, 2013). The style is emulated in the specialist problem-solving court approaches growing in popularity across a number of jurisdictions, including in the UK (Centre for Justice Innovation, 2015; Bowen and Whitehead, 2013;

Berman and Fox, 2009). This chapter moves now to discuss specialist problem-solving court approaches and locates these within the current transformations in criminal court justice.

Specialist problem-solving courts

Interest has been developing across jurisdictions in the benefits and value of specialised courts and problem-solving approaches as an alternative to the traditional adversarial court style of justice. This is in recognition of the weaknesses that exist within regular courtroom adjudication in equitably engaging all parties in the process, and of issues relating to strengthening offender accountability (Braithwaite, 1989). Alternative approaches are linked to the increasing tendency to accept that a significant degree of offending is linked to social lifestyle problems such as drugs and alcohol dependence, mental health issues, homelessness, disrupted upbringings and risks attached to early independence. They are conditions considered more usefully dealt with within therapeutic support and health treatment type arrangements, as opposed to criminal justice retributive styles. The emergence and growth in specialist drug courts, mental health courts, domestic and family violence courts, homelessness courts, the Koori 'indigenous sentencing courts' in Australia (Marchetti and Daly, 2007) and the 'Rangatahi' and 'Pacifica' courts operating in New Zealand (New Zealand Ministry of Justice, 2012; Waititi, 2012; Dickson, 2011) are some examples of these problem-solving court models. The latter two styles are specialised courts designed to fit more closely with the cultural identities of Aborigine, Maori and Pacific Islander young people who offend.

An underpinning principle of specialist problem-solving courts is 'therapeutic jurisprudence'. Therapeutic jurisprudence originates from the disciplines of psychology and mental health law (Winick, 2002; Wexler and Winick, 1996) and a defining feature is recognition of the role that the law, the courts and judicial actors can play in facilitating offenders' rehabilitation, as well as the potential to hamper a person's improvement. Nolan (2001) states that the commonly applied understanding of therapeutic jurisprudence is 'the therapeutic and anti-therapeutic consequences of laws, legal rules, and legal actions' (ibid.: 185).

The basic premise applied in this different approach to people who commit crime is the fact that some offender types are found to appear in courtrooms on a repeat and frequent basis. For instance, King (2011) writes in his paper on therapeutic jurisprudence that courts become 'dumping grounds' for people with drug addiction problems, mental health problems and homelessness issues. As such, he notes dissatisfaction from the judiciary and local communities at the 'revolving door' nature of the formal criminal justice system. He points out that there needs to be 'recognition that courts can be a vehicle for those who offend to address their underlying issues' (ibid.: 21). The team working model operationalised in specialist court design utilises the influence that a court judge can have on an offender's compliance with the sentence. This is alongside drawing upon a consensually agreed package of treatment between the offender and the court, integrating the support of relevant social care and welfare and health agencies (Ward, 2014).

Kaiser and Holtfreter (2016) write on the theoretical underpinnings driving the success of the specialised court model. They develop an 'integrated theory' incorporating the values of therapeutic jurisprudence and procedural justice. They argue that the two combined are the explanatory power behind the success of specialist courts. They take Tyler's conceptualisation of procedural justice – relating to perceptions of fairness of procedures in 'third party decision-making' and the way value is attached to opportunities for participation in the process – 'to state their case and provide their views to a decision-maker, regardless of whether those will influence the outcome' (ibid.: 49). Kaiser and Holtfreter analyse different studies that have assessed perceptions of fairness from the experiences of the clients of specialist courts. They cite a study by Frazer (2006) that asked defendants to evaluate their opinions of effective communication, treatment and helpfulness of the court actors – the judge, prosecutor, defence attorney and court officers. They found that 'judicial factors' were the best pre-dictors of perceived overall fairness. From their review of the studies, Kaiser and Holtfreter (2016) highlight the enabling features of connection, listening and the injection of a more human and responsive element into the court interactions. Thus, Kaiser and Holtfreter (2016) conclude that the success of the specialist problem-solving court model is in the therapeutic style in combination with court processes and procedures that the clients experience as fair and just. They go on to add 'The specialised court movement offers a guiding paradigm for the court system to consider their role in the rehabilitation of offenders' (ibid.: 46).

In the early stages of my book research, a judge working within a problem-solving court approach in a New Zealand criminal court gave his views on the value of this style, emphasising the strength of the person-centred focus. For him, achieving positive and motivated sentence compliance linked to showing an interest towards the person. He believed in the court judging role, in that it was 'important to show you're interested in people'.

In line with current developments in court reform, accompanied by magistrates' inclination to be active and engaged in their communities, the research brought me into contact with a group of youth court magistrates involved in a problem-solving approach with young offenders. This was initiated by a local youth offending team (YOT) who, alongside their remit in youth offender supervision, had devised a sentence review panel system that drew in magistrates in a judicial monitoring style. The youth offending team found that, after an early period of engagement, the motivation of some young people assigned to a 'youth rehabilitation order' (YRO) could begin to wane. A youth rehabilitation order is a court sanction applied to 10–17-year-olds guilty of certain offences. The order is overseen by statutory youth offending teams and has elements of punishment, restorative justice and reparation within it. It combines a multi-agency team approach to address the 'criminogenic' needs of the young person and supports participation in education, training or employment. The youth offending team had set up the problem-solving sentence review approach involving the magistrates to test whether injecting an element of judicial authority into the process would be effective at reinvigorating the order. Staff members from the youth offending team involved with the panels were interviewed and two review panels involving four youth court magistrates were observed between January and March 2015 (Ward and Warkel, 2015).[1]

Indeed, specialist problem-solving approaches are being promoted as a method in youth offender rehabilitation in the English justice system. The independent inquiry into the operation and effectiveness of the youth courts chaired by Lord Carlile (2014) acknowledged the early disadvantage of many young offenders. The report recommended testing problem-solving approaches in diverting children who offend from 'the formalities of the criminal justice process', in which it was stated that 'many flounder and don't understand' (ibid.: iv). The report mentioned the potential involvement of youth court magistrates in the progression of a young offender's rehabilitation pathway (ibid.: 63). Moreover, in 2016 the UK Secretary of State for Justice, Michael Gove, placed his support behind specialist problem-solving courts following a visit to drug courts in Texas in the USA.

The lead youth court magistrate involved in the review panels discussed his rationale for volunteering in them beyond his regular magisterial duties. He believed that there is value in judicial participation in the rehabilitation pathways of young offenders and beyond the point of dispensing the sentence. He commented on the strength of the combined approach of the panel, with support provided by the youth offending team staff together with the judicial 'gravitas' that the magistrates provide. He found the experience of being involved encouraging and, further, he considered that failing to embrace the successful results magistrates can help achieve through their judicial input would be a flaw in the overall objective of the youth justice system:

> [T]he way I see this is when a youth court passes an order for a young person to do whatever it is they're going to do, that order remains active until it is completed. Now for a magistrate to sentence a young person and then not to care a jot about what happens afterwards seems to fly in the face of what the magistracy and what society is all about…. Some members of the judiciary might say that once a sentencer has sentenced that is their job done unless the matter comes back to court. My view is that that is extremely clinical and it severs the social responsibility of the judicial exercise.
>
> (Youth Court magistrate, male, aged 53, 20 years' service)

Another of the youth court magistrates involved in the review panels saw them as useful for magistrates to gain a better understanding of young offenders' lives. She recounted the way that sometimes young people are seen in court on a repeat basis. To her this illustrates that the sanction assigned was not something the young person had 'been able to achieve'. Engaging with them in a review forum enables close communication and appreciating the barriers some young people face in complying with the conditions of the order. What was powerful from my observations of the panels was the stories told by the young people and the difficulties they encountered in their daily lives. For instance, being in transitional accommodation, as in the example of one young lad who was staying with an older sister in an outlying village, to where he cycled back each evening to meet his curfew time after his day's work in a local catering company. There was also the 17-year-old residing with his girlfriend and her children who became homeless on the relationship breaking down. The precariousness of these temporary set-ups and the impacts on a young person's ability to follow the conditions of a penalty if something in their wider life breaks down is important to highlight and it is my argument that they are issues that need more consideration in discussions on youth justice and offender sentencing and in devising more appropriate supportive measures for these young and vulnerable people.

This nuanced information is not typically drawn out in analyses of youth re-offending, but it is necessary to understand the real hardships that some young people's lives are embroiled in to set achievable sentence penalties. Flexibility surrounding breach of conditions should be built in to assist and acknowledge that breaches sometimes occur due to the enormous and early independence challenges they are experiencing. The young people obviously benefited from the interest being shown to them and their general well-being and progress by the youth offending team members and magistrates. It was often noted by the magistrates, in regard to defendants generally but young ones in particular, that it was quite likely 'the first time anyone had shown any interest in them'.

Through my involvement with the youth order review panels and from the existing research that identifies the problems of young offenders as linked to vulnerabilities faced in neglected upbringings and transitions to early and precarious independence, it is my argument that it is vitally important to bring about a more sympathetic response within youth justice. This is one that acknowledges the combined circumstances influencing a young person's offending pathway (Ward and Warkel, 2015; Porteous *et al.*, 2015). The youth order review panels, in the way that they are modelled with the input of youth court magistrates, are an example of the way this can be achieved. Moreover, they link with Kaiser and Holtfreter's (2016) appraisal of the success of specialist problem-solving approaches, with strength attached to court users' perceptions of fairness associated with a listening and engaged approach, with the offender's participation and voice being drawn out in the process.

With the interest that is emerging in the UK in regard to problem-solving approaches and their development with young people, these need to be designed along the lines of empathy and practical support, involving court justices who are committed to assisting with problems. It is important with models of this nature that the rehabilitative priority is retained and that the judicial court punishment does not expand beyond this priority (cf. Ward and Warkel, 2015). One of the youth court magistrates interviewed said that she initially had reservations about the idea behind this extended magistrate involvement. She considered that magistrates might interpret their role more keenly than it should be.

Specialist court practice was a feature of the magistrates' experiences in another court area where the research was conducted. This was with the operation of a dedicated drug court set up within the running of the main magistrates' court. Two magistrates were interviewed who worked in the drug court. They expressed a pride in the court and enjoyment in seeing the improvements brought about to a person's life.

Drug courts

The guiding philosophy and genesis of the drug court movement, established internationally (Nolan, 2001) and in the UK (Bean, 1998; McIvor, 2010; Kerr *et al.*, 2011; Donoghue, 2014b), links to the high prevalence of drugs-related acquisitive crime. Benefits are found in offering structured rehabilitation programmes alongside multi-disciplinary support for certain low-level offenders as an alternative to prison custody. The Roskill[2] drug court was established on this basis. Receiving a community-based 'drugs rehabilitation order' (DRO) formally located a defendant as a client of the drug court. Monthly review meetings with specially trained magistrates along with probation staff check on clients' progress towards maintaining abstinence from drug use and in efforts to alter patterns of offending. Regular drug testing is a part of the programme. The two magistrates working in the drug court saw great value in the therapeutic support offered. One explained the working approach of the Roskill court as follows:

> [T]he magistrates basically take an interest in them and if they're doing badly, you ask and they are serious about it, but actually a lot of them are doing quite well, because they want to do well and you get a chance to praise them, which for some people it's the first time they've ever been praised by somebody in authority. So on the other hand, what do I get out of it, I get out of it the satisfaction that I've possibly changed a life and I think very much the same in family court.
>
> (DDC magistrate, female, aged 69, 30 years' service)

The Roskill drug court model was also spoken about in the way it understands the complexity of drug dependence and the potential for relapse in drug rehabilitation pathways. Occasional failures in negative drug test results were not seen as grounds for further punishment but as critical points to communicate about the triggers behind the lapse. In this way the model can be interpreted as realistic in design for accepting the complexities of drug dependence and that subtle changes are achieved over time:

> [W]e say right what's happened, what's the problem? Sometimes it can be that they've been evicted and they've been living with friends.... The probation are always in attendance and we usually say to the probation, is there anything that can be helped, can you put them into a direction where housing can be looked at for them. And we help them in that way ... it's not

a criminal court it's a review court, so it is an informal court. They sit down and talk to us.... We are very proud of our drug courts.

(DDC magistrate, female, aged 69, 25 years' service)

Indeed, drug courts are established in a number of countries, and are large in number in the USA. Different drug court models exist. A report by the Transform Drug Policy Foundation (2013) on the US drug courts criticised them for cherry-picking 'easy' clients who are most likely to succeed in their rehabilitation, thus positively influencing programme outcome results. The report also criticised the punitive responses applied in some US drug courts models, which react to relapses in drug use by activating spells of time in prison custody. However, a large-scale evaluation of the US drug courts found overall positive results and lower levels of drug use among drug court participants (Rossman *et al.*, 2011). A general scepticism has been placed on drug courts by some for the limited results from evaluation outcome studies and with higher than desired rates of continued drug use reported among some drug court clients. Donoghue (2014b) writes on the development of drug courts in English justice system, linking them to notions of 'community justice'. She reviews the drug court literature and the English drug court model and notes the difference in design to the US model, with punitive sanctions for non-compliance not built in to the UK model in the same way.

Specialist drug courts in the style referred to in the Roskill drug court, which attempt to address criminal offending linked to drug dependence through structured health and welfare treatment, are surely a preferred approach. This is both for the limited impact other penalties have on destitute drug-dependent offenders, as highlighted in the comment by the magistrate earlier in this chapter in reference to the perpetual shoplifters with drug and alcohol issues, for whom most other penalties have failed or are deemed inappropriate. The intensive support provided by drug courts might be the help needed to break the 'revolving door' cycle of criminal offending.

An additional argument is it is essential within the development of specialist problem-solving court approaches, as already emphasised with the drug court example, that there can be occasional drug relapse and to view the approach as working with a person's rehabilitation over time. Evaluations of programme outcomes and measures of success that are based on short- rather than long-term outcomes are not able to account for the time required to reach stabilisation, and that progress is achieved in significant ways but over a supported period of time. Moreover, evaluations of drug courts need to take on the accounts of the magistrates and judges who are working with these therapeutic, supportive courtroom models with drug-dependent defendants for the insights they can provide on the engagement and commitment by the people who are given the chance to participate in these rehabilitation opportunities.

Magistrates as social justice innovators

Another example emerging from the magistrates' experiences that can be located within notions of social justice was from one magistrate, who had been involved in setting up a supported hostel for young males coming out of prison and with no secure accommodation to move to. Her awareness of the gaps in provision and the greater need for facilities of this nature linked to her years serving as a youth court magistrate, and through serving on the Independent Monitoring Board (IMB), which inspects prisons. This role took her on visits to the local secure Young Offender Institution (YOI), where incarcerated young men were communicated with. Both experiences, she reflected, exposed her to the reality and deep misery of some young offenders' personal life deficits, psycho-social immaturity and incapability, along with serious unmet welfare needs. These were behind her interest in setting up the hostel:

> It was informed because I was a youth magistrate and during the project I was also youth chair. I was extremely aware of the revolving door.... I saw what these kids were coming out to, which was nothing, there was nothing for them other than standing on the sidewalk with a poly bag of their possessions. And I thought there must be a better way to treat these kids and give them a chance, we can't write them off before they're 18, so that's why I did it, because I had the dual hat and I could see from my Independent Monitoring Board and my judicial hat what was happening to these kids.
>
> (Female, 69 years, 30 years' service)

Her comments on providing for these young men and encountering them in their attempts to adjust, went on to reveal how ill-equipped some were to even contend with the basic demands of being a functioning member of society. She noted this as particularly important knowledge for when government and criminal justice officials are setting out expectations for the pace of reform and achievements of young offenders in their rehabilitation. She found that the outcome measures called upon to deem the project a success were unrealistic, considering the highly disadvantaged status of the young men, and the length of time that is needed for basic life functioning skills to be mastered by young people such as these:

> To get progress out of a kid like that that's really damaged and come out of custody, the slightest thing like getting them to sit down and engage in a conversation, is actually progress. It's difficult to say they should all have jobs, they are nowhere near getting jobs, they need the social skills they need self-awareness, more than anything else they need self-esteem and they need to get their lives worked out and that takes time and there is no quick fix for these kids ... the Ministry of Justice wanted the sort of measurements that are unrealistic ... how many had got jobs, and how many were doing this, and how many are doing that?
>
> (Female, 69 years, 30 years' service)

What these examples and experiences point to is the importance, when assessing the success of specialist drug courts, youth offender review panels (Ward and Warkel, 2015) and other support initiatives such as the hostel for young men, of moving beyond standardised measures of success specifically focusing on recidivism rates as the sole criteria. Coulsfield (2004) asserted in his report on community penalties that it was imperative to account for the small incremental achievements offenders make in their reform journeys. These include the way structure and discipline are embraced, such as keeping to appointments, learning to read and write and gaining employment ready skills, which lead to reductions in offending, rather than focusing so intensely on the crude measure of two-year re-offending rates. Coulsfield stated that we need

> more sophisticated ways of measuring the effectiveness of sentences than two year re-offending rates. Reduction in frequency and seriousness of offending are also relevant, as is the acquisition of skills, which will also enable offenders to obtain employment – which is also associated with a reduction in offending.
>
> (Ibid.: 5)

Criminal court procedure as social justice

It was put forward at the beginning of this chapter that the theme of social justice and the way it can be connected to criminal justice within the context of lower criminal court operations would be applied to my research. Heffernan's theorisations are used here. This is the way that he takes the rules of criminal procedure within court adjudication to map onto conceptualisations of social justice. Within Heffernan's definition of criminal justice, in which he highlights the predominance of people in court who are economically and materially disadvantaged, he refers also to the official processes of criminal investigation and prosecution that are followed when someone is suspected of committing an offence and the 'fairness' of 'investigative and adjudicative procedures' (ibid.: 51). In providing an example, Heffernan focused on publicly funded legal aid. He emphasised that access to legal representation was so important that it should be considered another branch of welfare entitlement. This is alongside universal rights to education, health care and social care. He referred to the right to publicly funded legal aid as 'judicaid' and in particular 'to decisions about whether the state should pay for legal representation of criminal defendants'. (ibid.: 79). Within his enquiry, Heffernan asked what the 'implications are for criminal convictions if defendants have different resources available to them to contest their guilt' (ibid.: 53). He was applying his analysis to the significant level of economic deprivation among lower criminal court defendants and who are inequitably disadvantaged in mounting an effective defence if legal representation is not equally accessible to them as it is for people with financial means. McBarnet (1981) similarly referred to legal aid accessibility in her analysis of the 'two tiers of justice' in the criminal courts.

Access to legal representation is picked up in reference to my research because magistrates provided views from their courtroom experiences relating to legal aid eligibility. Issues of due process and fair procedure were commented on in their considerations of it.

Legal aid

In regard to the alterations being made to summary justice and the impact of these on magistrates' courtroom working, changes in the provision of state-funded legal aid and the narrowing of the eligibility band so that fewer defendants could qualify for subsidised advice was commented on. The magistrates similarly mentioned the legal aid budget cuts in connection to notions of fairness within the court process. They noted how the alterations to legal aid as brought about through amendments to legislation in the Legal Aid, Sentencing and Punishment of Offenders Act 2013 had resulted in seeing more unrepresented defendants in the courtroom. The following comment illustrates the view of one magistrate and his concerns that due process protections are being jeopardised alongside these changes:

> [O]ne of the things that is also happening at the moment is restrictions on legal aid, and to me legal aid is also part of due process. You know somebody is entitled to a fair trial, whatever they may have done, if anything, but they are entitled to a fair trial and legal advice is part of the process of having a fair trial. That to me is very worrying, where for example if you're not likely to be sent to prison, then you don't actually have a right to a solicitor's help in all cases. Some people that have got their own solicitors and will use them – fine, but there are minor cases where perhaps a solicitor would help and that's not available.
>
> (Male, aged 63 years, 12 years' service)

The system of free legal advice provided at court for those in need in the form of the duty solicitor scheme was acknowledged by the magistrates, and for the most part celebrated for the service and protection it provides to defendants. However, the magistrates highlighted how stretched legal aid lawyers are when providing support, especially in busy city-centre courts with the volumes of people who require it. Moreover, the large caseloads that legal aid law firms carry were identified as affecting the quality of case oversight and having a handle on a defendant's case when adjourned and trial cases returned to court:

> [T]here's normally a string of people queuing up for them because there's normally either one or at max 2 and you know when you've got perhaps 5 courts running and you know 10/15 cases, 20 cases in each court, there's quite a lot of that.
>
> (Male, aged 63 years, 12 years' service)

It was mentioned though by one magistrate that the increase in unrepresented clients that has emerged out of the restrictions to legal aid has led to more direct communication between them as justices and the defendants before them; this was considered positive. She discussed this as enabling a better dialogue and understanding of a defendant's circumstances, which she said also facilitated arriving at case conclusions more quickly. Although it was the view of just one, it contradicts reports in the wake of the legal aid cuts in 2013 suggesting case hearings would be slowed down with the legal detail needing to be explained to unrepresented clients. The following comment reflects the different experience in courtroom communication with unrepresented clients. It was not determined whether arriving at the point more quickly related to defendants implicating themselves through their 'colourful' stories, and bringing forth their guilty pleas more rapidly or whether a fuller version of their situation enabled a more direct route to assigning an appropriate rehabilitative sentence:

> I think sometimes we can get to the point a lot quicker when we haven't got the lawyer standing there. It depends on how you talk to the defendant.... I think it's much, much easier and you get a much more colourful story than having to have the intermediaries, especially in the low level cases. I think it's a good thing that we're dealing with people on their own.
>
> (Aged 65, woman 13 years' service)

The changes to legal aid eligibility were not evident from my courtroom observations. The majority of defendants I observed in court were legally represented and, for the few who were not, time was taken to enquire whether advice had been sought, and why rejected if it had been. The problem, however, lies with defendants who want to contest an allegation and who face high legal costs if they are above the means-tested earnings threshold and/or they do not pass the 'merits test'. Eligibility to legal aid under the merits test is not guaranteed unless the penalty for the alleged offence is likely to carry a term of imprisonment. The rate of guilty pleas is pronounced in the lower courts and the high legal costs incurred through mounting a contested trial are likely to be prohibitive for many, meaning some defendants choose not to contest the charges against them, in turn adding to the high volume of guilty pleas that are entered. This brings serious justice concerns into the court process, especially for innocent people who are wrongly accused or for those who have a legitimate defence to mount but are unable to afford the legal representation costs.

In addition to legal aid being raised as an area of concern in relation to fair procedures the availability of courtroom interpreters for defendants whose comprehension and verbal communication in the English language was also expressed. This is a particular feature of lower criminal court work in a city as diverse in population as London. Language interpreters are stationed within magistrates' courts to translate during courtroom proceedings. One magistrate expressed concerns relating to the way that this provision is changing and the gaps emerging in regard to due procedure along with it. Her emphasis was on the input of different and various interpreters in cases and the inconsistency in case oversight, chiefly in long, complicated cases, which is especially important if imprisonment and loss of liberty are at stake:

[A]t one time if you had a tricky case and you hadn't finished it, you could say to the interpreter will you be able to come back next time? ... and yes they could, but now you can't do that ... it is just another interpreter. Now it might be only a small difference, but for somebody who cannot understand the language to have the same person coming back in a long complicated case I would have thought was pretty helpful, but no they have another person coming back, and their interpretation skills might be different, but also they won't have formed a bond. I do think they form a bond, even if it is a slight bond with the person who is doing the interpreting, so there is kind of lack of personal involvement and continuity going on around it seems to me.

(Female, aged 70, 16 years' service)

Communicating directly with defendants during court proceedings was mentioned by another magistrate. She similarly referred to being able to get a better understanding of a defendant's situation when hearing it from them than through their defence lawyer. The magistrate who had previously worked as a probation officer and social worker explained sometimes finding it necessary to address a defendant directly and in her view she interpreted it as contributing to giving the defendant a sense of a fair hearing. She did though indicate that it is not an approach that is encouraged within regular court proceedings:

I sometimes find it quite difficult when somebody is represented and they clearly want to say something and I will sometimes stop and sometimes my clerk ... will say 'mam, he has a representative' and I say 'yes I understand that, but he wants to say something and I want to hear it, or we [the bench] want to hear it', so I think ... they get a good deal in court in terms of being listened to, in terms of putting their case.

(Aged 70, woman, 16 years' service)

The comments she is making in respect to effective communications with defendants links back to the point made earlier about the distinction drawn between the role of social work and the judicial role. Some magistrates saw the judicial role as one that needs to be clinically distanced from any concerns with the social welfare and rehabilitation elements of a defendant's case. But, from this magistrate's view, her outlook was the contrary. She saw her judicial role as inextricably linked to a social justice role. She found it difficult to take the bare facts of a case, which indeed might point to technical guilt but for which a justification or 'excuse' defence might be put:

[W]hen I first started I got criticised a number of times by chairs because they said 'you are not a Social Worker now Betty, you are a magistrate'.

And I said 'well I think I bring that to my work and I do want questions to be asked about the areas around that person in the dock'. It is not just a person who has committed a crime, you know we need to know a certain amount more and I think I probably was a bit of an irritant in that I wanted to ask quite a bit more than perhaps sometimes people thought you should do. I always felt it was reasonable.... I did my best to make some sort of difference to have as fair a system as possible, to give everyone a fair crack of the whip, and a fair hearing and to try and make sure that we made fair decisions.

(Female, aged 70, 16 years' service)

This links back to the keen interest that some magistrates have in playing a more proactive sentencing role and in defendants' achievements than the way the current, mechanistic, distanced one can be. It connects to the problem-solving justice approach embedded within the youth order reviews and drug court models whereby the roots of the problems connected to offending are of central interest and addressed. Opportunities are provided for lay magistrates to be involved in sentencer supervision models with these problem-solving approaches, which are argued to be more engaged and empowering models of offender rehabilitation. Moreover, they offer rewarding work in which justices are able to see improvements in the conduct of offenders and in turning their lives around and which satisfies court magistrates and judges in playing a more participatory role in sensitive and structured programmes of support.

This chapter has emphasised the lower-tier criminal courts as processing people with various social, economic and lifestyle disadvantages and that magistrates in their courtroom role are central to rehabilitative sentencing considerations. The chapter argues that the problem-solving approaches in the example of the youth order review panels and the drug court model as conducted in this therapeutic, supportive way intended can be interpreted as social justice models of criminal justice. Heffernan's (2000) theorisation of social justice and criminal justice highlights the predominance of people in court who are economically and materially disadvantaged. He argues for notions of social justice to be embedded within criminal court adjudication in his consideration of fair procedure within these formal processes. Heffernan asks the question within his theory whether the defence of 'rotten social background' can reasonably be used as mitigation. The magistrates separate their judicial role from social care and welfare consideration but they are centrally located in hearing in-depth details about people's daily lives and struggles, about their substance dependence battles, about defendants and their children's illnesses, complex care needs, the young person's struggle to find employment, the 50-year-old who can't read and the plight of homelessness. It is not being suggested that we redefine the role of the courts. But the way that rehabilitative sentencing and the different problem-solving courts with defendants whose lives are intertwined within misfortune and ill-health, who are given opportunities to rectify within therapeutic programmes of support, can be interpreted as embedding social justice principles into criminal court sentencing. With an adequate amount of resourcing and investment, these can go a long way in the expansion of more human, empowering rehabilitation responses, from which a great many court defendants would benefit.

If we take on the thesis that social justice elements can be embedded within criminal court justice, we can apply the idea that the criminal justice system, specifically the criminal courts, has a role to play in at least exposing and highlighting the real hardships that a large number of people in society have to contend with.

Notes

1 See Ward and Warkel (2015) for an evaluation of the youth order review panels operated by the youth offending team and including local youth court magistrates.
2 A fictitious name has been given to the drug court.

7   Conclusion

This book has set out to account for some of the key alterations occurring to summary justice within the lower criminal courts of the English justice system as they undergo various modernising transformations. These are in efforts to operate criminal courts that are responsive to the changing demands of the twenty-first century, as well as achieving an efficiently run and tightly managed criminal court service. In addition, a key focus within this examination has been on the experiences of lay magistrates in their judicial court working role and at this time of reform.

This concluding section brings together the main themes framing the research material presented in the preceding chapters and the main arguments drawn out from the analysis. As such, it revisits aspects of the court process in which fundamental alterations are being made that can be argued are accruing examples of managerial and technocratic justice. Lay justice and the experiences of magistrates in their lower court judicial decision-making role are returned to, with links made to the value of citizen participation in this work. This is at the same time that it is argued that we are seeing the increasing professionalisation of lower court justice, which goes some way towards magistrates being appraised as lay legal professionals. This chapter also briefly revisits the conceptual theory developed in Chapter 6 on the way that the lower criminal courts can be argued as embedding social justice principles. This is specifically in the example of the rehabilitative sentencing styles assigned to some offenders with health treatment and other lifestyle needs, and the specialist problem-solving court approaches that are growing in popularity with various offender groups across jurisdictions and in the UK. It is argued that enhanced notions of fair justice are a key feature of these approaches.

Lower criminal court modernisation

Criminal court transformations have been ongoing and evolving in different forms for some decades, but in the recent period they have gained in momentum alongside strategies of modernisation and reform and are underpinned by discourses of efficient public service delivery. In essence, this translates to running a well-managed, cost efficient criminal court system, with intentions to cut waste

and minimise delay in case progression, and is being advanced through the introduction of new technologies in courtroom proceedings. From my research into
the specific areas where modernising and streamlining alterations can be identified, it is argued that we are experiencing radical changes which can be interpreted as fundamentally changing the way justice is delivered. Moreover,
attention is drawn to where questions can be asked on whether sufficient consideration is given to procedural due process within these modernising changes.

The modernisation and streamlining changes are theorised within neo-liberal
economics and the introduction of managerial techniques brought into public-
sector management beginning in the 1980s under the Conservative leader Mar-
garet Thatcher, accelerated as an economic ideology under the Labour
government and the dominant political economy of the current Conservative
government. The Conservative Party's governing term coincided with the global
economic downturn, beginning in 2009, with resultant pressures placed on the
nation's finances and fiscal tightening applied across UK public institutions in
response.

The modernising and efficiency reforms being made to lower criminal court
justice focused on in the preceding chapters are speedy justice initiatives and the
introduction of tighter case management rules so that individual cases move
swiftly through the system; the incentivising of early guilty pleas to facilitate
those who are guilty to admit to it at the earliest point in proceedings; the closure
and amalgamation of courthouses across the English justice system, where
underused premises have been decommissioned and business amalgamated to
take place within fewer courthouses; and the use of live video link technology in
courtroom proceedings. This is in the way the police and victims give evidence
over remote live links and how defendants appear in court from within police
stations. These various alterations – some new, some reinvigorated – are bound
up within efficiency savings and tighter administration in court service delivery.
As such it can be argued that modernising strategies are to some extent syn-
onymous with efficiencies and economic savings.

Modernisations within court delivery are typically discussed within ideals of
delivering fair justice because the removal of delay and protracted, slow processes from the criminal justice process is both pragmatic and reasonable for
those who are going through the system. This relates to victims of crime, who
wait on occasions for long periods to see perpetrators brought to justice, but also
to concerns for defendants, who experience the stress of unresolved accusations
hanging over their head. Thus the improvements and benefits brought about
through reducing delay, backlog and system waste based on these ambitions are
laudable. However, it is also the case that considerable due process concerns can
be raised in some areas. Vulnerable defendants are identified as particularly sus-
ceptible within swift case processing developments.

Through my research, and indeed that of other criminal justice commentators,
issues are identified in the way the speedy justice initiatives and tighter case
management rules, which as far as possible reduce the number of adjournments
a case receives on its way to trial, can mean cases are rushed to conclusion

without giving adequate time for defendants to prepare. The continued emphasis on the extraction of early guilty pleas, which the magistrates and various critics note can especially affect vulnerable defendants who may not understand processes, as well as those with English language difficulties, are mentioned. The many courthouse closures across the English justice system are considered to weaken 'access to justice', with some communities now located a far distance from their nearest court. Worries have also been highlighted with the advancements being made in the use of live video link technologies in the way that defendants are produced over live links from police stations to courtrooms. This is found to impair communication between defendants and their legal representatives and it is noted that it is adjudication taking place from within the non-neutral space of police stations.

Possibly one of the most noteworthy developments within court modernising transformations in the English justice system in the recent period is the introduction of virtual courts in the way just described. Any removal of unnecessary waste from police, court and judicial staff time, and of burdensome financial costs, such as transporting arrestees from police station custody to court and the maintenance of court custody cell space, which denies investment in other areas of criminal justice, is important. For straightforward low-level cases of accusation and acceptance of guilt, the use of video link technology for these appearances can be argued as having real benefits. But, as Mulcahy (2011) has stressed, these developments are occurring without wider public discussion and empirical research with defendants who experience this style of court procedure. Mulcahy (2011) argued from her research examining space and power in reconfigurations of courthouse and courtroom architecture, which included remote courtroom appearances, that these shifts in court design must be understood in the context of 'changing notions of due process' (ibid.: 9). She highlighted issues of 'neutral justice' and 'open justice'. From my research into virtual court operation it is agreed that, so far, we do not know enough about the experiences and perceptions of fairness of the process as felt by the court users and whether adherence to due process procedures is being upheld. With this I am aligned with Mulcahy's (2011) call for a greater level of discussion and empirical research in respect to these advances.

Virtual courts in the form I describe are at an early stage of initiation and as such it is not yet possible to judge whether they are bringing unique modernised improvements or whether they can be appraised as too high a cost in terms of justice. It is essential that protections are in place for vulnerable and non-English-speaking defendants, who may be disadvantaged in this style of court delivery. Moreover, where requests are made to face criminal accusation and to mount an effective defence in open court in person in line with the principles of open and neutral justice these should be honoured.

Many of the courtroom alterations mentioned are designed to reduce delay and backlog, which is obviously a desirable objective in running public services, but they are also linked to financial cost savings where these are considered burdensome. It is my argument that it is essential cost and efficiency savings are not prioritised over and above the retention of due process protections that are an essential element of the rights of defendants. With the high importance attached to principles of fair justice, which, indeed, the English justice system is built on and takes pride in, we have to question at what price is justice?

It is my argument from this book research that careful attention is needed to maintain due process protections in this climate of enhanced streamlining and efficiently managed, fast-moving summary justice. In the context of dispensing criminal court justice, quickened processes based on expediency can threaten fair justice and introduce injustices.

Lay justice, magistrates and professionalisation

Another key focus of my research has been on the experiences of lay magistrates in their courtroom and justice administration role and at this time of reform. Lay magistrates play a fundamental role in criminal court processing in the English justice system. The lower courts preside over the vast bulk of all criminal prosecutions and the English justice system is unique in its reliance on lay citizens to administer proceedings in the court setting. Along with this, magistrates are tasked with extensive judicial powers including adjudicating on guilt and non-guilt in trial, making bail and remand decisions and sentencing using a broad range of fines and community and custodial penalties. Moreover, sentencing and bail and remand decisions are often being made in respect of offenders with complex health and lifestyle needs, language issues and financial problems, among other difficulties in their life circumstances.

Lay justice as it is practised in the English justice system is a style of judicial practice that is not replicated elsewhere, although lay participation in legal decision-making is growing in popularity across European and international jurisdictions. This is for the mounting belief in its potential to balance power in judicial systems and for strengthening public confidence in legal structures. Despite the central involvement of lay magistrates in court justice, little research enquires into their personal experience of performing in this work. My research sought reflection from serving magistrates on the contribution they make to the principle of lay justice, in addition to how they are adapting to the various transformations being made within the lower courts.

A main argument I make in relation to the work of lay magistrates draws on the analysis developed by McBarnet (1981), in which she stresses that an ideology of triviality surrounds the work of the lower magistrates' courts. McBarnet refutes this, and sets out that the view is held due to the lower courts mainly processing minor routine offences for which lower-scale penalties are handed out. My argument picks up on the perception of triviality as it pertains to the lower courts, and also argues to the contrary. Magistrates are equipped with a vast range of powers and are at the centre of dispensing important and extensive criminal justice decisions (cf. Sanders *et al.*, 2010) that have major transformative impacts on people's everyday lives. Corresponding with this extent of responsibility it is my contention that more attention needs to be paid to the work of the lower courts and on the high legal decision-making role lay justices perform within them.

The lay magistrates interviewed were particularly committed to the principle of lay justice that their participation contributes to and they were immensely proud in the judicial position they occupied. They believed that citizen participation is powerful for the fact the law is not solely administered and interpreted by professionals whose careers are steeped within legal and technical expertise. They consider that greater public confidence is brought to the system through this citizen participation style. Legally qualified judges also adjudicate in the lower courts of the English justice system, but the majority of this court work is conducted by lay magistrates. I am aligned with the system of lay justice as it exists in the English courts as a powerful and fair form of legal arbitration. My argument relating to the participation of lay magistrates in criminal court adjudication favours the shared legal decision-making approach designed to be carried out in benches of three. This is in contrast to the court decision-making style performed by single sitting professional judges, who make legal judgements in isolation and without collaborative input.

Indeed, magistrates' court justice is historically based on the principle of local justice, which is defined as justice dispensed by people who are drawn from local communities and who bring local area knowledge and understanding to court decision-making and sentencing. However, the notion of local justice is critiqued within my arguments as it applies to the current lay justice model of the English system. This is due to the fact that an increasing uniformity is being imposed within court sentencing, which constrains discretion and sees defendants with very different needs, abilities, opportunities and advantages being dealt with in the same way as every other. Thus the legal principle of 'equal justice' and the obligation that like cases be treated alike contradict the objectives of local justice. Local justice implies that individualised tailored sentencing and rehabilitation choices can be made based on localised knowledge and understanding of social issues and problems. However, the introduction of uniformity and structured sentencing is removing this discretion.

Connected to the argument that local justice is being undermined is the increasing professionalisation that is occurring within lower court work. The changes and alterations that are being introduced into the lower courts can be interpreted as an enhanced professionalisation of lower court justice. This is in the requirements on magistrates and judges to work in accordance with the Sentencing Guidelines, in addition to the expectations to perform complex case management so that cases progress through the system in a timely manner and within rules of criminal procedure. I have questioned within my discussions whether the level of professional involvement demanded in the lay justice role principally locates and defines magistrates as lay legal professions. This links to the point made by Malsch (2009) from her discussion of lay participation in criminal justice systems and the blurring between lay and professional status. It can be asked at what point are long-serving, experienced magistrates who are operating within tight legal decision-making rules and within time-bound courtroom administration structures considered lay legal professionals. My argument is that lay magistrates working in the lower criminal courts of the English justice system and the competences and responsibilities required of them establishes them as lay legal professionals.

In line with the argument just rehearsed I am committed to the research and analysis of Dignan and Wynne (1997), which draws on the professional and skilled status of serving lay magistrates. This is set alongside the ongoing critique that they are not sufficiently reflective of the local communities they are employed to serve. Dignan and Wynne ask a fundamental question that my research supports and is an argument I have advanced. This connects to the points just made relating to local justice being undermined and that it is no longer possible to argue that magistrates' court justice signifies this principle. Dignan and Wynne asked whether it is time to commit to what is required from lay justices in their court working role, which is that a 'suitably qualified panel' of people are needed to carry out this work. They argue that this is essentially what we have in the group of lay magistrates who serve in the courts, but that the strength of the lay justice system continues to be expressed based on community representation values, which indeed it is criticised for failing to achieve.

In drawing on the continued criticism of the lay magistracy in terms of the extent to which they can be considered truly representative of local communities, along with the increasing demands within courtroom management, case processing and the application of the Sentencing Guidelines, I am committed to the discussion of whether it is time to more realistically commit to the fact that a 'quasi-professional' magistracy is required. The role of a lay magistrate is quite evidently one of high professional expertise operationalised within tight case management and decision-making structures. But it continues to capitalise on the historic identity of lay justice as local justice performed by ordinary members of the community. The notion of local justice as the bedrock of lower court justice is becoming difficult to justify in light of the fact that criminal courthouses are located in fewer and fewer provincial and local areas and are presided over only by those in time-privileged positions, who are constrained in making local area knowledge decisions in respect to individual defendants. It is time to admit that lay magistrates dispensing lower court justice are essentially lay legal professionals but with the added value of shared decision-making in their tribunal benches of three.

My research was going on at a time when discussion was focused on improving the profile of serving magistrates in achieving greater diversity among them. This links to the justice principle of magistrates' court work being conducted by balanced benches of lay people drawn from a cross-section of society. Although my sample of magistrates was small and cannot be considered truly representative of the wider pool, it is likely that it is reflective. As other research has found, the magistrates interviewed in my research were predominately from professional social class backgrounds and some writings criticise this, implying that there has been an ongoing failure on the part of the magistracy to demonstrate that they reflect the communities they sit in judgement over. It is my argument that a broad cross-section of lay justices is of course desirable and must as far as possible be achieved so that courtroom justice is dispensed by people from local communities. However, it is not useful to continue with the arguments that magistrates are from a narrow social class and are not truly representative. What is more important is that the existing membership of the magistracy and their varied backgrounds, interests and experiences, as were evidenced among those participating in my research, are highlighted. Moreover, this is so that existing notions of exclusivity that might bar entry to the role are diminished. This might provide greater appeal for a wider, more diverse group to join. What is more important to emphasise in respect to those who dispense justice within the lower criminal courts is that it is conducted within procedures of fair justice and by people who have a real interest in the lives of the people coming before them.

From social justice to criminal justice

Another key focus of my research on the lower criminal courts and transformations within them, has centred on these courts mainly processing people who come from social and economically marginalised backgrounds, often with significant health and welfare needs, such as drug and alcohol dependence, mental disorder, low educational attainment and dysfunctional family contexts, whose offending trajectories are often overlapping with these situational life problems. This is obviously not entirely the picture but the arguments I pull together in this section relate to this feature of lower court justice administration.

Other criminal court researchers have noted the predominance of social disadvantage among lower court populations (Roach Anleu and Mack, 2005, 2007a, 2007b; Hudson, 2000, Heffernan, 2000), and theoretical developments have been advanced that link social justice issues to criminal justice policy and administration of the law. My analysis of the lower criminal courts draws on these conceptualisations. In doing this, I refer significantly to the work of Heffernan (2000). Heffernan applied the definition of social justice as the equal and unequal distribution of resources and opportunities in society. He highlighted the high prevalence of people appearing in the lower criminal courts who are examples of deep poverty and adverse backgrounds and connected these circumstances to unequal resource allocation across society. In his polemical essay he asks whether the adversity and social disadvantage that has come about through no fault of the person concerned can be used as a defence or justification in personal mitigation for some low-level criminal wrongdoing.

Obviously this cannot be achieved within the parameters of legal definitions and formal criminal law administration in any straightforward way. But it is my argument the rehabilitative sentencing that exists within the lower courts in the form of the therapeutic treatment and drugs rehabilitation programmes that some offenders are assigned to, as well as drugs courts, and the problem-solving approaches that are being favoured for young offenders (Carlile, 2014) can be interpreted as social justice components of criminal court work. This is in the way that issues of social and lifestyle disadvantage and offending are addressed in conjunction with each other and in supportive and encouraging ways.

In my research I connect the rehabilitative sentencing styles that are available for certain offender groups to be supported in addressing heath and other lifestyle needs in the form of drugs and alcohol rehabilitation orders and mental health orders etc. and the specialist problem-solving courts that have been established across a number of countries and, in the UK, are recognition of interconnected social lifestyle problems. As such, a key argument I draw out from my research is that social justice principles can be located within the context of the lower criminal court work and in particular in reference to these developments.

However, it is my argument that there is a real need within the contemporary criminal justice landscape to find ways of advancing these approaches more extensively. These are preferable responses for the greater potential they provide to achieve more successful outcomes and, importantly, in recognition that retributive criminal sanctions are inappropriate and futile for some offenders. This is especially the case for those with drugs and alcohol dependence issues or mental disturbance, and for young people from problematic childhood backgrounds. These are more sympathetic and humane responses towards people with health and other social care needs, who benefit from supportive and guided sentence penalties. Moreover, Kaiser and Holtfreter (2016) found that the success of specialist problem-solving courts can be explained in the integrated approach of therapeutic jurisprudence and procedural justice. The involvement of judicial actors in sentencer supervision styles and the greater participation in the rehabilitation process by defendants themselves are found to be powerful. Perceptions of fair criminal justice procedure are found in respect to these therapeutic, more compassionate styles of offender management and rehabilitation.

In addition, it is my argument that research analysis is needed which more usefully brings out the nuanced detail on the real lives of some people who face criminal sanctions in court, often for low-range transgressions, in a much stronger and more illustrative way. The full circumstances behind some criminal offending and the overlapping lifestyle circumstances are candidly exposed in lower criminal courtrooms and are research findings that can be extracted to bring a greater level of confidence and support for expanding rehabilitative responses to low-level offenders who would benefit from these supervised sentencing approaches.

The lower courts are sites in which we hear in-depth detail about people's daily lives and struggles, their addiction battles, their own and their children's illnesses, the young person's struggle to find employment, the 50-year-old who can't read, the plight of homelessness and the interface of these conditions with some people's offending. These accounts and, indeed, personal mitigating factors are powerfully learned through sitting in the public galleries of the lower criminal courts where people are tried who may be technically guilty of an offence but for whom it is patently obvious there are serious mental health or substance dependence problems that lie beneath the offending. This was intensely highlighted in the case of the 18-year-old girl mentioned in Chapter 3 just released from psychiatric care and in court accused of 'kicking out at a police officer' and the homeless, mentally unwell man charged with criminal damage. These are legal transgressions, but the nuance that is revealed within these interactions is illuminating for exposing personal and mitigating factors and from which it is my argument that rehabilitative alternatives must be available as more sensible sentencing options. This research detail can go further when we scrutinise how individual offenders experience the sentence penalty assigned to them and how achieving it interacts, interferes and disrupts regular family and sometimes children's lives. This was referred to in my illustration of the young people participating in the youth review panels, who revealed the precariousness of their personal lives that are underpinned by very early independence and as they struggle to hold down jobs and relationships, alongside achieving the demands of the youth court community penalties they have been assigned. More research analysis is needed that highlights the real difficulties that some people face in their lives, which become compounded by retributive punishment responses.

Ideals of social justice and the fair and equitable distribution of opportunity and access to resources emerge as central concepts in discourses of desirable social policy. Equally, the deficit of equal opportunity is present in understandings of 'broken society'. There is a place in our understandings of the criminal courts and the nature of the work carried out within them in the form of rehabilitative sentencing and problem-solving approaches for these fairer criminal justice styles to be articulated more strongly than they are. This is so that the courts become recognised for the part they play in embedding social justice principles into the broader fabric of society.

As other research on serving magistrates has found, the magistrates in my research came from highly skilled professional backgrounds and bring their previous occupational skills and expertise to the tasks demanded within the magisterial role; this includes those who bring experience from previous social care and social welfare professional backgrounds. A number of magistrates came from teaching, special education and social work backgrounds and their previous work experiences with problem families and youth with special needs bring a particular understanding to their court judging role and attitude towards defendants in court. This has been drawn out in the various responses provided by the magistrate previously employed as a probation officer and her interpretations of fairness in court interactions with defendants and other offender rehabilitation ideas. These are real strengths that can be drawn out in implementing rehabilitative sentencing and problem-solving models more extensively.

My book has brought together notions of social justice with criminal justice to remark that the vast bulk of people being processed through the lower criminal courts reveal examples of societal problems, either within family and upbringing deficits or with health treatment needs in substance dependence and mental health problems. It is not possible for the 'rotten social background' defence, as Heffernan refers to, to be designed into the criminal justice system but the problem-solving court approaches that are being established are a move worth pursuing and resourcing for the greater potential they demonstrate in addressing human need in more attentive, supportive and encouraging ways.

References

Adler, Z. (1987) *Rape On Trial*. London: Routledge.

Ardichvili, A. and Kuchinke, K. P. (2009) International Perspectives on the Meanings of Work and Working: Current Research and Theory. *Advances in Developing Human Resources*, 11, 2, 155–167.

Ashworth, A. (2013) Penalty Notices for Disorder and Summary Justice. *Criminal Law Review*, 11, 869–870.

Ashworth, A. and Redmayne, M. (2010) *The Criminal Process*. Oxford: Oxford University Press.

Ashworth, A. and Roberts, J. (2010) Sentencing: Theory, Principle and Practice, in M. Maguire, R. Morgan and R. Reiner (eds) *The Oxford Handbook of Criminology* (5th edn). Oxford: Oxford University Press.

Ashworth, A. and Zedner, L. (2014) *Preventive Justice*. Oxford: Oxford University Press.

Atkinson, R. (2012) Virtual Courts: More Speed, Less Justice. *Guardian*, 18 July.

Auld, R. (2001) *Review of the Criminal Courts of England and Wales: Report*. London: The Stationery Office.

Baldwin, J. (1976) The Social Composition of the Magistracy. *British Journal of Criminology*, 16, 2, 171–174.

Baldwin, J. (2008) Research on the Criminal Courts, in R. D. King and E. Wincup (eds) *Doing Research on Crime and Justice* (2nd edn). Oxford: Oxford University Press.

Baldwin, J. and McConville, M. (1977) *Negotiated Justice: Pressures to Plead Guilty*. London: Martin Robertson.

Barry, B. (2005) *Why Social Justice Matters*. Cambridge: Polity Press.

Bazelon, D. (1976) The Morality of the Criminal Law. *Southern California Law Review*, 49, 385–405.

BBC News (2012) *'Virtual' Courts Rolled Out Across Kent*. [Online] Available at: www. bbc.co.uk/news/uk-england-kent-19080208 [accessed 14 May 2014]

Bean, P. (1998) Transplanting the USA's Drug Courts to Britain. *Drugs: Education, Prevention and Policy*, 5, 101–104.

Bell, B. and Dadamo, C. (2006) Magistrates' Courts and the 2003 Reforms of the Criminal Justice System. *European Journal of Crime, Criminal Law and Criminal Justice*, 14, 4, 339–365.

Bell, E. (2011) *Criminal Justice and Neoliberalism*. London: Palgrave Macmillan.

Berman, G. and Fox, A. (2009) *Lasting Change or Passing Fad: Problem-solving Justice in England and Wales*. [Online] Available at: www.policyexchange.org.uk [accessed August 2013].

Bingham, T. (2010) *The Rule of Law*. London: Penguin.

Bohm, R. M. (2006) 'McJustice': On the McDonaldisation of Criminal Justice. *Justice Quarterly*, 23, 1, 127–146.

Bottoms, A. and McClean, J. D. (1976) [2013] *Defendants in the Criminal Process*. London: Routledge.

Bowen, P. and Whitehead, S. (2013) *Better Courts: Cutting Crime through Court Innovation*. Centre for Justice Innovation. [Online] Available at: www.justiceinnovation.org [accessed 11 February 2014].

Braithwaite, J. (1989) *Crime, Shame and Reintegration*. Cambridge: Cambridge University Press.

Brennan, W. J. (1985) *The Constitution of the US: Contemporary Ratification*. Speech given at Georgetown University, 2 October 1985.

Brown, S. (1991) *Magistrates at Work*. Bristol: Open University Press.

Bryman, A. (2012) *Social Research Methods* (4th edn). Oxford: Oxford University Press.

Burney, E. (1979) *J. P.: Magistrate, Court and Community*. London: Hutchinson.

Cammiss, S. and Stride, C. (2008) Modelling Mode of Trial. *British Journal of Criminology*, 48, 4, 482–501.

Carlen, P. (1974) *Magistrates' Justice*. Oxford: Martin Robertson.

Carlile of Berriew, Lord (2014) *Independent Parliamentarians' Inquiry into the Operation and Effectiveness of the Youth Court*. [Online] Available at: www.ncb.org.uk

Carpenter, J. and Myers, C. (2010) Why Volunteer? Evidence on the Role of Altruism, Image and Incentives. *Journal of Public Economics*, 94, 11–12, 911–920.

Cavadino, M., Dignan, J. and Mair, G. (2013) *The Penal System: An Introduction* (5th edn) London: Sage.

Centre for Justice Innovation (2015) *Better Courts: A Blueprint for Innovation*. London: Centre for Justice Innovation. [Online] Available at: www.justiceinnovation.org.uk [accessed 30 January 2016].

Chakrabarti, S. (2014) *On Liberty*. London: Allen Lane.

Chambers, M., McLeod, C. and Davis, R. (2014) *Future Courts: A New Vision for Summary Justice*. London: Policy Exchange. [Online] Available at: www.policyexchange.org.uk.

Cheng, K. K. (2013) Pressures to Plead Guilty: Factors Affecting Plea Decisions in Hong Kong Magistrates Courts. *British Journal of Criminology*, 53, 2, 257–275.

Church, T. W. (1985) Examining Local Legal Culture. *American Bar Foundation Research Journal*, 3, 449–518.

The Civil Liberties Trust (2002) *Magistrates' Courts and Public Confidence: A Proposal for Fair and Effective Reform of the Magistracy*. London: The Civil Liberties. [Online] Available at: www.liberty-human-rights.org.uk.

Clegg, S. R. (1990) *Modern Organisations: Organisation Studies in the Postmodern World*. London: Sage.

College of Policing (2015) *College of Policing Analysis: Estimating the Demand on the Police Service*. [Online] Available at: www.college.police.uk [accessed 7 January 2016].

Comfort, M. (2007) Punishment Beyond the Legal Offender. *Annual Review of Law and Social Science*, 3, 271–296.

The Conservative Party (2010) *Invitation to Join the Government of Britain: The Conservative Party Manifesto*. [Online] Available at: www.conservatives.com [accessed 28 May 2015].

The Conservative Party (2015) *Strong Leadership: A Clear Economic Plan, a Brighter, More Secure Future*. [Online] Available at: www.conservatives.com [accessed 28 May 2015].

Cook, D. (2006) *Criminal and Social Justice*. London: Sage.

Corcoran, M. (2014) The Market Revolution in Criminal Justice. *Criminal Justice Matters*, 97, 1, 2–3.

Corey, Z. and Hans, V. P. (2010) Japan's New Lay Judge System: Deliberative Democracy in Action. *Asia Pacific Law and Policy Journal*, 12, 73.

Coughlan, S. (2010) *Majority of Young Women in University*. BBC News.

Coulsfield, Lord (2004) *Crime, Courts and Confidence: Report on an Independent Inquiry into Alternatives to Prison*. London: The Stationery Office.

Courts and Tribunals Judiciary (2015) Judicial Diversity Statistics 2015: Serving Magistrates Statistics 2014–15. [Online] Available at: www.judiciary.gov.uk [accessed 20 August 2015].

Cox, N. (2010) The Future of the Magistracy. *Criminal Law and Justice Weekly*, 17 September. [Online] Available at: www.criminallawandjustice.co.uk [accessed 8 January 2016].

Crown Prosecution Service (2014) *Crown Prosecution Service Annual Report and Accounts 2012–13*. [Online] Available at: www.cps.gov.uk [accessed 6 May 2014].

Davies, M. (2005) A New Training Initiative for the Lay Magistracy in England and Wales – A Further Step Towards Professionalisation. *International Journal of the Legal Profession*, 12, 1, 93–119.

Davies, M., Croall, H. and Tyrer, J. (2015) *Criminal Justice: An Introduction to the Criminal Justice System in England and Wales* (5th edn). London: Pearson-Longman.

Davis, G. and Vennard, J. (2006) Racism in Court: The Experience of Ethnic Minority Magistrates. *Howard Journal of Criminal Justice*, 45, 5, 485–501.

Dean, J. (2010) Irresponsible to Roll Out Virtual Courts After Critical Report. *The Law Society Gazette*, 21 December. [Online] Available at: www.lawgazette.co.uk.

Delgado, R., Dunn, C., Brown, P., Lee, H. and Hubbert, D. (1985) Fairness and Formality: Minimising the Risk of Prejudice in Alternative Dispute Resolution. *Wisconsin Law Review*, 6, 1359–1404.

Department for Constitutional Affairs (2006) *Delivering Simple, Speedy, Summary Justice*. London: Department for Constitutional Affairs.

Department of Health (2009) *The Bradley Report: Lord Bradley's Review of People with Mental Health Problems or Learning Disabilities in the Criminal Justice System*. London: Department of Health.

Dhami, M. (2004) Conditional Bail Decision Making in the Magistrates' Court. *The Howard Journal*, 43, 1, 27–46.

Dickson, M. (2011) The Rangatahi Court. *Waikato Law Review*, 19, 2, 86–107.

Dignan, J. and Wynne, A. (1997) A Microcosm of the Local Community? *British Journal of Criminology*, 37, 2, 184–197.

Dodd, V. (2015) Police Will Have to Pick and Choose what they Prioritise. *Guardian*, 12 March.

Donoghue, J. C. (2014a) Reforming the Role of Magistrates: Implications for Summary Justice in England and Wales. *The Modern Law Review*, 77, 6, 928–963.

Donoghue, J. C. (2014b) *Transforming Criminal Justice: Problem-solving and Court Specialisation*. London: Routledge.

Douglas, R. N. and Laster, K. (1992) *Reforming the People's Court: Victorian Magistrates' Reactions to Change*. Australia: Criminology Research Council Funded Reports.

Durcan, G., Saunders, A. Gadsby, B. and Hazard, A. (2014) *The Bradley Report Five Years On: An Independent Review of Progress to Date and Priorities for Further Development*. London: Centre for Mental Health.

Easton, S. and Piper, C. (2012) *Sentencing and Punishment; The Quest for Justice* (3rd edn). Oxford: Oxford University Press.

Edwards, A. (2011) Will Defendants Survive Changes to Criminal Legal Aid? *Criminal Justice Matters*, 86, 1, 30–32.

Edwards, J. (2012) Introduction: Retrieving the Big Society, in J. Edwards (ed.) *Retrieving the Big Society*. London: Political Quarterly.

Ericson, R. V. and Baranek, P. M. (1982) *The Ordering of Justice: A Study of Accused Persons as Dependants in the Criminal Justice Process*. Toronto: University of Toronto Press.

Etzioni, A. (1993) *The Spirit of Community: The Reinvention of American Society*. New York: Touchstone.

European Academy Berlin (2012) *European Day of Lay Judges: Documentary of the Elaboration of the European Charter of Lay Judges*. [Online] Available at: www.eab. berlin.de [accessed 2 May 2016].

Evans, J. (2015) *Locked Out: Children Experiences of Visiting a Parent in Prison*. Ilford: Barnardo's.

Fabri, M. and Contini, F. (eds) (2001) *Justice and Technology in Europe: How ICT is Changing the Judicial Business*. Dordrecht: Kluwer.

Farrington, D. P., Loeber, R. and Ttofi, M. M. (2012) Risk and Protective Factors for Offending. *The Oxford Handbook of Crime Prevention*. Oxford: Oxford University Press.

Fassenfelt, J. (2012) The Magistracy and the Police, in R. Jethwa (ed.) *Upholding the Queen's Peace: Towards a New Consensus*. The Police Federation. [Online] Available at: www.polfed.org [accessed 23 April 2014].

Fassenfelt, J. (2013) Magistrates Must Be Seen and Heard if they Are to Retain Public Respect. *The Times*, 24 October.

Feeley, M. M. (1983) [2013] *Court Reform on Trial: Why Simple Solutions Fail*. New Orleans: Quid Pro Books.

Feeley, M. M. (1992) *The Process is the Punishment: Handling Cases in a Lower Criminal Court*. New York: Russell Sage Foundation.

Fix-Fierro, H. (2003) *Courts, Justice and Efficiency: A Socio-legal Study of Rationality*. New York: Hart.

Frazer, M. S. (2006) *The Impact of the Community Court Model on Defendant Perceptions of Fairness: A Case Study at the Red Hook Community Justice Centre*. New York, NY: Centre for Court Innovation.

Freiberg, A. (2005) Managerialism in Australian Criminal Justice: RIP for KPIs. *Monash University Law Review*, 31, 12–36.

Galligan, D. J. (1996) *Due Process and Fair Procedures: A Study of Administrative Procedures*. Oxford: Clarendon.

Garland, D. (2001) *The Culture of Control*. Oxford: Oxford University Press.

Garside, R. and Ford, M. (2015) *The Coalition Years: Criminal Justice in the United Kingdom: 2010 to 2015*. Centre for Crime and Justice Studies.

Gerry, F. and Harris, L. (2014) *Women in Prison: Is the Penal System Fit for Purpose?* London: Halsbury Law Review. Available at: www.halsburyslawexchange.co.uk.

Gibbs, P. (2013) *Managing the Magistrates' Courts*. Transform Justice. [Online] Available at: www.transformjustice.org.uk.

Gibbs, P. (2014a) *Fit for Purpose: Do Magistrates get the Training and Development they Need?* Transform Justice. [Online] Available at: www.transformjustice.org.uk [accessed 19 February 2016].

Gibbs, P. (2014b) *Magistrates: Representatives of the People*. Transform Justice. [Online] Available at: www.transformjustice.org.uk.

Gibbs, P. and Kirby, A. (2014) *Judged by Peers? The Diversity of Lay Magistrates in England and Wales*. Howard League 'What is Justice?' Working papers 6/2014. [Online] Available at: www.howardleague.org.

Gray, K. (2004) Evidence Before the ICC, in D. McGoldrick (ed.) *The Permanent International Criminal Court*. New York: Hart.

Green, D. (2014) *Modernising the Magistracy*. Speech given to Policy Exchange, 14 March 2014. [Online] Available at: www.policyexchange.org.uk [accessed 3 October 2015].

Grove, T. (2002) *The Magistrate's Tale*. London: Bloomsbury.

Halliday, J. (2001) *Making Punishments Work: Report of a Review of the Sentencing Framework for England and Wales*. London: Home Office.

Hallsworth, S. and Lea, J. (2011) Reconstructing Leviathan: Emerging Contours of the Security State. *Theoretical Criminology*, 15, 2, 141–157.

Haarhuis, C. K. and Niemeijer, B. (2006) Vanishing or Increasing Trials in the Netherlands? *Journal of Dispute Resolution*, 71.

Hans, V. P. (2008) *Jury Systems Around the World*. Cornell Law Faculty Publications Paper 305. [Online] Available at: http://scholarship.law.cornell.edu [accessed 30 March 2016].

Hans, V. P. (2007) Introduction: Citizens as Legal Decision-makers: An International Perspective. *Cornell International Law Journal*, 2, 303–306.

Hanson, N. (2004) Clerks Seek Justice. *Law Gazette*, 17 June. [Online] Available at: www.lawgazette.co.uk [accessed 10 June 2016].

Harkness, P. V. (2009) *The Lay Magistracy in New Zealand: Judicial Asset of Colonial Anachronism*. Unpublished PhD thesis, University of Auckland.

Harkness, P. V. (2015) *Reading the Riot Act: A 200-year History of Justices of the Peace in New Zealand*. New Zealand: Media Features.

Hedderman, C. and Moxon, D. (1992) *Magistrates' Court or Crown Court?: Mode of Trial Decisions and Sentencing*. Home Office Research Study No. 125. London: The Stationery Office.

Heffernan, W. (2000) Social Justice/Criminal Justice, in W. Heffernan and K. Kleinig (eds) (2000) *From Social Justice to Criminal Justice: Poverty and the Administration of Criminal Law*. Oxford: Oxford University Press.

Heffernan, W. and Kleinig, K. (eds) (2000) *From Social Justice to Criminal Justice: Poverty and the Administration of Criminal Law*. Oxford: Oxford University Press.

Herbert, A. (2004) Mode of Trial and the Influence of Local Justice. *Howard Journal of Criminal Justice*. 43, 1, 65–78.

H. M. Crown Prosecution Service Inspectorate (2016) *Transforming Summary Justice: An Early Perspective of the CPS Consultation*. London: H. M. Crown Prosecution Service Inspectorate. [Online] Available at: www.justiceinspectorates.gov.uk [accessed 28 March 2016].

H. M. Government (1998) *Human Rights Act*. London: The Stationery Office.

H. M. Government (2002) *Justice for All*. London: The Stationery Office.

H. M. Inspectorate of Constabulary (2014) *Crime Recording: Making the Victim Count – The Final Report of an Inspection of Crime Data Integrity in Police Forces in England and Wales*.

H. M. Inspectorate of Prisons (2012) *Remand Prisoners: A Thematic Review*. H. M. Inspectorate of Prisons. [Online] Available at: www.justice.gov.uk.

H. M. Government (2013) *Legal Aid, Sentencing and Punishment of Offenders Act.* [Online] Available at: www.legislation.gov.uk

H. M. Inspectorate of Prisons and H. M. Inspectorate of Constabulary (2015) *Report on Unannounced Inspection Visit to Police Custody Suites in Hertfordshire.* London: H. M Inspectorate of Prisons.

Hood, R. (1979) *Sentencing the Motoring Offender: A Study of Magistrates' Views and Practices.* London: Heinemann.

Hood, R. (1992) *Race and Sentencing: A Study in the Crown Court – A Report for the Commission for Racial Equality.* Oxford: Clarendon.

Hogan-Howe, B. (2014) Cuts without Reform put the Public at Risk. *Guardian,* 14 December.

Hucklesbury, A. (1997) Court Culture: An Explanation of Variations in the use of Bail by Magistrates' Courts. *Howard Journal of Criminal Justice,* 36, 2, 129–145.

Hudson, B. (2000) Punishing the Poor: Dilemmas of Justice and Difference, in W. Heffernan and K. Kleinig (eds) *From Social Justice to Criminal Justice: Poverty and the Administration of Criminal Law.* Oxford: Oxford University Press.

Hughes, J. (2015) Rebranding the Magistrates Association: A Fresh and Energetic Approach. *Magistrate,* April–May. The Magistrates Association.

Ipsos MORI (2011) *The Strength and Skills of the Judiciary in the Magistrates' Courts.* Ministry of Justice Research Series 9/11. London: Ministry of Justice.

Ivkovic, S. K. (1999) *Lay Participation in Criminal Trials: The Case of Croatia.* USA: Austin and Winfield.

Jackson, J. D. and Kovalev, N. P. (2006) Lay Adjudication and Human Rights in Europe. *Columbia Journal of European Law,* 13, 1, 83–124.

Jacobson, J., Hunter, G. and Kirby, A. (2015) *Inside Crown Court: Personal Experience and Questions of Legitimacy.* London: Policy Press.

Jehle, J. M. and Wade, M. (2006) *Coping with Overloaded Criminal Justice Systems: The Rise of Prosecutorial Power Across Europe.* Berlin/Heidelberg: Springer.

Jennings, J. (2012) Tocqueville and the Big Society, in J. Edwards (ed.) *Retrieving the Big Society.* London: Political Quarterly.

Jones, C. (1993) Auditing Criminal Justice. *British Journal of Criminology,* 33, 2, 187–202.

Judiciary of England and Wales (2015a) *Becoming a Magistrate in England and Wales: Guidance for Prospective Applicants.* [Online] Available at: www.gov.uk [accessed 5 August 2015].

Kaiser, K. A. and Holtfreter, K. (2016) Using Procedural Justice and Therapeutic Jurisprudence to Promote Offender Compliance and Rehabilitation. *Criminal Justice and Behaviour,* 43, 1, 45–62.

Kerr, J., Tompkins, C., Tomaszewski, W., Dickens, S., Grimshaw, R., Wright, N. and Barnard, M. (2011) *The Dedicated Drug Courts Pilot Evaluation Process Study.* Ministry of Justice Research Series 1/11.

King, M. S. (2011) Therapeutic Jurisprudence Initiatives in Australia and New Zealand and the Overseas Experience. *Journal of Judicial Administration,* 21, 1, 19–33.

King, M. and May, C. (1985) *Black Magistrates.* London: Cobden Trust.

Klug, F. (2015) *A Magna Carta for Humanity: Homing in on Human Rights.* London: Routledge.

Kramer, A. (2000) Poverty, Crime and Criminal Justice, in W. Heffernan and K. Kleinig (eds) *From Social Justice to Criminal Justice: Poverty and the Administration of Criminal Law.* Oxford: Oxford University Press.

Law Society (2012) *Virtual Court First Hearings*. [Online] Available at: www.lawsociety.org.uk [accessed 29 April 2014].

Lees, S. (2002) *Carnal Knowledge: Rape on Trial* (2nd edn). London: Women's Press.

Lempert, R. O. (2001) Citizen Participation in Judicial Decision-Making: Juries, Lay Judges and Japan. *St. Louis Warsaw Transatlantic Law Journal.*

Leveson, B. (2007) *The Approach to Summary Justice both in and out of Court*. London: Centre for Crime and Justice Studies. Available at: www.crimeandjustice.org.uk.

Leveson, B. (2015a) *Review of Efficiency in Criminal Proceedings*. London: Judiciary of England and Wales. [Online] Available at: www.judiciary.gov.uk

Leveson, B. (2015b) *Modernising Justice through Technology*. Keynote Lecture transcript, 24 June 2015.

Liberty (2013) *Liberty's Response to the MoJ's Consultation 'Transforming Legal Aid: Delivering a More Credible and Efficient System'*. [Online] Available at: www.liberty.org.uk [accessed 31 March 2015].

Lord Carlile of Berriew (2014) *Independent Parliamentarians' Inquiry into the Operation and Effectiveness of the Youth Court*. Available at: www.ncb.org.uk

Lowndes, J. (1999) *The Australian Magistracy: From Justices of the Peace to Judges and Beyond*. Judicial Conference of Australia Colloquium Papers. [Online] Available at: www.jca.asn.au [accessed 6 August 2015].

Mack, K. and Roach Anleu, S. (2007) 'Getting Through the List': Judgecraft and Legitimacy in the Lower Courts. *Social and Legal Studies*, 16, 341–361.

Malsch, M. (2009) *Democracy in the Courts: Lay Participation in European Criminal Justice Systems*. Farnham: Ashgate.

Marchetti, E. and Daly, K. (2007) Indigenous Sentencing Courts: Towards a Theoretical and Jurisprudential Model. *Sydney Law Review*, 29, 415–443.

Marlow, A. (2014) Thinking about the Fall in Crime. *Safer Communities*, 13, 2, 56–62.

Martinson, R. (1974) Questions and Answers about Prison Reform. *The Public Interest*, 35, 22–54.

Matthews, R. (2014) *Realist Criminology*. London: Palgrave Macmillan.

McBarnet, D. (1981a) Magistrates' Courts and the Ideology of Justice. *British Journal of Law and Society*, 8, 2, 181–197.

McBarnet, D. (1981b) *Conviction: Law the State and the Construction of Justice*. London: Palgrave Macmillan.

McEwan, J. (2011) From Adversarialism to Managerialism: Criminal Justice in Transition. *Legal Studies*, 31, 4, 519–546.

McEwan, J. (2013) Vulnerable Defendants and the Fairness of Trials. *Criminal Law Review*, 2, 100–113.

McIvor, G. (2010) Drug Courts: Lessons from the UK and Beyond, in A. Hucklesby and E. Wincup (eds) *Drug Interventions in Criminal Justice*. Maidenhead: Open University Press.

McLaughlin, E.; Muncie, J. and Hughes, G. (2001) The Permanent Revolution: New Labour, New Public Management and the Modernisation of Criminal Justice. *Criminology and Criminal Justice*, 1, 3, 301–318.

Mawby, R. C. and Worrall, A. (2013) *Doing Probation Work: Identity in a Criminal Justice Occupation*. London: Routledge.

Ministry of Justice (2010) *Breaking the Cycle: Effective Punishment, Rehabilitation and Sentencing of Offenders*. London: Ministry of Justice.

Ministry of Justice (2011a) *Virtual Courts Bring Swifter Justice*. [Online] Available at: www.gov.uk/government/news [accessed 20 May 2014].

Ministry of Justice (2011b) *Modernising the Criminal Justice System: The CJS Efficiency Programme.* [Online] Available at: www.gov.uk.

Ministry of Justice (2012) *Swift and Sure Justice: The Government's Plans for Reform of the Criminal Justice System.* London: The Stationery Office.

Ministry of Justice (2013a) *Transforming the Criminal Justice System: A Strategy and Action Plan to Reform the CJS.* [Online] Available at: www.gov.uk.

Ministry of Justice (2013b) *Transforming Legal Aid: Delivering a More Credible and Efficient System.* [Online] Available at: https://consult.justice.gov.uk [accessed 24 June 2013].

Ministry of Justice (2013c) *Penalty Notices for Disorder.* London: Ministry of Justice.

Ministry of Justice (2013d) *Courts Statistics Quarterly January to March 2013.* London: Ministry of Justice.

Ministry of Justice (2014a) *Statistics on Women and the Criminal Justice System 2013.* London: Ministry of Justice.

Ministry of Justice (2014b) *Chris Grayling: Reform of the Courts and Tribunals: Press Release.* [Online] Available at: www.gov.uk [accessed 6 April 2014].

Ministry of Justice (2014c) *Criminal Court Statistics Quarterly, England and Wales July to September 2013.* Ministry of Justice Statistical Bulletin. [Online] Available at: www.gov.uk/government/uploads [accessed 17 May 2016].

Ministry of Justice (2014d) *Transforming the Criminal Justice System: Strategy and Action Plan – Implementation Update.* [Online] Available at: www.gov.uk [accessed 5 June 2015].

Ministry of Justice (2015a) *Proposal on the Provision of Court and Tribunal Estate in England and Wales.* London: Ministry of Justice. [Online] Available at: http://consult.justice.gov.uk [accessed 14 August 2015].

Ministry of Justice (2015b) *Criminal Justice Statistics Quarterly Update to March 2015.* Ministry of Justice Statistical Bulletin. [Online] Available at: www.gov.uk/government/uploads [accessed 24 August 2015].

Ministry of Justice (2015c) Criminal Justice Statistics Overview Table [spreadsheet].

Minson, S., Nadin, R. and Earle, J. (2015) *Sentencing of Mothers: Improving the Sentencing Process and Outcome for Women with Dependent Children.* London: Prison Reform Trust.

Morgan, R. (2008) *Summary Justice: Fast but Fair?* Kings College Centre for Crime and Justice Studies. [Online] Available at: www.crimeandjustice.org.uk.

Morgan, R. (2012) Extending the Office of Magistrate in England and Wales, in D. Faulkner (ed.) *The Magistracy at the Crossroads.* Hook: Waterside.

Morgan, R. (2013) The Magistracy: Secure Epitome of the Big Society? *Criminal Justice Matters*, 91, 1, 8–9.

Morgan, R. and Russell N. (2000) *The Judiciary in the Magistrates' Courts.* Home Office and LC Occasional Paper 66. London: Home Office.

Mulcahy, L. (2008) The Unbearable Lightness of Being? Shifts Towards the Virtual Trial. *Journal of Law and Society*, 35, 4, 464–489.

Mulcahy, L. (2011) *Legal Architecture: Justice, Due Process and the Place of Law.* London: Routledge.

Newburn, T. (2007) *Criminology.* Cullompton: Willan.

New Zealand Ministry of Justice (2012) *Evaluation of the Early Outcomes of Nga Kooti Rangatahi.* Wellington: Ministry of Justice. www.justice.govt.nz [accessed 14 February 2016].

Nolan, J. (2001) *Reinventing Justice: The Drug Court Movement.* Princeton, NJ: Princeton University Press.

Office for Criminal Justice Reform (2010) *Virtual Courts: Information for Defence Representatives*. [Online] Available at: www.justice.gov.uk [accessed 29 April 2014].

O'Malley, P. (2008) Neoliberalism and Risk in Criminology, in T. Anthony and C. Cunneen (eds) *The Critical Criminology Companion*. Sydney: Federation.

Packer, H. (1968) *The Limits of the Criminal Sanction*. Stanford, CA: Stanford University Press.

Padfield, N., Morgan, R. and Maguire, M. (2012) Out of Court, Out of Sight? Criminal Sanctions and Non-Judicial Decision-Making, in M. Maguire, R. Morgan and R. Reiner (eds) *The Oxford Handbook of Criminology* (5th edn). Oxford: Oxford University Press.

Parker, H., Sumner, M. and Jarvis, G. (1989) *Unmasking the Magistrates*. Bristol: Open University Press.

Peay, J. (2012) Mentally Disordered Offenders, Mental Health, and Crime, in M. Maguire, R. Morgan and R. Reiner (eds) *The Oxford Handbook of Criminology* (5th edn). Oxford: Oxford University Press.

Pedroso, J. and Trincão, C. (2008) The (Re)birth of the Justice of the Peace: Democratic or Technocratic Justice Reform? The Experiences of Italy, Spain, Brazil and Portugal. *Beyond Law*, 27, 91–108.

Pen, J. (2015) The Rise and Rise of Technocratic Justice. *Alternative Law Journal*, 40, 2, 132–133.

Platt, B. (2015) Inspector, Strategic Criminal Justice Department, Kent Police. Personal Communication.

Plotnikoff, J. and Woolfson, R. (1999) *Preliminary Hearing: Video Link Evaluation of Pilot Projects: Final Report*.

Porteous, D., Adler, J. and Davidson, J. (2015) *The Development of Specialist Support Services for Young People who have Offended and who have also been Victims of Crime, Abuse or Violence: Final Report*. London: Greater London Authority. [Online] Available at: www.london.gov.uk [accessed 22 June 2015].

Porteous, D. (2015) *Troubled Lives: Supporting Offenders who Are also Victims*. Middlesex Minds blogspot. [Online] Available at: www.mdxminds.com [accessed 21 June 2015].

Prison Reform Trust (2011) *Prison Reform Trust Submission to the Ministry of Justice: Breaking the Cycle: Effective Punishment, Rehabilitation and Sentencing of Offenders*. Prison Reform Trust. [Online] Available at: www.prisonreformtrust.org [accessed 25 May 2015].

Prison Reform Trust (2015) *Bromley Briefings Prison Factfile*. [Online] Available at: www.prisonreformtrust.org.uk.

Raine, J. (2000) Whither Local Justice? *Criminal Justice Matters*, 40, 1, 19–20.

Raine, J. W. (2005) Courts, Sentencing and Justice in a Changing Political and Managerial Context. *Public Money and Management*, 25, 5, 290–298.

Raine, J. and Willson, M. (1993) *Managing Criminal Justice*. Harlow: Harvester Wheatsheaf.

Raine, J. W. and Willson, M. (1995) New Public Management and Criminal Justice. *Public Money and Management*, 15, 1, 35–40.

Ridout, F. (2010) Virtual Courts, Virtual Justice. *Criminal Law and Justice Weekly*, 24 September.

Roach Anleu, S., Bergman Blix, S., Mack, K. and Wettergren, A. (2015) Observing Judicial Work and Emotions: Using Two Researchers. *Qualitative Research* DOI: 10.1177/1468794115579475.

Roach Anleu, S. and Mack, K. (2005) Magistrates' Everyday Work and Emotional Labour. *Journal of Law and Society*, 32, 4, 590–614.

Roach Anleu and Mack, K. (2007a) Magistrates, Magistrates Courts and Social Change. *Law and Policy*, 29, 2, 183–209.

Roach Anleu, S. and Mack, K. (2007b) Australian Magistrates, Therapeutic Jurisprudence and Social Change, in G. Reinhardt and A. Cannon (eds) *Transforming Legal Processes in Court and Beyond: A Collection of Refereed Papers from the 3rd International Conference on Therapeutic Jurisprudence*. The Australian Institute of Judicial Administration. [Online] Available at: www.aija.org.au [accessed 1 April 2015].

Roach Anleu, S. and Mack, K. (2009) Intersections Between In-court Procedures and the Prosecution of Guilty Pleas. *Australian and New Zealand Journal of Criminology*, 42, 1, 1–23.

Roach Anleu, S. and Mack, K. (2014) Job Satisfaction in the Judiciary. *Work, Employment and Society*, 28, 5, 683–701.

Roach Anleu, S., Mack, S. and Mack, K. (2013) Social Change in the Australian Judiciary, in K. Carrington, M. Ball, E. O'Brien and J. Tauri (eds) *Crime, Justice and Social Democracy*. London: Palgrave Macmillan.

Roberts, J. (2011) Sentencing Guidelines and Judicial Discretion: Evolution of the Duty of Courts to Comply in England and Wales. *British Journal of Criminology*, 51, 6, 997–1013.

Roberts, J. (2010) Sentencing Guidelines in England and Wales: A Review of Recent Developments. *Criminal Justice Matters*, 82, 41–42.

Robson, G. (2014) Clouds over the Lower Courts. *Criminal Law and Justice Weekly*, 178 (16/17/18 April). [Online] Available at: www.criminallawandjustice.co.uk.

Rock, P. (1991) Witnesses and Space in a Crown Court. *British Journal of Criminology*, 31, 31, 266–279.

Rock, P. (1993) *The Social World of an English Crown Court*. Oxford: Clarendon.

Rossman, S. B., Rempel, M., Roman, J. K., Zweig, J. M., Linquist, C. H., Green, M., Mitchell Downey, P., Yahner, J., Bhati, A. S. and Farole, D. J. (2011) *The Multi-site Adult Drug Court Evaluation: The Impact of Drug Courts*. Washington, DC: Urban Institute Justice Policy Center.

Rowden, E. (2013) Virtual Courts and Putting 'Summary' back into 'Summary Justice': Merely Brief or Unjust?, in J. Simon, N. Temple, and R. Tobe (Eds.) *Architecture and Justice: Judicial Meanings in the Public Realm*. Ashgate Publishing Co. UK.

Rowden, E., Wallace, A., Tait, D., Hanson, M. and Jones, D. (2013) *Gateways to Justice: Design and Operational Guidelines for Remote Participation in Court Proceedings*. Sydney: University of Western Sydney Press. [Online] Available at: www.uws.edu.au/justice/justice/publications.

Rumgay, J. (1995) Custodial Decision Making in a Magistrates' Court: Court Culture and Immediate Situational Factors. *British Journal of Criminology*, 35, 201–217.

Samuels, J. (2013) *Sentencer Supervision: Concept and Practicality*. Paper delivered at the Howard League for Penal Reform 'What is Justice?' conference.

Sanders, A. and Young, R. (2007) *Criminal Justice* (3rd edn). Oxford: Oxford University Press.

Sanders, A., Young, R. and Burton, M. (2010) *Criminal Justice* (4th edn). Oxford: Oxford University Press.

Savage, S. and Bretherwick, D. (2011) Lay Justice or Professional Justice, in T. Ellis and S. Savage (eds) *Debates in Criminal Justice: Key Themes and Issues*. London: Routledge.

Schabas, W. A. (2005) Genocide Trials and *Gacaca* Courts. *Journal of International Criminal Justice*, 3, 1–17.

Schein, E. H. (2010) *Organisational Culture and Leadership* (4th edn). Jossey-Bass.

Seago, P., Walker, C. and Wall, D (2000) The Development of the Professional Magistracy in England and Wales. *Criminal Law Review*, August 631–651.

Senior Presiding Judge for England and Wales (2010) *Proposal on the Provision of Court Services in England and Wales*. [Online] Available at: www.judiciary.gov.uk [accessed 29 May 2015].

Sharpe, M. (2014) Bar Lowered to 'Car Boot' Legal Aid. *New Zealand Sunday Star Times*, 16 March, A6.

Shute, S., Hood, R. and Seemungal, F. (2005) *A Fair Hearing? Ethnic Minorities in the Criminal Court*. Cullompton: Willan.

Slapper, G. (2010) Pay-as-you-go Street Justice. *Journal of Criminal Law*, 74, 1, 1–3.

Social Exclusion Unit (2002) *Reducing Re-offending by Ex-prisoners: Report by the Social Exclusion Unit*. London: Social Exclusion Unit.

Sommerlad, H. (2004) Some Reflections on the Relationship Between Citizenship, Access to Justice and the Reform of Legal Aid. *Journal of Law and Society*, 31, 3, 345–368.

Sommerlad, H. (2008) Reflections on the Reconfiguration of Access to Justice. *International Journal of the Legal Profession*, 15, 3, 179–193.

Stenson, K. and Edwards, A. (2001) Crime Control and Liberal Government: The Third Way and the Return to the Local, in K. Stenson and R. R. Sullivan (eds) Crime, Risk and Justice: *The Politics of Crime Control in Neo-liberal Democracies*. Cullompton: Willan.

Smith, T. (2013) The 'Quiet Revolution' in Criminal Defence: How the Zealous Advocate Slipped into the Shadow. *International Journal of the Legal Profession*, 20, 1, 111–137.

Tarling, R. (1979) *Sentencing Practice in Magistrates Courts*. London: The Stationery Office.

Tarling, R. (2006) Sentencing Practice in Magistrates' Courts Revisited. *The Howard Journal*, 45, 1, 29–41.

Terry, M., Johnson, S. and Thompson, P. (2010) *Virtual Court Pilot: Outcome Evaluation*. Ministry of Justice Research Series 21/10.

Thomas, C. (2010) *Are Juries Fair?* Ministry of Justice Research Series 1/10. London: Home Office.

Transform Drug Policy Foundation (2013) *A Cause for Celebration or a Misguided Attempt at Progress*. [Online] Available at: Transform-drugs.blogspot.co.uk [accessed 26 April 2016].

Travers, M. (2007) Sentencing in the Children's Court: an Ethnographic Perspective. *Youth Justice*, 7, 1, 21–35.

Travis, A. (2013) Ten Thousand Violent Crime Cases Dealt with by 'Community Resolution' Methods. *Guardian*.

Tyler, T. R. (2000) Social Justice: Outcome and Procedure. *International Journal of Psychology*, 35, 2, 117–125.

Tyler, T. R. (2008) Procedural Justice and the Courts. *Court Review*, 44, 25–31.

Tyler, T. R. (2010) Legitimacy in Corrections. *Criminology and Public Policy*, 9, 1, 127–134.

Van Dijk, J., Tseloni, A. and Farrell, G. (2012) *The International Crime Drop: New Directions in Research*. London: Palgrave Macmillan.

Vennard, J. (1982) *Contested Trials in the Magistrates' Courts*. Home Office Research Study 71. London: The Stationery Office.

Vidmar, N. (2002) Juries and Lay Assessors in the Commonwealth. *Criminal Law Forum*, 13, 4, 385–407.

Wacquant, L. (2009) *Punishing the Poor: The Neoliberal Government of Social Security*. London: Duke University Press.

Waititi, H. (2012) *Toitū Te Mana Rangatahi: Marae-based Youth Courts – Negotiating Pathways for Rangatahi Offending*. MSc thesis, Victoria University of New Zealand. [Online] Available at: www.researcharchive.vuw.ac.nz [accessed 7 August 2015].

Ward, J. (2013) The Punishment of Drug Possession Cases in the Magistrates' Courts: Time for a Rethink. *European Journal on Criminal Policy and Research*, 19, 4, 289–307.

Ward, J. (2014) *Are Problem-solving Courts the Way Forward for Justice?* Howard League 'What is Justice?' Working papers 2/2014. [Online] Available at: www. howardleague.org.

Ward, J. (2015) Transforming 'Summary Justice' through Police-led Prosecution and 'Virtual Courts' – Is 'Procedural Due Process' Being Undermined? *British Journal of Criminology*, 55, 2, 341–358.

Ward, J. and Warkel, K. (2015) *Northampton Youth Offending Service Review Panel Evaluation*. London: Middlesex University. [Online] Available at: www.mdx.ac.uk.

Wexler, D. B. and Winick, B. J. (1996) *Law in a Therapeutic Key: Developments in Therapeutic Jurisprudence*. Durham, NC: Carolina Academic Press.

Wilson, M. (2007) The Dawn of Criminal Jury Trials in Japan. *Wisconsin International Law Journal*, 24, 4, 835–870.

Winick, B. (2002) Therapeutic Jurisprudence and Problem-solving Courts. *Fordham Urban Law Journal*, 30, 3, 1056–1104.

Young, J. (1999) *The Exclusive Society: Exclusion, Crime and Difference in Late Modernity*. London: Sage.

Young, J. (2011) *A Virtual Day in Court: Design Thinking and Virtual Courts*. The Royal Society of Arts. [Online] Available at: www.thersa.org [accessed 8 May 2014].

Index

Page numbers in *italics* denote tables.